THE WORLD'S CLASSICS

TRAVELS WITH A DONKEY IN THE CEVENNES

and

SELECTED TRAVEL WRITINGS

ROBERT LOUIS STEVENSON, only child of Thomas Stevenson, engineer and lighthouse-keeper, and Margaret Balfour, daughter of a Scots minister, was born in Edinburgh in 1850. In 1871 he exchanged the study of engineering for the law. From 1876 he pursued a full-time literary career, beginning as an essayist and travel writer with the publication of *An Inland Voyage* (1878), *Edinburgh: Picturesque Notes* (1878), *Travels with a Donkey* (1879), and *Virginibus Puerisque* (1881). Stevenson is probably best remembered for *Treasure Island* (his first widespread success, 1883), *Kidnapped*, and *Dr Jekyll and Mr Hyde* (both published in 1886). Temperament and ill health prompted Stevenson to travel widely on the Continent, in the United States, and in the South Seas where he settled in 1889–90 until his death in Samoa on 3 December 1894.

EMMA LETLEY lectures and writes on nineteenth- and twentieth-century literature. She has edited R. L. Stevenson's *The Master of Ballantrae*, *Treasure Island*, *Kidnapped*, and *Catriona* and *The Strange Case of Dr Jekyll and Mr Hyde*, and *Weir of Hermiston* for World's Classics.

THE WORLD'S CLASSICS

ROBERT LOUIS STEVENSON

Travels with a Donkey in the Cevennes

and Selected Travel Writings

Edited with an Introduction by
EMMA LETLEY

Oxford New York
OXFORD UNIVERSITY PRESS

Oxford University Press, Walton Street, Oxford OX2 6DP

Oxford New York Toronto
Delhi Bombay Calcutta Madras Karachi
Kuala Lumpur Singapore Hong Kong Tokyo
Nairobi Dar es Salaam Cape Town
Melbourne Auckland Madrid

and associated companies in
Berlin Ibadan

Oxford is a trade mark of Oxford University Press

Editorial material © Emma Letley 1992

First published as a World's Classics paperback 1992

British Library Cataloguing in Publication Data
Data available

Library of Congress Cataloging in Publication Data
Stevenson, Robert Louis, 1850-1894.
Travels with a donkey in the Cevennes, and selected travel
writings / Robert Louis Stevenson; edited with an introduction by
Emma Letley.
p. cm.—(World's classics)
Includes bibliographical references.
1. Stevenson, Robert Louis, 1850-1894– Journeys—France –Cévennes
Mountains. 2. Cévennes Mountains (France)—Description and travel.
3. Authors, Scottish— 19th century—Biography. 4. Voyages and
travels. I. Letley, Emma. II. Title. III. Series.
PR5488.T8 1992 828'.803—dc20 91-47569

ISBN 0-19-282629-8

3 5 7 9 10 8 6 4 2

Printed in Great Britain by
BPCC Paperbacks Ltd
Aylesbury, Bucks

CONTENTS

CONTENTS

INTRODUCTION

Writing in the *Athenaeum* in June 1878, Sidney Colvin had this to say about R.L.S.'s first published book, *An Inland Voyage*:

But the interest of a book of travels depends in all cases on the character of the traveller much more than on the extent of his travels, and the most trivial journey related by one man will be better worth reading than the most perilous explorations and hair-breadth escapes of another.

Colvin understood, too, that one of this writer's great strengths was his ability in landscape painting: 'It is a landscape-writing like the landscape painting of the Japanese'; and perhaps most important of all, he appreciated Stevenson's 'Natural liking for and fellow-feeling with the French character'.[1]

The canoe journey in the two sail-powered skiffs named *Cigarette* and *Arethusa* was a central event of Stevenson's life in 1876; for some years he had shared his friends' (notably Sir Walter Simpson's and R. A. M. (Bob) Stevenson's) enthusiasm for canoeing; the eccentric Scots barrister 'Rob Roy' MacGregor had been responsible for making it a popular sport on the Firth of Forth at Edinburgh some ten years previously. In France, too, canoes had become part of the life at Grez, the artists' colony near Paris where R.L.S. spent some time. The idea for the journey came, however, most probably from J. L. Molloy's *Our Autumn Holiday on French Rivers* (1874), an account of a journey up the Seine and down the Loire in a four-oared outrigger.

The cruise itself, which took the two friends, Simpson and R.L.S., from Antwerp to Pontoise, was not an unmitigated pleasure and Stevenson admits in a letter of 9 September 1876 that the weather had been intolerable from the start, squally with showers and a cold wind. It had been

[1] As quoted in *Robert Louis Stevenson: The Critical Heritage*, ed. Paul Maixner (1981), 50–1.

tempting to give up the whole enterprise, 'if it had not been for professional purposes; for an easy book may be written and sold, with mighty little brains about it, where the journey is of a certain seriousness and can be named'.[2]

The book, although no masterpiece and at times immature in its posturing (he likes the *idea* of himself as a traveller rather too much on occasion), was quite well received and formed a landmark in Stevenson's literary career. Recent critical work on R.L.S. has focused on the fact that he was a travel writer first and foremost and well before he became known as a writer of fiction, and *Inland Voyage* is his first travel book;[3] it was also the start of his literary relationship with France. He has the Scot's characteristic affinity with and for the French and things French, and according to some critics he even wrote like a Frenchman. His stepson, Lloyd Osbourne, wrote that what most pleased Stevenson in the French was 'their universal indulgence towards all sexual problems—their clear-sighted toleration of everything affecting the relations of men and women'. In this matter they were, he felt, the most civilized nation in Europe. The British might be better governed, but their outlook was 'blinkered by caste, puritanism and prejudice'. Later in his life Stevenson even felt that he would have loved to have been a French writer. Again to Lloyd, he commented:

How the French misuse their freedom; see nothing worth writing about but the eternal triangle; while we, who are muzzled like dogs, but who are infinitely wider in outlook, are condemned to avoid half the life that passes us by. What books Dickens could have written had he been permitted! Think of Thackeray as unfettered as Flaubert or Balzac! What books I might have written myself! But they give us a little box of toys, and say to us, 'You mustn't play with anything but these.'[4]

[2] Graham Balfour, *The Life of Robert Louis Stevenson* (1901), i. 143.

[3] For recent critical comment see, in particular, James Wilson, 'Landscape with Figures', in *Robert Louis Stevenson*, ed. Andrew Noble (1983), and Robert Louis Stevenson, *The Lantern Bearers*, ed. Jeremy Treglown (1988), Introduction.

[4] Quoted in Nicholas Rankin, *Dead Man's Chest: Travels after Robert Louis Stevenson* (1988), 86.

Inland Voyage is full of Stevenson's characteristic enthusiasm for French life. In the Sambre and Oise Canal section of the book he tells, for example, how he ventured to praise his hosts' way of life on a barge:

Now, what I like so much in France is the clear, unflinching recognition by everybody of his own luck. They all know on which side their bread is buttered, and take a pleasure in showing it to others, which is surely the better part of religion. And they scorn to make poor mouth over their poverty, which I take to be the better part of manliness. (pp. 47–8)

And, of course, Stevenson appreciates the style of the French. The skiffs, *Cigarette* and *Arethusa*, have been complimented for their grace (they are compared with violins):

Was not this a graceful little ovation? Where this people finds the secret of its pretty speeches I cannot imagine; unless the secret should be none other than a sincere desire to please! But then no disgrace is attached in France to saying a thing neatly; whereas in England, to talk like a book is to give in one's resignation to Society. (p. 58)

Inland Voyage ends on this note:

Now we were to return, like the voyager in the play, and see what rearrangements fortune had perfected the while in our surroundings; what surprises stood ready made for us at home; and whither and how far the world had voyaged in our absence. You may paddle all day long; but it is when you come back at nightfall, and look in at the familiar room, that you find Love or Death awaiting you before the stove; and the most beautiful adventures are not those we go to seek. (p. 107)

There was a great and beautiful adventure waiting for R.L.S. when he and Sir Walter Simpson returned to Grez after their Inland Voyage. Before this date, artists' colonies like the one at Grez 'had been nearly as free of the female element as were afterwards the early novels of Stevenson himself';[5] at this time, however, Fanny Osbourne, an American lady, and her children, retreating from an un-

[5] Balfour, *Life*, i. 145.

happy marriage to a Kentucky lawyer were living there in some poverty, and Stevenson soon fell in love with her.

The parting with Fanny when she returned to the United States was very painful indeed. R.L.S. could not think of marriage at this stage; he was not earning a living and parental disapproval of a liaison with a woman ten years his senior, and soon to be a divorcée, meant that he was loath to ask for their support. In these circumstances it is not surprising that an underlying theme of Stevenson's best-known travel-book, *Travels with a Donkey*, is the absence of Fanny (he had undertaken the 'Travels' shortly after her departure to California). He admitted as much in a letter to Bob Stevenson in April 1879: 'lots of it is mere protestations to F, most of which I think you will understand.'[6] The Dedication to Colvin, after invoking the great virtues of friendship, hints that the submerged theme will be known to his friends: 'Every book is, in an intimate sense, a circular letter to the friends of him who writes it. They alone take his meaning; they find private messages, assurances of love, and expressions of gratitude dropped for theme in every corner' (p. 122).

His wish for a companion expressed within the text itself clearly suggests that during the journey he missed Fanny very much indeed. He has spent 'A Night among the Pines':

I thought I had re-discovered one of those truths which are revealed to savages and hid from political economists: at the least I had discovered a new pleasure for myself. And yet even while I was exulting in my solitude I became aware of a strange lack. I wished a companion to lie near me in the starlight, silent and not moving, but ever within touch. For there is a fellowship more quiet even than solitude, and which, rightly understood, is solitude made perfect. And to live out of doors with the woman a man loves is of all lives the most complete and free. (p. 188)

In the midst of this very difficult situation Stevenson went to Monastier, a town in the mountains near the source of the Loire, and worked hard on *New Arabian Nights* and *Edinburgh: Picturesque Notes* (ironically the distance from home

[6] As quoted in Maixner, *Robert Louis Stevenson*, 62.

afforded by exile allowed him, as did later the even greater distance of the South Seas, to write with much more assurance of his native country and his native city). He completed his work in Monastier, made some sketches of the nearby countryside, and then, on 23 September, set out with his donkey on his eleven days' journey through the Cevennes. It was, as Fanny Stevenson tells us, a journey much more to his taste than the Inland Voyage, 'having elements of romance the former lacked'. It appealed to the imagination of a 'lantern-bearer'.[7]

During the journey Stevenson followed his usual practice and kept a diary; this was his preferred method with travel writing—to keep a diary and, if need be, add to it later. The diary, now published as *The Cevennes Journal*, shows revealing differences from the text of the *Travels*. Stevenson was well aware of his public and of the need to tailor his image accordingly. Apart from a number of stylistic revisions, there are certain significant omissions: Stevenson left out details of just how cruel he had had to be to the recalcitrant donkey in order to make her move a little faster; he also omitted to record exactly how affected he had been by his experiences at the Trappist Monastery of Our Lady of the Snows—the very moving prayers in the *Journal*, for example, find no place in the *Travels*. This characteristic prayer for friends is one such:

God who has given us the love of women, and the friendship of men keep alive in our hearts the sense of old fellowship and tenderness; make offences to be forgotten and services remembered; protect those whom we love in all things and follow them with kindness, so that they may lead simple and unsuffering lives, and in the end may die easily with quiet minds.[8]

Stevenson kept his emotional tracks well covered and, for the published version, clearly felt that such personal reflections were part of 'an emotional "autobiography" ' he was

---

[7] Mrs R. L. Stevenson, 'Prefatory Note' (Tusitala edn. 1923–4), *The Works of Robert Louis Stevenson*, xvii.

[8] *R.L.S. The Cevennes Journal: Notes on a Journey through the French Highlands*, ed. Gordon Golding (1978), 69.

unprepared to share with his readers at this stage in his life.[9] He takes on instead a very different persona, as he dismisses the more intensely felt moments of the *Journal*, stating that, after the Compline Service, he was not surprised that he made his escape 'into the court with somewhat whirling fancies, and stood like a man bewildered in the windy starry night' (p. 175). In the published *Travels* he reacts with some violence to the calm of the monastery; but this, too, the comparison with the *Journal* suggests, may simply be a part of his chosen, constructed self-image.

Material, too, is added to the *Journal* before the work becomes the *Travels*; in particular, Stevenson adds a large amount of descriptive matter about the Camisards, those eighteenth-century Protestant rebels who resisted the French Government. The Camisards, the history and terrain with which they are associated were full of Scots reverberations for Stevenson. All his life, influenced from his earliest years by the stories of his nurse, he had been fascinated by the Covenanters and the tales of the religious struggles in seventeenth-century Scotland—one of his earliest projects was an essay, or perhaps a series of essays (there is no surviving version), on the Covenanters, and to the end of his life he was planning a novel of the 'Killing Time' (surviving only as the fragment *Heathercat*)—and in the Camisards he found a parallel with their struggles.

The rewriting involved in turning the diary into the *Travels* was done during December 1878 and January 1879 in Edinburgh and the book was published in June 1879. It reached a wider audience than had *An Inland Voyage*, and on the whole the critical reception was more favourable. The *Voyage* had called forth some criticism of a certain affectation, what Meredith called Stevenson's 'Osric's vein'. He was careful to maintain a more even and natural style in the *Travels*, and it repaid him well, as Grant Allan in the *Fortnightly Review* remarked:

His *Inland Voyage* struck the keynote of his literary gamut; and the new volume of travel with which he now favours us, has the

---

[9] Richard Holmes, *Footsteps: Adventures of a Romantic Biographer* (1985), 33

self-same happy ring, the self-same light and graceful touch, as if Mr. Stevenson were rather a Frenchman born out of due place, than a Scotsman of the Scots.

Stevenson's work sometimes prompted comments about a certain lack of godliness: his iconoclasm, unconventionality, and Bohemian stance brought him into confrontation with the Edinburgh literary establishment, the strict Presbyterian atmosphere of his home, and, in particular, with his father. The young Louis's *Travels* was guilty on this account: 'The book has the same fault as the "Inland Voyage" for there are three or four irreverent uses of the name God which offend me and must offend many others.' There was some criticism, too, of his alleged cruelty to Modestine (despite Stevenson's efforts to modify this for the published book), including this from an anonymous reviewer in the *Spectator*:

Nothing can be less amusing than to hear how he was obliged to carry his own packages, after fruitless efforts to overload his donkey, unless it is the vivid description he gives of each blow, as it descended on the creature's back. Mr. Stevenson in other works has shown so refined a taste, that it is strange how he can dwell with such placid content on the suffering that he owns to have inflicted on his companion. Raw legs and bleeding skin do not move him in the least.[10]

An essential part of Stevenson's travels was always the book that could and would be made out of them; he travelled self-consciously with this aim as his comments about the dreadful conditions of his 'Inland Voyage' make clear. There is a telling section, too, in the *Travels with a Donkey*: 'For my part I travel not to go anywhere, but to go: I travel for travel's sake. The great affair is to move; to feel the needs and hitches of our life a little more nearly, to get down off this feather-bed of civilisation, and to find the globe granite underfoot and strewn with cutting flints' (p. 163), but the parallel diary entry belies this simple motivation: 'I travel for travel's sake. And to write about it

---

[10] Review quoted in Maixner, *Robert Louis Stevenson*, 65, 64, 72.

'afterwards, if only the public will be so condescending as to read.'[11] To Stevenson, as another omitted diary passage has it, 'A voyage is a piece of autobiography at best'. He is a much more literary, self-conscious, and, in this, a more modern travel writer than the comments in the *Travels* would suggest.

A further perspective on this complex of attitudes towards travel-writing is found in Stevenson's essays: of those which pre-date the *Travels*, 'Roads', first published in 1873, was Stevenson's first paid contribution to a periodical. The essay had been planned during a walk with Colvin in Suffolk earlier in the year, and it sounds a keynote of R.L.S.'s attitude to travel:

And now we come to that last and most subtle quality of all, to that sense of prospect, of outlook, that is brought so powerfully to our minds by a road. In real nature as well as in old landscapes, beneath that impartial daylight in which a whole variegated plain is plunged and saturated, the line of the road leads the eye forth with the vague sense of desire up to the green limit of the horizon. Travel is brought home to us, and we visit in spirit every grove and hamlet that tempts us in the distance. *Sehnsucht*—the passion for what is ever beyond—is livingly expressed in that white riband of possible travel that severs the uneven country: not a ploughman following his plough up the shining furrow, not the blue smoke of any cottage in a hollow, but is brought to us with a sense of nearness and attainability by this wavering line of junction. (p. 240)

Stevenson was, of course, a traveller by temperament; he could not bear even the notion of a life of inaction (Fanny Stevenson attributes this to his 'Scottish unrest'):

For a long while he was fain to content himself with inactive roving. To the end of his life he found the keenest pleasure in the study of a map, especially one of roads. Like Branwell Brontë, of whom he could never speak without emotion, he would sit poring over maps, making imaginary journeys. Like Young Brontë, too, he knew the hours when the railway trains of London and

Paris started, and when outgoing ships left English and French ports.[12]

Other journeys were occasioned by less happy circumstances, however. His invalidism has been overstressed by his critics—how could a very sickly man possibly have survived the appalling conditions on ship and railroad described in *The Amateur Emigrant?*—but invalid he was, troubled throughout his life by respiratory problems and threatened with tuberculosis. In 1873 he became very ill and, after the intervention of Colvin, saw a doctor who insisted that he go and rest, alone, in France. Menton, a coastal town near Nice, was a favourite resort of consumptives in the 1870s, but R.L.S. did not find it an inspiring setting. He did not relish being 'among the wounded soldiery of mankind . . . all shut up together in some basking angle of the Riviera, walking a dusty promenade or sitting in dusty olive-yards within earshot of interminable and unchanging surf' (p. 309). From this experience in the South of France came the essay, 'Ordered South'. It is impossible, as Henry James commented, to read it 'attentively without feeling that it is personal; the reflections it contains are from experience, not from fancy'.[13] Although the places are beautiful,

In his heart of hearts he has to confess that it is not beautiful for him . . . He is like an enthusiast leading about with him a stolid, indifferent tourist. There is some one by who is out of sympathy with the scene, and is not moved up to the measure of the occasion; and that some one is himself . . . He seems to himself to touch things with muffled hands and to see them through a veil . . . Many a white town that sits far out on the promontory, many a comely fold of wood on the mountain-side, beckons and allures his imagination day after day, and is yet as inaccessible to his feet as the clefts and gorges of the clouds. (pp. 245–6, 250)

The essay is a fascinating commentary on the 'imprisoned life' of the Victorian invalid confined by his disabilities and,

[12] Mrs R. L. Stevenson, Prefatory Note, *Works* (Tusitala edn.), vol. xvii p. xiv.
[13] *Henry James and Robert Louis Stevenson: A Record of Friendship and Criticism*, edited with an introduction by Janet Adam Smith (1948), 142.

as in this passage, forced into a splitting and division of self. (Always fascinated by all kinds of duality and doubling, Stevenson repays comparison here with Borges.[14])

'Ordered South' is the response of an ailing man to one part of France; very different are those reactions registered in essays R.L.S. wrote about the village of Barbizon and the Forest of Fontainebleau—'Forest Notes' was based on his visit to the latter in March and April 1875 and was written during the following Summer. It registers enchantment with the place and its charm (indeed, to such an extent that retrospectively R.L.S. felt the essay was 'too sweet to be wholesome').[15] He was also delighted to spend time in a place where there was a kind of moral abeyance:

You forget all your scruples and live a while in peace and freedom, and for the moment only. For here, all is absent that can stimulate to moral feeling. Such people as you see may be old, or toil-worn, or sorry; but you see them framed in the forest, like figures on a painted canvas; and for you, they are not people in any living and kindly sense. (p. 285)

The forest had been a source of freedom and inspiration since the early nineteenth century: 'Half the famous writers of modern France have had their word to say about Fontainebleau' (p. 284); and both Barbizon and the village of Grez where Stevenson spent much time had been peopled by writers and artists. Theodore Rousseau had settled at Barbizon in 1836, and Jean François Millet in 1849. The members of the Barbizon community were socialist in politics, advocates of the natural life, and fought to preserve the forest.

Shortly after the death of Millet in 1875, Stevenson was 'A consistent Barbizonian' (p. 296), at a time when there was a lively group of artists living as part of the community. This was, R.L.S. felt later an essentially French enterprise:

Painters, sculptors, writers, singers, I have seen all of these in Barbizon; and some were sulky and some blatant and inane; but one and all entered at once into the spirit of the association. This

[14] Nicholas Rankin develops this comparison in *Dead Man's Chest*, 85–6.
[15] See *Works* (Tusitala edn.), xxxii. 23.

singular society is purely French, a creature of French virtues, and possibly of French defects. It cannot be imitated by the English. (p. 300)

This 'purely artistic society' was an excellent place for the young artist at that stage of his life when he was 'too much occupied with style to be aware of the necessity for any matter'. He could work at his trade and think only 'of his material and nothing else'. This was an opportunity absent at home:

Here, in England, too many painters and writers dwell dispersed, unshielded, among the intelligent bourgeois. These, when they are not merely indifferent, prate to him about the lofty aims and moral influence of art. And this is the lad's ruin. For art is, first of all, and last of all, a trade. (p. 292)

The young Lloyd Osbourne, writing of R.L.S. at this period and of his attitude to the bourgeoisie, remarks that it was the custom of all members of the Barbizon group, living in the spell of the *vie de Bohème* to 'rail at the respectable and well-to-do; R.L.S.'s favourite expression was "a common banker", used as one might refer to a common labourer'. Lloyd came to feel that such people were to be despised: 'They belonged to a strange race called Philistines, and were sternly to be kept in their place. If any had dared to install them in the Hotel Chevillon they would have found it a nest of hornets.'[16]

Away from the bourgeoisie, the young artist was 'saturated in an atmosphere of style . . . He enjoyed a strenuous idleness . . . and still floating like music through his brain, foresights of great works that Shakespeare might be proud to have conceived, headless epics, glorious torsos of drama, and words that were alive with import' (pp. 300–1). There was, however, a drawback: 'in such a place, it was hardly possible to write.'

The need to have an appropriate place to write is a recurring preoccupation in the travel writings; it is some-

---

[16] Lloyd Osbourne, 'Stevenson at Twenty-Six', in *Works* (Tusitala edn.), vol. xvii, p. x.

thing of which R.L.S. is very much aware even when confined, for reasons of health, in his 'mountain prison' in the Alps. The *Swiss Notes*, which resulted from this experience in the winter of 1880–1, as well as offering an insight into their author's rebellions about confinement, also draw attention to one of his great strengths as an essayist, what Henry James called his 'note of visibility' and Jeremy Treglown has more recently termed his 'painterly' quality. Indeed, the interest of the essays is focused in considerable part on looking at landscape.[17] This ability is present throughout Stevenson's travel writings; in the longer texts and the essays included in this volume, in his American writings following the *Travels with a Donkey* (and published as *The Silverado Squatters* and *The Amateur Emigrant*), and in his travel works written towards the end of his life from the South Seas. The texts in this edition pre-date the great flowering of Stevenson's fictional art (with the exception, that is, of *Treasure Island* which was written in the same year as the *Swiss Notes* pieces), but there is no doubt that the fine scene-painting of these essays is crucial, too, to the effects of his fiction—notably to the seascapes of *Treasure Island*, to the Scottish scenes of *Kidnapped* and *Catriona* (1886 and 1893), and to the Scottish and North American scenes of The *Master of Ballantrae* (1889). There is in fact no clear-cut division between Stevenson's skill in travel writing and in fiction; as he wrote in an essay on Whitman, 'There is a sense of course in which all true books are books of travel . . . '.[18]

---

[17] *Henry James and Robert Louis Stevenson*, 258; Treglown, Introduction to *The Lantern Bearers*, p. xiv.
[18] 'Walt Whitman' (Tusitala edn.), xxvii. 62.

NOTE ON THE TEXTS

The texts are those included in the Tusitala Edition (1923–4); in the case of *An Inland Voyage* and *Travels with a Donkey* these have been checked and amended with the first book editions. In the case of the essays these have been checked with the first periodical versions.

SELECT BIBLIOGRAPHY

Place of publication London unless stated otherwise.

BIBLIOGRAPHY

GEORGE H. FORD (ed.), *Victorian Fiction: A Second Guide to Research* (Cambridge, Mass., 1978) [includes a chapter on R.L.S. by Robert Kiely].

GEORGE L. MCKAY, *The Stevenson Library of Edwin J. Beinecke*, 6 vols. (New Haven, Conn., 1958).

W. F. PRIDEAUX, *Bibliography of Robert Louis Stevenson* (1903; revised edn., 1917).

ROGER G. SWEARINGEN, *The Prose Writings of Robert Louis Stevenson: A Guide* (1980).

EDITIONS

Collected Editions of the works of R.L.S. include:

The Edinburgh Edition, ed. Sidney Colvin (1894–8).

The Pentland Edition, with bibliographical notes by Edmund Gosse (1906–7).

The Swanston Edition, with an Introduction by Andrew Lang (1911–12).

The Vailima Edition, ed. Lloyd Osbourne, with Prefatory Notes by Fanny van de Grift Stevenson (1922–3).

The Tusitala Edition (1923–4).

LETTERS

Vailima Letters (1895).

The Letters of Robert Louis Stevenson to His Family and Friends, ed. Sidney Colvin (1899; new edn., 1911).

Henry James and Robert Louis Stevenson: A Record of Friendship and Criticism, ed. Janet Adam Smith (1948).

R.L.S.: Stevenson's Letters to Charles Baxter, ed. De Lancey Ferguson and Marshall Waingrow (New Haven, Conn., 1956).

BIOGRAPHY

GRAHAM BALFOUR, *The Life of Robert Louis Stevenson* (1901).

JENNI CALDER, *R.L.S.: A Life Study* (1980).

ELSIE NOBLE CALDWELL, *Last Witness for Robert Louis Stevenson* (Norman, Okla., 1960).

DAVID DAICHES, *Robert Louis Stevenson and His World* (1973).

J. C. FURNAS, *Voyage to Windward* (1951).

J. A. HAMMERTON, *In the Track of R. L. Stevenson and Elsewhere in Old France* (Bristol and London, 1907).

JAMES POPE HENNESSY, *Robert Louis Stevenson* (1974).

RICHARD HOLMES, *Footsteps: Adventures of a Romantic Biographer* (1985).

NICHOLAS RANKIN, *Dead Man's Chest: Travels After Robert Louis Stevenson* (1989).

CRITICISM AND BACKGROUND

ALANNA KNIGHT, *Robert Louis Stevenson Treasury* (1985).

PAUL MAIXNER (ed.) *Robert Louis Stevenson: The Critical Heritage* (1981).

GEORGE L. MCKAY, *Some Notes on Robert Louis Stevenson, His Finances and His Agents and Publishers* (New Haven, Conn., 1958).

ANDREW NOBLE (ed.), *Robert Louis Stevenson* (1983).

A CHRONOLOGY OF
ROBERT LOUIS STEVENSON

1850 Born in Edinburgh, 13 November.

1862 3 Excursions with his parents to Germany, the Riviera, and Italy.

1867 Enters Edinburgh University.

1871 Makes decision to abandon engineering and study law.

1872 Passes preliminary examinations for the Scottish Bar.

1873 Crisis with his father over agnosticism; following this, and a bout of ill health, goes to Suffolk to stay with his Balfour cousins. Meets Frances Sitwell, one of the most important influences on his life until his marriage. Beginning of his friendship with Sidney Colvin. Further ill health sends R.L.S. south to France at the end of the year; Stevenson's first paid periodical essay, 'Roads' published in the *Portfolio* in December.

1874 At Menton in France. Returns to Edinburgh in May and resumes reading for the Bar. Contributes to the *Cornhill Magazine*. 'Ordered South' published in *Macmillan's Magazine*.

1875 Meets W. E. Henley in Edinburgh. Called to the Scottish Bar but does not practise as an advocate. Visits France and joins his cousin, Bob Stevenson, at the artists' colony at Barbizon, Fontainebleau, in March and April 1875. Contributes to *Vanity Fair* and the *Academy*.

1876 Makes a canoe trip in September around the canals of northern France, later to be recorded in *An Inland Voyage*. Meets Fanny Osbourne, a married women with two children, from Indiana. Publication of 'Forest Notes' in May, 'Walking Tours' in *Cornhill Magazine* in June.

1877 Divides year between Edinburgh, London, and Fontainebleau. Publication of 'An Old Song' in *London*. Rewrites his journal for *An Inland Voyage*.

1878   Fanny returns to her husband in California in August
        and eventually divorce proceedings begin. Soon after
        her departure R.L.S. goes on travels with his donkey,
        Modestine, in the Cevennes. Publication of *An Inland
        Voyage* in April and *Edinburgh: Picturesque Notes*.

1879   Divides time between London, Scotland, and France.
        Very ill in March and April. Sets off on journey to
        join Fanny in America. *Travels with a Donkey* published.

1880   Marries Fanny in San Francisco in May. They stay in
        the Californian mountains and then return to Scot-
        land. Publication of *Deacon Brodie*, R.L.S.'s first play
        in collaboration with W. E. Henley.

1881   At Braemar, writes fifteen chapters of *Treasure Island*.
        Visits Davos in Switzerland where *Treasure Island* is
        completed. Publication of *Virginibus Puerisque*. Publica-
        tion of *Swiss Notes* in the *Pall Mall Gazette*.

1882   At Davos, then he and Fanny move to Hyères, France,
        their main home from March 1883 to July 1884.
        Publication of *Familiar Studies of Men and Books* and *New
        Arabian Nights*.

1883   Publication of *The Silverado Squatters* and *Treasure Island*.
        Serialization of *The Black Arrow* in *Young Folks* (June to
        October).

1884   Illness at Nice in January and further serious ill health
        in May. The Stevensons return to England at about
        the same time as an outbreak of cholera at Hyères.
        They go to Bournemouth, their home from Septem-
        ber of this year until August 1887. Publication of
        Austin Guinea and *Beau Austin*, both in collaboration
        with W. E. Henley. In May 'Fontainebleau: Village
        Communities of Painters' appears in the *Magazine of
        Art*.

1885   Moves to 'Skerryvore', Bournemouth (the house was
        a wedding present from Thomas Stevenson to his
        daughter-in-law). Henry James spends a long visit in
        Bournemouth. Publication of *A Child's Garden of Verses*;
        Prince Otto; *More New Arabian Nights*; *The Dynamiter*, with
        Fanny Stevenson; *Macaire*, with W. E. Henley.

1886   Publication of *The Strange Case of Dr Jekyll and Mr Hyde*,
        Stevenson's first large-scale British and American suc-

cess, and *Kidnapped* (previously serialized in *Young Folks*, May–July 1886).

1887   Thomas Stevenson dies in May. In August, R.L.S. sails for America with his mother, Fanny, and Lloyd. For reasons of health stays at Saranac in the Adirondack Mountains. Publication of *The Merry Men and Other Tales and Fables*; *Underwoods*; *Memories and Portraits*; and *A Memoir of Fleeming Jenkin*.

1888   Scribner's, Stevenson's American publishers, commission a volume on the South Seas. Voyage on the yacht *Casco* to the Marquesas, the Paumotus, Tahiti, and then to Hawaii. Publication of *The Black Arrow* and *The Misadventures of John Nicholson*.

1889   Mrs Thomas Stevenson returns to Scotland. R.L.S., Fanny, and Lloyd remain in Honolulu. Voyage on the trading schooner *Equator* to the Gilbert Islands and then to Samoa. Publication of *The Wrong Box*, with Lloyd, and *The Master of Ballantrae*. Buys estate at Opolu, Samoa.

1890   A third voyage in the trading steamer *Janet Nicholl* in the Eastern and Western Pacific. Further ill health, including a serious haemorrhage, leads the Stevensons to realize that R.L.S. can never again leave a tropical climate. In October they take up residence at Opolu. Publication of *In the South Seas* and *Ballads*.

1892   Becomes involved in Samoan politics. Publication of *A Footnote to History*, *Across the Plains*, and *The Wrecker*.

1893   War breaks out in Samoa. Stevenson supports Mataafa. Visits Honolulu. Publication of *Island Nights' Entertainments* and *Catriona*.

1894   The tribe of Mataafa build 'The Road of Loving Hearts' in gratitude to R.L.S. for helping their cause. Publication of *The Ebb-Tide*. Dies on 3 December of cerebral haemorrhage. *Weir of Hermiston* published posthumously.

AN INLAND VOYAGE

'Thus sang they in the English boat.'

MARVELL*

PREFACE TO THE FIRST EDITION

To equip so small a book with a preface is, I am half afraid, to sin against proportion. But a preface is more than an author can resist, for it is the reward of his labours. When the foundation stone is laid, the architect appears with his plans, and struts for an hour before the public eye. So with the writer in his preface: he may have never a word to say, but he must show himself for a moment in the portico, hat in hand, and with an urbane demeanour.

It is best, in such circumstance, to represent a delicate shade of manner between humility and superiority: as if the book had been written by some one else, and you had merely run over it and inserted what was good. But for my part I have not yet learned the trick to that perfection; I am not yet able to dissemble the warmth of my sentiments towards a reader; and if I meet him on the threshold, it is to invite him in with country cordiality.

To say truth, I had no sooner finished reading this little book in proof than I was seized upon by a distressing apprehension.

It occurred to me that I might not only be the first to read these pages, but the last as well; that I might have pioneered this very smiling tract of country all in vain, and find not a soul to follow in my steps. The more I thought, the more I disliked the notion; until the distaste grew into a sort of panic terror, and I rushed into this Preface, which is no more than an advertisement for readers.

What am I to say for my book? Caleb and Joshua* brought back from Palestine a formidable bunch of grapes; alas! my book produces naught so nourishing; and for the matter of that, we live in an age when people prefer a definition to any quantity of fruit.

I wonder, would a negative be found enticing? for, from the negative point of view, I flatter myself this volume has a certain stamp. Although it runs to considerably upwards of two hundred pages, it contains not a single reference to the imbecility of God's universe, nor so much as a single hint that I could have made a better one myself—I really do not know where my head can have been. I seemed to have forgotten all that makes it glorious to be man. 'T is an omission that renders the book philosophically unimportant; but I am in hopes the eccentricity may please in frivolous circles.

To the friend who accompanied me I owe many thanks already, indeed I wish I owed him nothing else; but at this moment I feel towards him an almost exaggerated tenderness. He, at least, will become my reader—if it were only to follow his own travels alongside of mine.

R. L. S.

DEDICATION

TO
SIR WALTER GRINDLAY SIMPSON*
BART.

My dear 'Cigarette,'

It was enough that you should have shared so liberally in the rains and portages of our voyage; that you should have had so hard a paddle to recover the derelict 'Arethusa' on the flooded Oise; and that you should thenceforth have piloted a mere wreck of mankind to Origny Sainte-Benoîte and a supper so eagerly desired. It was perhaps more than enough, as you once somewhat piteously complained, that I should have set down all the strong language to you, and kept the appropriate reflections for myself. I could not in decency expose you to share the disgrace of another and more public shipwreck. But now that this voyage of ours is going into a cheap edition, that peril, we shall hope, is at an end, and I may put your name on the burgee.

But I cannot pause till I have lamented the fate of our two ships. That, sir, was not a fortunate day when we projected the possession of a canal barge; it was not a fortunate day when we shared our day-dream with the most hopeful of day-dreamers. For a while, indeed, the world looked smilingly. The barge was procured and christened, and, as the 'Eleven Thousand Virgins of Cologne,' lay for some months, the admired of all admirers, in a pleasant river and under the walls of an ancient town; M. Mattras, the accomplished carpenter of Moret, had made her a centre of emulous labour; and you will not have forgotten the amount of sweet champagne consumed in the inn at the bridge end, to give zeal to the workmen and speed to the work. On the financial aspect, I would not willingly dwell. The 'Eleven Thousand Virgins of Cologne' rotted in the stream where she was beautified. She felt not the impulse of the breeze; she was never harnessed to the patient track-horse. And when at length she was sold, by the indignant carpenter of Moret, there were sold along with

her the 'Arethusa' and the 'Cigarette,' she of cedar, she, as we knew
so keenly on a portage, of solid-hearted English oak. Now these historic
vessels fly the tricolour and are known by new and alien names.

R. L. S.

ANTWERP TO BOOM

We made a great stir in Antwerp Docks. A stevedore and a lot of dock porters took up the two canoes, and ran with them for the slip. A crowd of children followed cheering. The *Cigarette* went off in a splash and a bubble of small breaking water. Next moment the *Arethusa* was after her. A steamer was coming down, men on the paddle-box shouted hoarse warnings, the stevedore and his porters were bawling from the quay. But in a stroke or two the canoes were away out in the middle of the Scheldt, and all steamers, and stevedores, and other 'long-shore vanities were left behind.

The sun shone brightly; the tide was making four jolly miles an hour; the wind blew steadily, with occasional squalls. For my part, I had never been in a canoe under sail in my life; and my first experiment out in the middle of this big river was not made without some trepidation. What would happen when the wind first caught my little canvas? I suppose it was almost as trying a venture into the regions of the unknown as to publish a first book, or to marry. But my doubts were not of long duration; and in five minutes you will not be surprised to learn that I had tied my sheet.

I own I was a little struck by this circumstance myself; of course, in company with the rest of my fellow-men, I had always tied the sheet in a sailing-boat; but in so little and crank a concern as a canoe, and with these charging squalls, I was not prepared to find myself follow the same principle; and it inspired me with some contemptuous views of our regard for life. It is certainly easier to smoke with the sheet fastened; but I had never before weighed a comfortable pipe of tobacco against an obvious risk, and gravely elected for the comfortable pipe. It is a commonplace, that we cannot answer for ourselves before we have been tried. But it is not so common a reflection, and surely more consoling, that we usually find ourselves a great deal braver and better than we thought. I believe this is every one's experience: but an apprehension that they may belie themselves in the future prevents mankind from trumpeting this cheerful sentiment abroad. I wish sincerely, for it would have saved me much trouble, there had been some one to put me in a good heart about life when I was younger; to tell me how dangers are most portentous on a distant sight; and how the good in a man's spirit will not suffer itself to be overlaid, and rarely or never deserts him in the hour of need. But we are all for tootling on the sentimental flute in literature; and not a man among us will go to the head of the march to sound the heady drums.

It was agreeable upon the river. A barge or two went past laden with hay. Reeds and willows bordered the stream; and cattle and grey, venerable horses came and hung their mild heads over the embankment. Here and there was a pleasant village among trees, with a noisy shipping-yard; here and there a villa in a lawn. The wind served us well up the Scheldt and thereafter up the Rupel; and we were running pretty free when we began to sight the brickyards of Boom, lying for a long way on the right bank of the river. The left bank was still green and pastoral, with alleys of trees along the embankment, and here and there a flight of steps to serve a ferry, where perhaps there sat a woman with her elbows on her knees, or an old gentleman with a staff and silver spectacles. But Boom and its brickyards grew smokier and shabbier with every minute; until a great church with a clock, and a wooden bridge over the river, indicated the central quarters of the town.

Boom is not a nice place, and is only remarkable for one thing: that the majority of the inhabitants have a private opinion that they can speak English, which is not justified by fact. This gave a kind of haziness to our intercourse. As for the Hôtel de la Navigation, I think it is the worst feature of the place. It boasts of a sanded parlour, with a bar at one end, looking on the street; and another sanded parlour, darker and colder, with an empty bird-cage and a tricolour subscription box by way of sole adornment, where we made shift to dine in the company of three uncommunicative engineer apprentices and a silent bagman. The food, as usual in Belgium, was of a nondescript occasional character; indeed I have never been able to detect anything in the nature of a meal among this pleasing people; they seem to peck and trifle with viands all day long in an amateur spirit: tentatively French, truly German, and somehow falling between the two.

The empty bird-cage, swept and garnished, and with no trace of the old piping favourite, save where two wires had been pushed apart to hold its lump of sugar, carried with it a sort of graveyard cheer. The engineer apprentices would have nothing to say to us, nor indeed to the bagman; but talked low and sparingly to one another, or raked us in the gaslight with a gleam of spectacles. For though handsome lads, they were all (in the Scots phrase) barnacled.*

There was an English maid in the hotel, who had been long enough out of England to pick up all sorts of funny foreign idioms, and all sorts of curious foreign ways, which need not here be specified. She spoke to us very fluently in her jargon, asked us information as to the manners of the present day in England, and obligingly corrected us when we attempted to answer. But as we were dealing with a woman, perhaps our information was not so much thrown away as it appeared. The sex likes to pick up knowledge and yet preserve its superiority. It is good policy, and almost necessary in the circumstances. If a man finds a woman admires him, were it only for his acquaintance with geography, he will begin at once to build upon the admiration. It is only by unintermittent snubbing that the pretty ones can keep us in our place. Men, as Miss Howe or Miss Harlowe* would have said, 'are such *encroachers*.' For my part, I am body and soul with the women; and after a well-married couple, there is nothing so beautiful in the world as the myth of the divine huntress. It is no use for a man to take to the woods; we know him; St. Anthony tried the same thing long ago, and had a pitiful time of it by all accounts. But there is this about some women, which overtops the best gymnosophist among men, that they suffice to themselves, and can walk in a high and cold zone without the countenance of any trousered being. I declare, although the reverse of a professed ascetic, I am more obliged to women for this ideal than I should be to the majority of them, or, indeed, to any but one, for a spontaneous kiss. There is nothing so encouraging as the spectacle of self-sufficiency. And when I think of the slim and lovely maidens, running the woods all night to the note of Diana's horn; moving among the old oaks, as fancy-free as they; things of the forest and the starlight, not touched by the commotion of man's hot and turbid life—although there are plenty other ideals that I should prefer—I find my heart beat at the thought of this one. 'Tis to fail in life, but to fail with what a grace! That is not lost which is not regretted. And where—here slips out the male—where would be much of the glory of inspiring love, if there were no contempt to overcome?

ON THE WILLEBROEK CANAL

Next morning, when we set forth on the Willebroek Canal, the rain began heavy and chill. The water of the canal stood at about the drinking temperature of tea; and under this cold aspersion, the surface was covered with steam. The exhilaration of departure, and the easy motion of the boats under each stroke of the paddles, supported us through this misfortune while it lasted; and when the cloud passed and the sun came out again, our spirits went up above the range of stay-at-home humours. A good breeze rustled and shivered in the rows of trees that bordered the canal. The leaves flickered in and out of the light in tumultuous masses. It seemed sailing weather to eye and ear; but down between the banks, the wind reached us only in faint and desultory puffs. There was hardly enough to steer by. Progress was intermittent and unsatisfactory. A jocular person, of marine antecedents, hailed us from the tow-path with a '*C'est vite, mais c'est long.*'*

The canal was busy enough. Every now and then we met or overtook a long string of boats, with great green tillers; high sterns with a window on either side of the rudder, and perhaps a jug or a flower-pot in one of the windows; a dingy following behind; a woman busied about the day's dinner, and a handful of children. These barges were all tied one behind the other with tow ropes, to the number of twenty-five or thirty; and the line was headed and kept in motion by a steamer of strange construction. It had neither paddle-wheel nor screw; but by some gear not rightly comprehensible to the unmechanical mind, it fetched up over its bow a small bright chain which lay along the bottom of the canal, and paying it out again over the stern, dragged itself forward, link by link, with its whole retinue of loaded scows. Until one had found out the key to the enigma, there was something solemn and uncomfortable in the progress of one of these trains, as it moved gently along the water with nothing to mark its advance but an eddy alongside dying away into the wake.

Of all the creatures of commercial enterprise, a canal barge is by far the most delightful to consider. It may spread its sails, and then you see it sailing high above the tree-tops and the windmill, sailing on the aqueduct, sailing through the green corn-lands: the most picturesque of things amphibious. Or the horse plods along at a foot-pace as if there were no such thing as business in the world; and the man dreaming at the tiller sees the same spire on the horizon all day long. It is a mystery how things ever get to their destination at this rate; and to see the barges waiting their turn at a lock, affords a fine lesson of how easily the world may be taken. There should be many contented spirits on board, for such a life is both to travel and to stay at home.

The chimney smokes for dinner as you go along; the banks of the canal slowly unroll their scenery to contemplative eyes; the barge floats by great forests and through great cities with their public buildings and their lamps at night; and for the bargee, in his floating home, 'travelling abed,' it is merely as if he were listening to another man's story or turning the leaves of a picture book in which he had no concern. He may take his afternoon walk in some foreign country on the banks of the canal, and then come home to dinner at his own fireside.

There is not enough exercise in such a life for any high measure of health; but a high measure of health is only necessary for unhealthy people. The slug of a fellow, who is never ill nor well, has a quiet time of it in life, and dies all the easier.

I am sure I would rather be a bargee than occupy any position under Heaven that required attendance at an office. There are few callings, I should say, where a man gives up less of his liberty in return for regular meals. The bargee is on shipboard; he is master in his own ship; he can land whenever he will; he can never be kept beating off a lee-shore a whole frosty night when the sheets are as hard as iron; and so far as I can make out, time stands as nearly still with him as is compatible with the return of bedtime or the dinner-hour. It is not easy to see why a bargee should ever die.

Half-way between Willebroek and Villevorde, in a beautiful reach of canal like a squire's avenue, we went ashore to lunch. There were two eggs, a junk of bread, and a bottle of wine on board the *Arethusa*; and two eggs and an Etna cooking apparatus on board the *Cigarette*. The master of the latter boat smashed one of the eggs in the course of disembarkation; but observing pleasantly that it might still be cooked *à la papier*, he dropped it into the Etna, in its covering of Flemish newspaper. We landed in a blink of fine weather; but we had not been two minutes ashore before the wind freshened into half a gale, and the rain began to patter on our shoulders. We sat as close about the Etna as we could. The spirits burned with great ostentation; the grass caught flame every minute or two, and had to be trodden out; and before long there were several burnt fingers of the party. But the solid quantity of cookery accomplished was out of proportion with so much display; and when we desisted, after two applications of the fire, the sound egg was a little more than loo-warm; and as for *à la papier*, it was a cold and sordid *fricassée* of printer's ink and broken egg-shell. We made shift to roast the other two by putting them close to the burning spirits, and that with better success. And then we uncorked the bottle of wine, and sat down in a ditch with our canoe aprons over our knees. It rained smartly. Discomfort, when it is honestly uncomfortable and makes no nauseous pretensions to the contrary, is a vastly humorous business; and people well steeped and stupefied in the open air are in a good vein for laughter. From this point of view, even egg *à la papier* offered by way of food may pass muster as a sort of accessory to the fun. But this manner of jest, although it may be taken in good part, does not invite repetition; and from that time forward the Etna voyaged like a gentleman in the locker of the *Cigarette*.

It is almost unnecessary to mention that when lunch was over and we got aboard again and made sail, the wind promptly died away. The rest of the journey to Villevorde we still spread our canvas to the unfavouring air, and with now and then a puff, and now and then a spell of paddling, drifted along from lock to lock between the orderly trees.

It was a fine, green, fat landscape, or rather a mere green water-lane going on from village to village. Things had a settled look, as in places long lived in. Crop-headed children spat upon us from the bridges as we went below, with a true conservative feeling. But even more conservative were the fishermen, intent upon their floats, who let us go by without one glance. They perched upon sterlings and buttresses and along the slope of the embankment, gently occupied. They were indifferent like pieces of dead nature. They did not move any more than if they had been fishing in an old Dutch print. The leaves fluttered, the water lapped, but they continued in one stay, like so many churches established by law. You might have trepanned every one of their innocent heads and found no more than so much coiled fishing line below their skulls. I do not care for your stalwart fellows in india-rubber stockings breasting up mountain torrents with a salmon rod; but I do dearly love the class of man who plies his unfruitful art forever and a day by still and depopulated waters.

At the last lock, just beyond Villevorde, there was a lock mistress who spoke French comprehensibly, and told us we were still a couple of leagues from Brussels. At the same place the rain began again. It fell in straight, parallel lines, and the surface of the canal was thrown up into an infinity of little crystal fountains. There were no beds to be had in the neighbourhood. Nothing for it but to lay the sails aside and address ourselves to steady paddling in the rain.

Beautiful country houses, with clocks and long lines of shuttered windows, and fine old trees standing in groves and avenues, gave a rich and sombre aspect in the rain and the deepening dusk to the shores of the canal. I seem to have seen something of the same effect in engravings: opulent landscapes, deserted and overhung with the passage of storm. And throughout we had the escort of a hooded cart, which trotted shabbily along the tow-path, and kept at an almost uniform distance in our wake.

THE ROYAL SPORT NAUTIQUE

The rain took off near Laeken. But the sun was already down; the air was chill; and we had scarcely a dry stitch between the pair of us. Nay, now we found ourselves near the end of the *Allée Verte*, and on the very threshold of Brussels, we were confronted by a serious difficulty. The shores were closely lined by canal boats waiting their turn at the lock. Nowhere was there any convenient landing place; nowhere so much as a stableyard to leave the canoes in for the night. We scrambled ashore and entered an *estaminet* where some sorry fellows were drinking with the landlord. The landlord was pretty round with us; he knew of no coach-house or stable-yard, nothing of the sort; and seeing we had come with no mind to drink, he did not conceal his impatience to be rid of us. One of the sorry fellows came to the rescue. Somewhere in the corner of the basin there was a slip, he informed us, and something else besides, not very clearly defined by him, but hopefully construed by his hearers.

Sure enough there was the slip in the corner of the basin; and at the top of it two nice-looking lads in boating clothes. The *Arethusa* addressed himself to these. One of them said there would be no difficulty about a night's lodging for our boats; and the other, taking a cigarette from his lips, inquired if they were made by Searle and Son. The name was quite an introduction. Half-a-dozen other young men came out of a boat-house bearing the superscription ROYAL SPORT NAUTIQUE, and joined in the talk. They were all very polite, voluble, and enthusiastic; and their discourse was interlarded with English boating terms, and the names of English boat-builders and English clubs. I do not know, to my shame, any spot in my native land where I should have been so warmly received by the same number of people. We were English boating-men, and the Belgian boating-men fell upon our necks. I wonder if French Huguenots were as cordially greeted by English Protestants

when they came across the Channel out of great tribulation.* But, after all, what religion knits people so closely as
a common sport?

The canoes were carried into the boat-house; they were
washed down for us by the club servants, the sails were
hung out to dry, and everything made as snug and tidy as
a picture. And in the meanwhile we were led upstairs by
our new-found brethren, for so more than one of them
stated the relationship, and made free of their lavatory. This
one lent us soap, that one a towel, a third and fourth helped
us to undo our bags. And all the time such questions, such
assurances of respect and sympathy! I declare I never knew
what glory was before.

'Yes, yes, the *Royal Sport Nautique* is the oldest club in
Belgium.'

'We number two hundred.'

'We'—this is not a substantive speech, but an abstract of
many speeches, the impression left upon my mind after a
great deal of talk; and very youthful, pleasant, natural, and
patriotic it seems to me to be—'We have gained all races,
except those where we were cheated by the French.'

'You must leave all your wet things to be dried.'

'O! *entre frères!* In any boat-house in England we should
find the same.' (I cordially hope they might.)

'*En Angleterre, vous employez des sliding-seats, n'est-ce pas?*'

'We are all employed in commerce during the day; but
in the evening, *voyez vous, nous sommes sérieux.*'

These were the words. They were all employed over the
frivolous mercantile concerns of Belgium during the day;
but in the evening they found some hours for the serious
concerns of life. I may have a wrong idea of wisdom, but
I think that was a very wise remark. People connected with
literature and philosophy are busy all their days in getting
rid of second-hand notions and false standards. It is their
profession, in the sweat of their brows, by dogged thinking,
to recover their old fresh view of life, and distinguish what
they really and originally like from what they have only
learned to tolerate perforce. And these Royal Nautical
Sportsmen had the distinction still quite legible in their

hearts. They had still those clean perceptions of what is nice and nasty, what is interesting and what is dull, which envious old gentlemen refer to as illusions. The nightmare illusion of middle age, the bear's hug of custom gradually squeezing the life out of a man's soul, had not yet begun for these happy-starred young Belgians. They still knew that the interest they took in their business was a trifling affair compared to their spontaneous, long-suffering affection for nautical sports. To know what you prefer, instead of humbly saying Amen to what the world tells you you ought to prefer, is to have kept your soul alive. Such a man may be generous; he may be honest in something more than the commercial sense; he may love his friends with an elective, personal sympathy, and not accept them as an adjunct of the station to which he has been called. He may be a man, in short, acting on his own instincts, keeping in his own shape that God made him in; and not a mere crank in the social engine-house, welded on principles that he does not understand, and for purposes that he does not care for.

For will anyone dare to tell me that business is more entertaining than fooling among boats? He must have never seen a boat, or never seen an office, who says so. And for certain the one is a great deal better for the health. There should be nothing so much a man's business as his amusements. Nothing but money-grubbing can be put forward to the contrary; no one but

> Mammon, the least erected spirit that fell
> From Heaven,*

durst risk a word in answer. It is but a lying cant that would represent the merchant and the banker as people disinterestedly toiling for mankind, and then most useful when they are most absorbed in their transactions; for the man is more important than his services. And when my Royal Nautical Sportsman shall have so far fallen from his hopeful youth that he cannot pluck up an enthusiasm over anything but his ledger, I venture to doubt whether he will be near so nice a fellow, and whether he would welcome, with so good a grace, a couple of drenched Englishmen paddling into Brussels in the dusk.

When we had changed our wet clothes and drunk a glass of pale ale to the club's prosperity, one of their number escorted us to a hotel. He would not join us at our dinner, but he had no objection to a glass of wine. Enthusiasm is very wearing; and I begin to understand why prophets were unpopular in Judæa, where they were best known. For three stricken hours did this excellent young man sit beside us to dilate on boats and boat-races; and before he left, he was kind enough to order our bedroom candles.

We endeavoured now and again to change the subject; but the diversion did not last a moment: the Royal Nautical Sportsman bridled, shied, answered the question, and then breasted once more into the swelling tide of his subject. I call it his subject; but I think it was he who was subjected. The *Arethusa*, who holds all racing as a creature of the devil, found himself in a pitiful dilemma. He durst not own his ignorance for the honour of Old England, and spoke away about English clubs and English oarsmen whose fame had never before come to his ears. Several times, and once, above all, on the question of sliding-seats, he was within an ace of exposure. As for the *Cigarette*, who has rowed races in the heat of his blood, but now disowns these slips of his wanton youth, his case was still more desperate; for the Royal Nautical proposed that he should take an oar in one of their eights on the morrow, to compare the English with the Belgian stroke. I could see my friend perspiring in his chair whenever that particular topic came up. And there was yet another proposal which had the same effect on both of us. It appeared that the champion canoeist of Europe (as well as most other champions) was a Royal Nautical Sportsman. And if we would only wait until the Sunday, this infernal paddler would be so condescending as to accompany us on our next stage. Neither of us had the least desire to drive the coursers of the sun against Apollo.

When the young man was gone, we countermanded our candles, and ordered some brandy and water. The great billows had gone over our heads. The Royal Nautical Sportsmen were as nice young fellows as a man would wish to see, but they were a trifle too young and a thought too nautical for us. We began to see that we were old and cynical; we liked ease and the agreeable rambling of the human mind about this and the other subject; we did not want to disgrace our native land by messing an eight, or toiling pitifully in the wake of the champion canoeist. In short, we had recourse to flight. It seemed ungrateful, but we tried to make that good on a card loaded with sincere compliments. And, indeed, it was no time for scruples; we seemed to feel the hot breath of the champion on our necks.

AT MAUBEUGE

Partly from the terror we had of our good friends the Royal Nauticals, partly from the fact that there were no fewer than fifty-five locks between Brussels and Charleroi, we concluded that we should travel by train across the frontier, boats and all. Fifty-five locks in a day's journey was pretty well tantamount to trudging the whole distance on foot, with the canoes upon our shoulders, an object of astonishment to the trees on the canal side, and of honest derision to all right-thinking children.

To pass the frontier, even in a train, is a difficult matter for the *Arethusa*. He is, somehow or other, a marked man for the official eye. Wherever he journeys, there are the officers gathered together. Treaties are solemnly signed, foreign ministers, ambassadors, and consuls sit throned in state from China to Peru, and the Union Jack flutters on all the winds of heaven. Under these safeguards, portly clergymen, school-mistresses, gentlemen in grey tweed suits, and all the ruck and rabble of British touristry pour unhindered, *Murray** in hand, over the railways of the Continent, and yet the slim person of the *Arethusa* is taken in the meshes, while these great fish go on their way rejoicing. If he travels without a passport, he is cast, without any figure about the matter, into noisome dungeons: if his papers are in order, he is suffered to go his way, indeed, but not until he has been humiliated by a general incredulity. He is a born British subject, yet he has never succeeded in persuading a single official of his nationality. He flatters himself he is indifferent honest; yet he is rarely known for anything better than a spy, and there is no absurd and disreputable means of livelihood but has been attributed to him in some heat of official or popular distrust...

For the life of me I cannot understand it. I, too, have been knolled to church and sat at good men's feasts, but I bear no mark of it. I am as strange as a Jack Indian to their official spectacles. I might come from any part of the globe, it seems, except from where I do. My ancestors have laboured in vain, and the glorious Constitution cannot protect me in my walks abroad. It is a great thing, believe me, to present a good normal type of the nation you belong to.

Nobody else was asked for his papers on the way to Maubeuge, but I was; and although I clung to my rights, I had to choose at last between accepting the humiliation and being left behind by the train. I was sorry to give way, but I wanted to get to Maubeuge.

Maubeuge is a fortified town with a very good inn, the *Grand Cerf*. It seemed to be inhabited principally by soldiers and bagmen; at least, these were all that we saw, except the hotel servants. We had to stay there some time, for the canoes were in no hurry to follow us, and at last stuck hopelessly in the custom-house until we went back to liberate them. There was nothing to do, nothing to see. We had good meals, which was a great matter, but that was all.

The *Cigarette* was nearly taken up upon a charge of drawing the fortifications: a feat of which he was hopelessly incapable. And besides, as I suppose each belligerent nation has a plan of the other's fortified places already, these precautions are of the nature of shutting the stable door after the steed is away. But I have no doubt they help to keep up a good spirit at home. It is a great thing if you can persuade p ple that they are somehow or other partakers in a mystery. It makes them feel bigger. Even the Freemasons, who have been shown up to satiety, preserve a kind of pride; and not a grocer among them, however honest, harmless, and empty-headed he may feel himself to be at bottom, but comes home from one of their *cœnacula** with a portentous significance for himself.

It is an odd thing how happily two people, if there are two, can live in a place where they have no acquaintance. I think the spectacle of a whole life in which you have no part paralyses personal desire. You are content to become a mere spectator. The baker stands in his door; the colonel with his three medals goes by to the *café* at night; the troops drum and trumpet and man the ramparts, as bold as so many lions. It would task language to say how placidly you behold all this. In a place where you have taken some root you are provoked out of your indifference; you have a hand in the game; your friends are fighting with the army. But in a strange town, not small enough to grow too soon familiar, nor so large as to have laid itself out for travellers, you stand so far apart from the business that you positively forget it would be possible to go nearer; you have so little human interest around you that you do not remember yourself to be a man. Perhaps, in a very short time, you would be one no longer. Gymnosophists go into a wood, with all nature seething around them, with romance on every side; it would be much more to the purpose if they took up their abode in a dull country town where they should see just so much of humanity as to keep them from desiring more, and only the stale externals of man's life. These externals are as dead to us as so many formalities, and speak a dead language in our eyes and ears. They have no more meaning than an oath or a salutation. We are so much accustomed to see married couples going to church of a Sunday that we have clean forgotten what they represent; and novelists are driven to rehabilitate adultery, no less, when they wish to show us what a beautiful thing it is for a man and a woman to live for each other.

One person in Maubeuge, however, showed me something more than his outside. That was the driver of the hotel omnibus: a mean enough looking little man, as well as I can remember, but with a spark of something human in his soul. He had heard of our little journey, and came to me at once in envious sympathy. How he longed to travel! he told me. How he longed to be somewhere else, and see the round world before he went into the grave! 'Here I am,' said he. 'I drive to the station. Well. And then I drive back again to the hotel. And so on every day and all the week round. My God, is that life?' I could not say I thought it was—for him. He pressed me to tell him where I had been, and where I hoped to go; and as he listened, I declare the fellow sighed. Might not this have been a brave African traveller, or gone to the Indies after Drake? But it is an evil age for the gypsily inclined among men. He who can sit squarest on a three-legged stool, he it is who has the wealth and glory.

I wonder if my friend is still driving the omnibus for the *Grand Cerf*! Not very likely, I believe; for I think he was on the eve of mutiny when we passed through, and perhaps our passage determined him for good. Better a thousand times that he should be a tramp, and mend pots and pans by the wayside, and sleep under trees, and see the dawn and the sunset every day above a new horizon. I think I hear you say that it is a respectable position to drive an omnibus? Very well. What right has he who likes it not to keep those who would like it dearly out of this respectable position? Suppose a dish were not to my taste, and you told me that it was a favourite among the rest of the company, what should I conclude from that? Not to finish the dish against my stomach, I suppose.

Respectability is a very good thing in its way, but it does not rise superior to all considerations. I would not for a moment venture to hint that it was a matter of taste; but I think I will go as far as this: that if a position is admittedly unkind, uncomfortable, unnecessary, and superfluously useless, although it were as respectable as the Church of England, the sooner a man is out of it, the better for himself, and all concerned.

ON THE SAMBRE CANALISED

TO QUARTES

About three in the afternoon the whole establishment of the *Grand Cerf* accompanied us to the water's edge. The man of the omnibus was there with haggard eyes. Poor cage-bird! Do I not remember the time when I myself haunted the station, to watch train after train carry its complement of freemen into the night, and read the names of distant places on the time-bills with indescribable longings?

We were not clear of the fortifications before the rain began. The wind was contrary, and blew in furious gusts; nor were the aspects of nature any more clement than the doings of the sky. For we passed through a blighted country, sparsely covered with brush, but handsomely enough diversified with factory chimneys. We landed in a soiled meadow among some pollards, and there smoked a pipe in a flaw of fair weather. But the wind blew so hard we could get little else to smoke. There were no natural objects in the neighbourhood, but some sordid workshops. A group of children, headed by a tall girl, stood and watched us from a little distance all the time we stayed. I heartily wonder what they thought of us.

At Hautmont, the lock was almost impassable, the landing-place being steep and high, and the launch at a long distance. Near a dozen grimy workmen lent us a hand. They refused any reward; and, what is much better, refused it handsomely, without conveying any sense of insult. 'It is a way we have in our countryside,' said they. And a very becoming way it is. In Scotland, where also you will get services for nothing, the good people reject your money as if you had been trying to corrupt a voter. When people take the trouble to do dignified acts, it is worth while to take a little more, and allow the dignity to be common to all concerned. But in our brave Saxon countries, where we plod threescore years and ten in the mud, and the wind keeps singing in our ears from birth to burial, we do our good and bad with a high hand and almost offensively; and make even our alms a witness-bearing and an act of war against the wrong.

After Hautmont, the sun came forth again and the wind went down; and a little paddling took us beyond the iron works and through a delectable land. The river wound among low hills, so that sometimes the sun was at our backs, and sometimes it stood right ahead and the river before us was one sheet of intolerable glory. On either hand meadows and orchards bordered, with a margin of sedge and water flowers, upon the river. The hedges were of great height, woven about the trunks of hedgerow elms; and the fields, as they were often very small, looked like a series of bowers along the stream. There was never any prospect; sometimes a hill-top with its trees would look over the nearest hedgerow, just to make a middle distance for the sky; but that was all. The heaven was bare of clouds. The atmosphere, after the rain, was of enchanting purity. The river doubled among the hillocks, a shining strip of mirror glass; and the dip of the paddles set the flowers shaking along the brink.

In the meadows wandered black and white cattle fantastically marked. One beast, with a white head and the rest of the body glossy black, came to the edge to drink, and stood gravely twitching his ears at me as I went by, like some sort of preposterous clergyman in a play. A moment after I heard a loud plunge, and, turning my head, saw the clergyman struggling to shore. The bank had given way under his feet.

Besides the cattle, we saw no living things except a few birds and a great many fishermen. These sat along the edges of the meadows, sometimes with one rod, sometimes with as many as half a score. They seemed stupefied with contentment; and, when we induced them to exchange a few words with us about the weather, their voices sounded quiet and far away. There was a strange diversity of opinion among them as to the kind of fish for which they set their lures; although they were all agreed in this, that the river was abundantly supplied. Where it was plain that no two of them had ever caught the same kind of fish, we could not help suspecting that perhaps not any one of them had ever caught a fish at all. I hope, since the afternoon was so lovely, that they were one and all rewarded; and that a silver booty went home in every basket for the pot. Some of my friends would cry shame on me for this; but I prefer a man, were he only an angler, to the bravest pair of gills in all God's waters. I do not affect fishes unless when cooked in sauce; whereas an angler is an important piece of river scenery, and hence deserves some recognition among canoeists. He can always tell you where you are, after a mild fashion; and his quiet presence serves to accentuate the solitude and stillness, and remind you of the glittering citizens below your boat.

The Sambre turned so industriously to and fro among his little hills that it was past six before we drew near the lock at Quartes. There were some children on the towpath, with whom the *Cigarette* fell into a chaffing talk as they ran along beside us. It was in vain that I warned him. In vain I told him, in English, that boys were the most dangerous creatures; and if once you began with them, it was safe to end in a shower of stones. For my own part, whenever anything was addressed to me, I smiled gently and shook my head, as though I were an inoffensive person inadequately acquainted with French. For, indeed, I have had such an experience at home that I would sooner meet many wild animals than a troop of healthy urchins.

But I was doing injustice to these peaceable young Hainaulters. When the *Cigarette* went off to make inquiries, I got out upon the bank to smoke a pipe and superintend the boats, and became at once the centre of much amiable curiosity. The children had been joined by this time by a young woman and a mild lad who had lost an arm; and this gave me more security. When I let slip my first word or so in French, a little girl nodded her head with a comical grown-up air. 'Ah, you see,' she said, 'he understands well enough now; he was just making believe.' And the little group laughed together very good-naturedly.

They were much impressed when they heard we came from England; and the little girl proffered the information that England was an island 'and a far way from here—*bien loin d'ici.*'

'Ay, you may say that: a far way from here,' said the lad with one arm.

I was nearly as homesick as ever I was in my life; they seemed to make it such an incalculable distance to the place where I first saw the day.

They admired the canoes very much. And I observed one piece of delicacy in these children which is worthy of record. They had been deafening us for the last hundred yards with petitions for a sail; ay, and they deafened us to the same tune next morning when we came to start; but then, when the canoes were lying empty, there was no word of any such petition. Delicacy? or perhaps a bit of fear for the water in so crank a vessel? I hate cynicism a great deal worse than I do the devil; unless perhaps, the two were the same thing? And yet 'tis a good tonic; the cold tub and bath-towel of the sentiments; and positively necessary to life in cases of advanced sensibility.

From the boats they turned to my costume. They could not make enough of my red sash; and my knife filled them with awe.

'They make them like that in England,' said the boy with one arm. I was glad he did not know how badly we make them in England nowadays. 'They are for people who go away to sea,' he added, 'and to defend one's life against great fish.'

I felt I was becoming a more and more romantic figure to the little group at every word. And so I suppose I was. Even my pipe, although it was an ordinary French clay, pretty well 'trousered,' as they call it, would have a rarity in their eyes, as a thing coming from so far away. And if my feathers were not very fine in themselves, they were all from over seas. One thing in my outfit, however, tickled them out of all politeness; and that was the bemired condition of my canvas shoes. I suppose they were sure the mud at any rate was a home product. The little girl (who was the genius of the party) displayed her own sabots in competition; and I wish you could have seen how gracefully and merrily she did it.

The young woman's milk-can, a great amphora of hammered brass, stood some way off upon the sward. I was glad of an opportunity to divert public attention from myself and return some of the compliments I had received. So I admired it cordially both for form and colour, telling them, and very truly, that it was as beautiful as gold. They were not surprised. The things were plainly the boast of the country-side. And the children expatiated on the costliness of these amphoræ, which sell sometimes as high as thirty francs apiece; told me how they were carried on donkeys, one on either side of the saddle, a brave caparison in themselves; and how they were to be seen all over the district, and at the larger farms in great number and of great size.

PONT-SUR-SAMBRE

WE ARE PEDLARS

The *Cigarette* returned with good news. There were beds to be had some ten minutes' walk from where we were, at a place called Pont. We stowed the canoes in a granary, and asked among the children for a guide. The circle at once widened round us, and our offers of reward were received in dispiriting silence. We were plainly a pair of Bluebeards to the children; they might speak to us in public places, and where they had the advantage of numbers; but it was another thing to venture off alone with two uncouth and legendary characters, who had dropped from the clouds upon their hamlet this quiet afternoon, sashed and be-knived, and with a flavour of great voyages. The owner of the granary came to our assistance, singled out one little fellow, and threatened him with corporalities; or I suspect we should have had to find the way for ourselves. As it was, he was more frightened at the granary man than the strangers, having perhaps had some experience of the former. But I fancy his little heart must have been going at a fine rate, for he kept trotting at a respectful distance in front, and looking back at us with scared eyes. Not otherwise may the children of the young world have guided Jove or one of his Olympian compeers on an adventure.

A miry lane led us up from Quartes, with its church and bickering windmill. The hinds were trudging homewards from the fields. A brisk little old woman passed us by. She was seated across a donkey between a pair of glittering milk-cans, and, as she went, she kicked jauntily with her heels upon the donkey's side, and scattered shrill remarks among the wayfarers. It was notable that none of the tired men took the trouble to reply. Our conductor soon led us out of the lane and across country. The sun had gone down, but the west in front of us was one lake of level gold. The path wandered a while in the open, and then passed under a trellis like a bower indefinitely prolonged. On either hand were shadowy orchards; cottages lay low among the leaves and sent their smoke to heaven; every here and there, in an opening, appeared the great gold face of the west.

I never saw the *Cigarette* in such an idyllic frame of mind. He waxed positively lyrical in praise of country scenes. I was little less exhilarated myself; the mild air of the evening, the shadows, the rich lights, and the silence made a symphonious accompaniment about our walk; and we both determined to avoid towns for the future and sleep in hamlets.

At last the path went between two houses, and turned the party out into a wide, muddy high-road, bordered as far as the eye could reach on either hand by an unsightly village. The houses stood well back, leaving a ribbon of waste land on either side of the road, where there were stacks of firewood, carts, barrows, rubbish heaps, and a little doubtful grass. Away on the left, a gaunt tower stood in the middle of the street. What it had been in past ages I know not: probably a hold in time of war; but nowadays it bore an illegible dial-plate in its upper parts, and near the bottom an iron letter-box.

The inn to which we had been recommended at Quartes was full, or else the landlady did not like our looks. I ought to say, that with our long, damp india-rubber bags, we presented rather a doubtful type of civilisation: like rag-and-bone men, the *Cigarette* imagined. 'These gentlemen are pedlars?'—*Ces messieurs sont des marchands?*—asked the landlady. And then, without waiting for an answer, which I suppose she thought superfluous in so plain a case, recommended us to a butcher who lived hard by the tower and took in travellers to lodge.

Thither went we. But the butcher was flitting, and all his beds were taken down. Or else he didn't like our look. As a parting shot, we had 'These gentlemen are pedlars?'

It began to grow dark in earnest. We could no longer distinguish the faces of the people who passed us by with an inarticulate good-evening. And the householders of Pont seemed very economical with their oil, for we saw not a single window lighted in all that long village. I believe it is the longest village in the world; but I dare say in our predicament every space counted three times over. We were much cast down when we came to the last auberge, and, looking in at the dark door, asked timidly if we could sleep there for the night. A female voice assented, in no very friendly tones. We clapped the bags down and found our way to chairs.

The place was in total darkness, save a red glow in the chinks and ventilators of the stove. But now the landlady lit a lamp to see her new guests; I suppose the darkness was what saved us another expulsion, for I cannot say she looked gratified at our appearance. We were in a large bare apartment adorned with two allegorical prints of Music and Painting, and a copy of the law against Public Drunkenness. On one side there was a bit of a bar, with some half-a-dozen bottles. Two labourers sat waiting supper, in attitudes of extreme weariness; a plain-looking lass bustled about with a sleepy child of two, and the landlady began to derange the pots upon the stove and set some beefsteak to grill.

'These gentlemen are pedlars?' she asked sharply; and that was all the conversation forthcoming. We began to think we might be pedlars, after all. I never knew a population with so narrow a range of conjecture as the innkeepers of Pont-sur-Sambre. But manners and bearings have not a wider currency than bank-notes. You have only to get far enough out of your beat, and all your accomplished airs will go for nothing. These Hainaulters could see no difference between us and the average pedlar. Indeed, we had some grounds for reflection while the steak was getting ready, to see how perfectly they accepted us at their own valuation, and how our best politeness and best efforts at entertainment seemed to fit quite suitably with the character of packmen. At least it seemed a good account of the profession in France, that even before such judges we could not beat them at our own weapons.

At last we were called to table. The two hinds (and one of them looked sadly worn and white in the face, as though

sick with over-work and under-feeding) supped off a single
plate of some sort of bread-berry* some potatoes in their
jackets, a small cup of coffee sweetened with sugar candy,
and one tumbler of swipes.* The landlady, her son, and
the lass aforesaid took the same. Our meal was quite a
banquet by comparison. We had some beefsteak, not so
tender as it might have been, some of the potatoes, some
cheese, an extra glass of the swipes, and white sugar in our
coffee.

You see what it is to be a gentleman—I beg your pardon,
what it is to be a pedlar. It had not before occurred to me
that a pedlar was a great man in a labourer's ale-house;
but now that I had to enact the part for the evening, I
found that so it was. He has in his hedge quarters somewhat
the same pre-eminence as the man who takes a private
parlour in a hotel. The more you look into it, the more
infinite are the class distinctions among men; and possibly,
by a happy dispensation there is no one at all at the bottom
of the scale; no one but can find some superiority over
somebody else, to keep up his pride withal.

We were displeased enough with our fare. Particularly
the *Cigarette*; for I tried to make believe that I was amused
with the adventure, tough beefsteak and all. According to
the Lucretian maxim,* our steak should have been fla-
voured by the look of the other people's bread-berry; but
we did not find it so in practice. You may have a head
knowledge that other people live more poorly than yourself,
but it is not agreeable—I was going to say, it is against the
etiquette of the universe—to sit at the same table and pick
your own superior diet from among their crusts. I had not
seen such a thing done since the greedy boy at school with
his birthday cake. It was odious enough to witness, I could
remember; and I had never thought to play the part myself.
But there, again, you see what it is to be a pedlar.

There is no doubt that the poorer classes in our country
are much more charitably disposed than their superiors in
wealth. And I fancy it must arise a great deal from the
comparative indistinction of the easy and the not so easy
in these ranks. A workman or a pedlar cannot shutter

himself off from his less comfortable neighbours. If he treats himself to a luxury, he must do it in the face of a dozen who cannot. And what should more directly lead to charitable thoughts? . . . Thus the poor man, camping out in life, sees it as it is, and knows that every mouthful he puts in his belly has been wrenched out of the fingers of the hungry.

But at a certain stage of prosperity, as in a balloon ascent, the fortunate person passes through a zone of clouds, and sublunary matters are thenceforward hidden from his view. He sees nothing but the heavenly bodies, all in admirable order and positively as good as new. He finds himself surrounded in the most touching manner by the attentions of Providence, and compares himself involuntarily with the lilies and the skylarks. He does not precisely sing, of course; but then he looks so unassuming in his open landau! If all the world dined at one table, this philosophy would meet with some rude knocks.

PONT-SUR-SAMBRE

THE TRAVELLING MERCHANT

Like the lackeys in Molière's farce,* when the true noble-
man broke in on their high life below stairs, we were
destined to be confronted with a real pedlar. To make the
lesson still more poignant for fallen gentlemen like us, he
was a pedlar of infinitely more consideration than the sort
of scurvy fellows we were taken for; like a lion among mice,
or a ship of war bearing down upon two cock-boats. Indeed,
he did not deserve the name of pedlar at all; he was a
travelling merchant.

I suppose it was about half-past eight when this worthy,
Monsieur Hector Gilliard of Maubeuge, turned up at the
ale-house door in a tilt cart drawn by a donkey, and cried
cheerily on the inhabitants. He was a lean, nervous flibber-
tigibbet of a man, with something the look of an actor and
something the look of a horse-jockey. He had evidently
prospered without any of the favours of education, for he
adhered with stern simplicity to the masculine gender, and
in the course of the evening passed off some fancy futures
in a very florid style of architecture. With him came his
wife, a comely young woman, with her hair tied in a yellow
kerchief, and their son, a little fellow of four, in a blouse
and military *képi*. It was notable that the child was many
degrees better dressed than either of the parents. We were
informed he was already at a boarding-school; but the
holidays having just commenced, he was off to spend them
with his parents on a cruise. An enchanting holiday occupation, was it not? to travel all day with father and mother
in the tilt cart full of countless treasures; the green country
rattling by on either side, and the children in all the villages
contemplating him with envy and wonder. It is better fun,
during the holidays, to be the son of a travelling merchant,
than son and heir to the greatest cotton spinner in creation.

And as for being a reigning prince,—indeed, I never saw
one if it was not Master Gilliard!

While M. Hector and the son of the house were putting
up the donkey and getting all the valuables under lock and
key, the landlady warmed up the remains of our beefsteak
and fried the cold potatoes in slices, and Madame Gilliard
set herself to waken the boy, who had come far that day,
and was peevish and dazzled by the light. He was no sooner
awake than he began to prepare himself for supper by
eating galette, unripe pears, and cold potatoes—with, so far
as I could judge, positive benefit to his appetite.

The landlady, fired with motherly emulation, awoke her
own little girl, and the two children were confronted.
Master Gilliard looked at her for a moment, very much as
a dog looks at his own reflection in a mirror before he
turns away. He was at that time absorbed in the galette.
His mother seemed crestfallen that he should display so
little inclination towards the other sex, and expressed her
disappointment with some candour and a very proper
reference to the influence of years.

Sure enough a time will come when he will pay more
attention to the girls, and think a great deal less of his
mother; let us hope she will like it as well as she seemed
to fancy. But it is odd enough; the very women who profess
most contempt for mankind as a sex, seem to find even its
ugliest particulars rather lively and high-minded in their
own sons.

The little girl looked longer and with more interest,
probably because she was in her own house, while he was
a traveller and accustomed to strange sights. And, besides,
there was no galette in the case with her.

All the time of supper there was nothing spoken of but
my young lord. The two parents were both absurdly fond
of their child. Monsieur kept insisting on his sagacity; how
he knew all the children at school by name, and when this
utterly failed on trial, how he was cautious and exact to a
strange degree, and if asked anything, he would sit and
think—and think, and if he did not know it, 'my faith, he
wouldn't tell you at all—*ma foi, il ne vous le dira pas.*' Which

is certainly a very high degree of caution. At intervals, M. Hector would appeal to his wife, with his mouth full of beefsteak, as to the little fellow's age at such or such a time when he had said or done something memorable; and I noticed that Madame usually pooh-poohed these inquiries. She herself was not boastful in her vein; but she never had her fill of caressing the child; and she seemed to take a gentle pleasure in recalling all that was fortunate in his little existence. No school-boy could have talked more of the holidays which were just beginning and less of the black school-time which must inevitably follow after. She showed, with a pride perhaps partly mercantile in origin, his pockets preposterously swollen with tops and whistles and string. When she called at a house in the way of business, it appeared, he kept her company; and, whenever a sale was made, received a sou out of the profit. Indeed, they spoiled him vastly, these two good people. But they had an eye to his manners, for all that, and reproved him for some little faults in breeding which occurred from time to time during supper.

On the whole, I was not much hurt at being taken for a pedlar. I might think that I ate with greater delicacy, or that my mistakes in French belonged to a different order; but it was plain that these distinctions would be thrown away upon the landlady and the two labourers. In all essential things we and the Gilliards cut very much the same figure in the ale-house kitchen. M. Hector was more at home, indeed, and took a higher tone with the world; but that was explicable on the ground of his driving a donkey-cart, while we poor bodies tramped afoot. I dare say the rest of the company thought us dying with envy, though in no ill sense, to be as far up in the profession as the new arrival.

And of one thing I am sure; that everyone thawed and became more humanised and conversible as soon as these innocent people appeared upon the scene. I would not very readily trust the travelling merchant with any extravagant sum of money, but I am sure his heart was in the right place. In this mixed world, if you can find one or two sensible places in a man—above all, if you should find a whole family living together on such pleasant terms—you may surely be satisfied, and take the rest for granted; or, what is a great deal better, boldly make up your mind that you can do perfectly well without the rest, and that ten thousand bad traits cannot make a single good one any the less good.

It was getting late. M. Hector lit a stable lantern and went off to his cart for some arrangements, and my young gentleman proceeded to divest himself of the better part of his raiment and play gymnastics on his mother's lap, and thence on to the floor, with accompaniment of laughter.

'Are you going to sleep alone?' asked the servant lass.

'There's little fear of that,' says Master Gilliard.

'You sleep alone at school,' objected his mother. 'Come, come, you must be a man.'

But he protested that school was a different matter from the holidays; that there were dormitories at school; and silenced the discussion with kisses: his mother smiling, no one better pleased than she.

There certainly was, as he phrased it, very little fear that he should sleep alone, for there was but one bed for the trio. We, on our part, had firmly protested against one man's accommodation for two; and we had a double-bedded pen in the loft of the house, furnished, beside the beds, with exactly three hat-pegs and one table. There was not so much as a glass of water. But the window would open, by good fortune.

Some time before I fell asleep the loft was full of the sound of mighty snoring; the Gilliards and the labourers and the people of the inn, all at it, I suppose, with one consent. The young moon outside shone very clearly over Pont-sur-Sambre, and down upon the ale-house where all we pedlars were abed.

ON THE SAMBRE CANALISED

TO LANDRECIES

In the morning, when we came downstairs the landlady pointed out to us two pails of water behind the street door. *'Voilà de l'eau pour vous débarbouiller,'** says she. And so there we made shift to wash ourselves, while Madame Gilliard brushed the family boots on the outer doorstep, and M. Hector, whistling cheerily, arranged some small goods for the day's campaign in a portable chest of drawers, which formed a part of his baggage. Meanwhile the child was letting off Waterloo crackers* all over the floor.

I wonder, by-the-bye, what they call Waterloo crackers in France; perhaps Austerlitz* crackers. There is a great deal in the point of view. Do you remember the Frenchman who, travelling by way of Southampton, was put down in Waterloo Station, and had to drive across Waterloo Bridge? He had a mind to go home again, it seems.

Pont itself is on the river, but whereas it is ten minutes' walk from Quartes by dry land, it is six weary kilomètres by water. We left our bags at the inn and walked to our canoes through the wet orchards unencumbered. Some of the children were there to see us off, but we were no longer the mysterious beings of the night before. A departure is much less romantic than an unexplained arrival in the golden evening. Although we might be greatly taken at a ghost's first appearance, we should behold him vanish with comparative equanimity.

The good folk of the inn at Pont, when we called there for the bags, were overcome with marvelling. At the sight of these two dainty little boats, with a fluttering Union Jack on each, and all the varnish shining from the sponge, they began to perceive that they had entertained angels unawares.* The landlady stood upon the bridge, probably lamenting she had charged so little; the son ran to and fro, and called out the neighbours to enjoy the sight; and we paddled away from quite a crowd of rapt observers. These gentlemen pedlars, indeed! Now you see their quality too late.

The whole day was showery, with occasional drenching plumps. We were soaked to the skin, then partially dried in the sun, then soaked once more. But there were some calm intervals, and one notably, when we were skirting the forest of Mormal, a sinister name to the ear, but a place most gratifying to sight and smell. It looked solemn along the river-side, drooping its boughs into the water, and piling them up aloft into a wall of leaves. What is a forest but a city of nature's own, full of hardy and innocuous living things, where there is nothing dead and nothing made with the hands, but the citizens themselves are the houses and public monuments? There is nothing so much alive, and yet so quiet, as a woodland; and a pair of people, swinging past in canoes, feel very small and bustling by comparison.

And surely, of all smells in the world, the smell of many trees is the sweetest and most fortifying. The sea has a rude pistolling sort of odour, that takes you in the nostrils like snuff, and carries with it a fine sentiment of open water and tall ships; but the smell of a forest, which comes nearest to this in tonic quality, surpasses it by many degrees in the quality of softness. Again, the smell of the sea has little variety, but the smell of a forest is infinitely changeful; it varies with the hour of the day, not in strength merely, but in character; and the different sorts of trees, as you go from one zone of the wood to another, seem to live among different kinds of atmosphere. Usually the resin of the fir predominates. But some woods are more coquettish in their habits; and the breath of the forest of Mormal, as it came aboard upon us that showery afternoon, was perfumed with nothing less delicate than sweetbriar.

I wish our way had always lain among woods. Trees are the most civil society. An old oak that has been growing where he stands since before the Reformation, taller than many spires, more stately than the greater part of mountains, and yet a living thing, liable to sicknesses and death, like you and me: is not that in itself a speaking lesson in history? But acres on acres full of such patriarchs contiguously rooted, their green tops billowing in the wind, their stalwart younglings pushing up about their knees; a whole forest, healthy and beautiful, giving colour to the light, giving perfume to the air; what is this but the most imposing piece in nature's repertory? Heine wished to lie like Merlin under the oaks of Broceliande. I should not be satisfied with one tree; but if the wood grew together like a banyan grove, I would be buried under the tap-root of the whole; my parts should circulate from oak to oak; and my consciousness should be diffused abroad in all the forest, and give a common heart to that assembly of green spires, so that it, also, might rejoice in its own loveliness and dignity. I think I feel a thousand squirrels leaping from bough to bough in my vast mausoleum; and the birds and the winds merrily coursing over its uneven, leafy surface.

Alas! the forest of Mormal is only a little bit of a wood, and it was but for a little way that we skirted by its boundaries. And the rest of the time the rain kept coming in squirts and the wind in squalls, until one's heart grew weary of such fitful, scolding weather. It was odd how the showers began when we had to carry the boats over a lock and must expose our legs. They always did. This is a sort of thing that readily begets a personal feeling against nature. There seems no reason why the shower should not come five minutes before or five minutes after, unless you suppose an intention to affront you. The *Cigarette* had a mackintosh which put him more or less above these contrarieties. But I had to bear the brunt uncovered. I began to remember that nature was a woman. My companion, in a rosier temper, listened with great satisfaction to my jeremiads, and ironically concurred. He instanced, as a cognate matter, the action of the tides, 'which,' said he, 'was altogether designed for the confusion of canoeists, except in so far as it was calculated to minister to a barren vanity on the part of the moon.'

At the last lock, some little way out of Landrecies, I refused to go any farther; and sat in a drift of rain by the side of the bank, to have a reviving pipe. A vivacious old man, whom I take to have been the devil, drew near, and questioned me about our journey. In the fulness of my heart I laid bare our plans before him. He said it was the silliest enterprise that ever he heard of. Why, did I not know, he asked me, that it was nothing but locks, locks, locks, the whole way? not to mention that, at this season of the year, we would find the Oise quite dry? 'Get into a train, my little young man,' said he, 'and go you away home to your parents.' I was so astounded at the man's malice that I could only stare at him in silence. A tree would never have spoken to me like this. At last I got out with some words. We had come from Antwerp already, I told him, which was a good long way; and we should do the rest in spite of him. Yes, I said, if there were no other reason, I would do it now, just because he had dared to say we could not. The pleasant old gentleman looked at me sneeringly, made an allusion to my canoe, and marched off, wagging his head.

I was still inwardly fuming when up came a pair of young fellows who imagined I was the *Cigarette's* servant, on a comparison, I suppose, of my bare jersey with the other's mackintosh, and asked me many questions about my place and my master's character. I said he was a good enough fellow, but had this absurd voyage on the head. 'Oh, no, no,' said one, 'you must not say that; it is not absurd; it is very courageous of him.' I believe these were a couple of angels sent to give me heart again. It was truly fortifying to reproduce all the old man's insinuations, as if they were original to me in my character of a malcontent footman, and have them brushed away like so many flies by these admirable young men.

When I recounted this affair to the *Cigarette*, 'They must have a curious idea of how English servants behave,' says he, dryly, 'for you treated me like a brute beast at the lock.'

I was a good deal mortified; but my temper had suffered, it is a fact.

AT LANDRECIES

At Landrecies the rain still fell and the wind still blew; but we found a double-bedded room with plenty of furniture, real water-jugs with real water in them, and dinner: a real dinner, not innocent of real wine. After having been a pedlar for one night, and a butt for the elements during the whole of the next day, these comfortable circumstances fell on my heart like sunshine. There was an English fruiterer at dinner, travelling with a Belgian fruiterer; in the evening at the *café* we watched our compatriot drop a good deal of money at corks,* and I don't know why, but this pleased us.

It turned out that we were to see more of Landrecies than we expected; for the weather next day was simply bedlamite. It is not the place one would have chosen for a day's rest, for it consists almost entirely of fortifications. Within the ramparts a few blocks of houses, a long row of barracks, and a church, figure, with what countenance they may, as the town. There seems to be no trade, and a shop-keeper from whom I bought a sixpenny flint and steel was so much affected that he filled my pockets with spare flints into the bargain. The only public buildings that had any interest for us were the hotel and the *café*. But we visited the church. There lies Marshal Clarke. But as neither of us had ever heard of that military hero, we bore the associations of the spot with fortitude.

In all garrison towns, guard-calls, and *réveillés*, and such-like, make a fine, romantic interlude in civic business. Bugles, and drums, and fifes are of themselves most excellent things in nature, and when they carry the mind to marching armies and the picturesque vicissitudes of war they stir up something proud in the heart. But in a shadow of a town like Landrecies, with little else moving, these points of war made a proportionate commotion. Indeed, they were the only things to remember. It was just the place to hear the round going by at night in the darkness, with the solid tramp of men marching, and the startling reverberations of the drum. It reminded you that even this place was a point in the great warfaring system of Europe, and might on some future day be ringed about with cannon smoke and thunder, and make itself a name among strong towns.

The drum, at any rate, from its martial voice and notable physiological effect, nay, even from its cumbrous and comical shape, stands alone among the instruments of noise. And if it be true, as I have heard it said, that drums are covered with asses' skin, what a picturesque irony is there in that! As if this long-suffering animal's hide had not been sufficiently belaboured during life, now by Lyonnese costermongers, now by presumptuous Hebrew prophets, it must be stripped from his poor hinder quarters after death, stretched on a drum, and beaten night after night round the streets of every garrison town in Europe. And up the heights of Alma and Spicheren,* and wherever death has his red flag a-flying, and sounds his own potent tuck upon the cannons, there also must the drummer boy, hurrying with white face over fallen comrades, batter and bemaul this slip of skin from the loins of peaceable donkeys.

Generally a man is never more uselessly employed than when he is at this trick of bastinadoing asses' hide. We know what effect it has in life, and how your dull ass will not mend his pace with beating. But in this state of mummy and melancholy survival of itself, when the hollow skin reverberates to the drummer's wrist, and each dub-a-dub goes direct to a man's heart, and puts madness there, and that disposition of the pulses which we, in our big way of talking, nickname Heroism,—is there not something in the nature of a revenge upon the donkey's persecutors? Of old, he might say, you drubbed me up hill and down dale and I must endure; but now that I am dead those dull thwacks that were scarcely audible in country lanes have become stirring music in front of the brigade, and for every blow that you lay on my old great-coat, you will see a comrade stumble and fall.

Not long after the drums had passed the *café*, the *Cigarette* and the *Arethusa* began to grow sleepy, and set out for the hotel, which was only a door or two away. But although we had been somewhat indifferent to Landrecies, Landrecies had not been indifferent to us. All day, we learned, people had been running out between the squalls to visit our two boats. Hundreds of persons, so said report, although it fitted ill with our idea of the town,—hundreds of persons had inspected them where they lay in a coal-shed. We were becoming lions in Landrecies, who had been only pedlars the night before in Pont.

And now, when we left the *café*, we were pursued and overtaken at the hotel door by no less a person than the *Fuge de Paix* a functionary, as far as I can make out, of the character of a Scots Sheriff-Substitute. He gave us his card and invited us to sup with him on the spot, very neatly, very gracefully, as Frenchmen can do these things. It was for the credit of Landrecies, said he; and although we knew very well how little credit we could do the place, we must have been churlish fellows to refuse an invitation so politely introduced.

The house of the judge was close by; it was a well-appointed bachelor's establishment, with a curious collection of old brass warming-pans upon the walls. Some of these were most elaborately carved. It seemed a picturesque idea for a collector. You could not help thinking how many nightcaps had wagged over these warming-pans in past generations; what jests may have been made and kisses taken while they were in service; and how often they had been uselessly paraded in the bed of death. If they could only speak, at what absurd, indecorous, and tragical scenes had they not been present?

The wine was excellent. When we made the judge our compliments upon a bottle, 'I do not give it you as my worst,' said he. I wonder when Englishmen will learn these hospitable graces. They are worth learning; they set off life and make ordinary moments ornamental.

There were two other Landrecienses present. One was the collector of something or other, I forget what; the other, we were told, was the principal notary of the place. So it happened that we all five more or less followed the law. At this rate, the talk was pretty certain to become technical. The *Cigarette* expounded the Poor Laws very magisterially. And a little later I found myself laying down the Scotch law of illegitimacy, of which I am glad to say I know nothing. The collector and the notary, who were both married men, accused the judge, who was a bachelor, of having started the subject. He deprecated the charge, with a conscious, pleased air, just like all the men I have ever seen, be they French or English. How strange that we should all, in our unguarded moments, rather like to be thought a bit of a rogue with the women!

As the evening went on the wine grew more to my taste; the spirits proved better than the wine; the company was genial. This was the highest water mark of popular favour on the whole cruise. After all, being in a judge's house, was there not something semi-official in the tribute? And so, remembering what a great country France is, we did full justice to our entertainment. Landrecies had been a long while asleep before we returned to the hotel; and the sentries on the ramparts were already looking for a day-break.

SAMBRE AND OISE CANAL

CANAL BOATS

Next day we made a late start in the rain. The judge politely escorted us to the end of the lock under an umbrella. We had now brought ourselves to a pitch of humility, in the matter of weather, not often attained except in the Scottish Highlands. A rag of blue sky or a glimpse of sunshine set our hearts singing; and when the rain was not heavy we counted the day almost fair.

Long lines of barges lay one after another along the canal, many of them looking mighty spruce and shipshape in their jerkin of Archangel tar picked out with white and green. Some carried gay iron railings and quite a parterre of flower-pots. Children played on the decks, as heedless of the rain as if they had been brought up on Loch Carron side; men fished over the gunwale, some of them under umbrellas; women did their washing; and every barge boasted its mongrel cur by way of watch-dog. Each one barked furiously at the canoes, running alongside until he had got to the end of his own ship, and so passing on the word to the dog aboard the next. We must have seen something like a hundred of these embarkations in the course of that day's paddle, ranged one after another like the houses in a street; and from not one of them were we disappointed of this accompaniment. It was like visiting a menagerie, the *Cigarette* remarked.

These little cities by the canal side had a very odd effect upon the mind. They seemed, with their flower-pots and smoking chimneys, their washings and dinners, a rooted piece of nature in the scene; and yet if only the canal below were to open, one junk after another would hoist sail or harness horses and swim away into all parts of France; and the impromptu hamlet would separate, house by house, to the four winds. The children who played together to-day by the Sambre and Oise Canal, each at his own father's threshold, when and where might they next meet?

For some time past the subject of barges had occupied a great deal of our talk, and we had projected an old age on the canals of Europe. It was to be the most leisurely of progresses, now on a swift river at the tail of a steamboat, now waiting horses for days together on some inconsiderable junction. We should be seen pottering on deck in all the dignity of years, our white beards falling into our laps. We were ever to be busied among paint- pots, so that there should be no white fresher and no green more emerald than ours in all the navy of the canals. There should be books in the cabin, and tobacco jars, and some old Burgundy as red as a November sunset and as odorous as a violet in April. There should be a flageolet whence the *Cigarette*, with cunning touch, should draw melting music under the stars; or perhaps, laying that aside, upraise his voice—somewhat thinner than of yore, and with here and there a quaver, or call it a natural grace note—in rich and solemn psalmody.

All this, simmering in my mind, set me wishing to go aboard one of these ideal houses of lounging. I had plenty to choose from, as I coasted one after another and the dogs bayed at me for a vagrant. At last I saw a nice old man and his wife looking at me with some interest, so I gave them good day and pulled up alongside. I began with a remark upon their dog, which had somewhat the look of a pointer; thence I slid into a compliment on Madame's flowers, and thence into a word in praise of their way of life.

If you ventured on such an experiment in England you would get a slap in the face at once. The life would be shown to be a vile one, not without a side shot at your better fortune. Now, what I like so much in France is the clear, unflinching recognition by everybody of his own luck. They all know on which side their bread is buttered, and take a pleasure in showing it to others, which is surely the better part of religion. And they scorn to make a poor mouth over their poverty, which I take to be the better part of manliness. I have heard a woman in quite a better position at home, with a good bit of money in hand, refer to her own child with a horrid whine as 'a poor man's child.' I would not say such a thing to the Duke of Westminster. And the French are full of this spirit of independence. Perhaps it is the result of republican institutions, as they call them. Much more likely it is because there are so few people really poor that the whiners are not enough to keep each other in countenance.

The people on the barge were delighted to hear that I admired their state. They understood perfectly well, they told me, how Monsieur envied them. Without doubt Monsieur was rich, and in that case he might make a canal-boat as pretty as a villa—*joli comme un château*. And with that they invited me on board their own water villa. They apologised for their cabin; they had not been rich enough to make it as it ought to be.

'The fire should have been here, at this side,' explained the husband. 'Then one might have a writing-table in the middle—books—and' (comprehensively) 'all. It would be quite coquettish—*ça serait tout-à-fait coquet.*' And he looked about him as though the improvements were already made. It was plainly not the first time that he had thus beautified his cabin in imagination; and when next he makes a hit, I should expect to see the writing-table in the middle.

Madame had three birds in a cage. They were no great thing, she explained. Fine birds were so dear. They had sought to get a *Hollandais* last winter in Rouen (Rouen? thought I; and is this whole mansion, with its dogs, and birds, and smoking chimneys, so far a traveller as that? and as homely an object among the cliffs and orchards of the Seine as on the green plains of Sambre?)—they had sought to get a *Hollandais* last winter in Rouen; but these cost fifteen francs apiece—picture it—fifteen francs!

'*Pour un tout petit oiseau*—For quite a little bird,' added the husband.

As I continued to admire, the apologetics died away, and the good people began to brag of their barge and their happy condition in life, as if they had been Emperor and

Empress of the Indies. It was, in the Scots phrase, a good hearing, and put me in good-humour with the world. If people knew what an inspiriting thing it is to hear a man boasting, so long as he boasts of what he really has, I believe they would do it more freely and with a better grace.

They began to ask about our voyage. You should have seen how they sympathised. They seemed half ready to give up their barge and follow us. But these *canaletti* are only gypsies semi-domesticated. The semi-domestication came out in rather a pretty form. Suddenly Madame's brow darkened. '*Cependant*,' she began, and then stopped; and then began again by asking me if I were single.

'Yes,' said I.

'And your friend who went by just now?'

He also was unmarried.

Oh, then, all was well. She could not have wives left alone at home; but since there were no wives in the question, we were doing the best we could.

'To see about one in the world,' said the husband, '*il n'y a que ça*—there is nothing else worth while. A man, look you, who sticks in his own village like a bear,' he went on, 'very well, he sees nothing. And then death is the end of all. And he has seen nothing.'

Madame reminded her husband of an Englishman who had come up this canal in a steamer.

'Perhaps Mr Moens in the *Ytene*,' I suggested.

'That's it,' assented the husband. 'He had his wife and family with him, and servants. He came ashore at all the locks and asked the name of the villages, whether from boatmen or lock-keepers; and then he wrote, wrote them down. Oh, he wrote enormously! I suppose it was a wager.'

A wager was a common enough explanation for our own exploits, but it seemed an original reason for taking notes.

THE OISE IN FLOOD

Before nine next morning the two canoes were installed on a light country cart at Etreux; and we were soon following them along the side of a pleasant valley full of hop-gardens and poplars. Agreeable villages lay here and there on the slope of the hill: notably, Tupigny, with the hop-poles hanging their garlands in the very street, and the houses clustered with grapes. There was a faint enthusiasm on our passage; weavers put their heads to the windows; children cried out in ecstasy at sight of the two 'boaties'—*barquettes*; and bloused pedestrians, who were acquainted with our charioteer, jested with him on the nature of his freight.

We had a shower or two, but light and flying. The air was clean and sweet among all these green fields and green things growing. There was not a touch of autumn in the weather. And when, at Vadencourt, we launched from a little lawn opposite a mill, the sun broke forth and set all the leaves shining in the valley of the Oise.

The river was swollen with the long rains. From Vadencourt all the way to Origny it ran with ever-quickening speed, taking fresh heart at each mile, and racing as though it already smelt the sea. The water was yellow and turbulent, swung with an angry eddy among half-submerged willows, and made an angry clatter along stony shores. The course kept turning and turning in a narrow and well-timbered valley. Now the river would approach the side, and run gliding along the chalky base of the hill, and show us a few open colza fields among the trees. Now it would skirt the garden walls of houses, where we might catch a glimpse through a doorway, and see a priest pacing in the chequered sunlight. Again, the foliage closed so thickly in front that there seemed to be no issue; only a thicket of willows, overtopped by elms and poplars, under which the river ran flush and fleet, and where a kingfisher flew past like a piece of the blue sky. On these different manifestations the sun poured its clear and catholic looks. The shadows lay as solid on the swift surface of the stream as on the stable meadows. The light sparkled golden in the dancing poplar leaves, and brought the hills into communion with our eyes. And all the while the river never stopped running or took breath; and the reeds along the whole valley stood shivering from top to toe.

There should be some myth (but if there is, I know it not) founded on the shivering of the reeds. There are not many things in nature more striking to man's eye. It is such an eloquent pantomime of terror; and to see such a number of terrified creatures taking sanctuary in every nook along the shore is enough to infect a silly human with alarm. Perhaps they are only a-cold, and no wonder, standing waist-deep in the stream. Or, perhaps, they have never got accustomed to the speed and fury of the river's flux, or the miracle of its continuous body. Pan once played upon their forefathers; and so, by the hands of his river, he still plays upon these later generations down all the valley of the Oise; and plays the same air, both sweet and shrill, to tell us of the beauty and the terror of the world.

The canoe was like a leaf in the current. It took it up and shook it, and carried it masterfully away, like a Centaur carrying off a nymph. To keep some command on our direction required hard and diligent plying of the paddle. The river was in such a hurry for the sea! Every drop of water ran in a panic, like so many people in a frightened crowd. But what crowd was ever so numerous or so single-minded? All the objects of sight went by at a dance measure; the eyesight raced with the racing river; the exigencies of every moment kept the pegs screwed so tight that our being quivered like a well-tuned instrument, and the blood shook off its lethargy, and trotted through all the highways and byways of the veins and arteries, and in and out of the heart, as if circulation were but a holiday journey and not the daily moil of threescore years and ten. The reeds might nod their heads in warning, and with tremulous gestures tell how the river was as cruel as it was strong and cold, and how death lurked in the eddy underneath the willows. But the reeds had to stand where they were; and those who stand still are always timid advisers. As for us, we could have shouted aloud. If this lively and beautiful river were, indeed, a thing of death's contrivance, the old ashen rogue had famously outwitted himself with us. I was living three to the minute. I was scoring points against him every stroke of my paddle, every turn of the stream. I have rarely had better profit of my life.

For I think we may look upon our little private war with death somewhat in this light. If a man knows he will sooner or later be robbed upon a journey, he will have a bottle of the best in every inn, and look upon all his extravagances as so much gained upon the thieves. And above all, where, instead of simply spending, he makes a profitable investment for some of his money, when it will be out of risk of loss. So every bit of brisk living, and above all when it is healthful, is just so much gained upon the wholesale filcher, death. We shall have the less in our pockets, the more in our stomachs, when he cries, 'Stand and deliver.' A swift stream is a favourite artifice of his, and one that brings him in a comfortable thing per annum; but when he and I come to settle our accounts I shall whistle in his face for these hours upon the upper Oise.

Towards afternoon we got fairly drunken with the sunshine and the exhilaration of the pace. We could no longer contain ourselves and our content. The canoes were too small for us; we must be out and stretch ourselves on shore. And so in a green meadow we bestowed our limbs on the grass, and smoked deifying tobacco, and proclaimed the world excellent. It was the last good hour of the day, and I dwell upon it with extreme complacency.

On one side of the valley, high upon the chalky summit of the hill, a ploughman with his team appeared and disappeared at regular intervals. At each revelation he stood still for a few seconds against the sky, for all the world (as the *Cigarette* declared) like a toy Burns who should have just ploughed up the Mountain Daisy.* He was the only living thing within view, unless we are to count the river.

On the other side of the valley a group of red roofs and a belfry showed among the foliage. Thence some inspired bell-ringer made the afternoon musical on a chime of bells. There was something very sweet and taking in the air he played, and we thought we had never heard bells speak so intelligibly or sing so melodiously as these. It must have been to some such measure that the spinners and the young maids sang, 'Come away, Death,'* in the Shakespearian Illyria. There is so often a threatening note, something blatant and metallic, in the voice of bells, that I believe we have fully more pain than pleasure from hearing them; but these, as they sounded abroad, now high, now low, now with a plaintive cadence that caught the ear like the burthen of a popular song, were always moderate and tunable, and seemed to fall in with the spirit of still, rustic places, like the noise of a waterfall or the babble of a rookery in spring. I could have asked the bell-ringer for his blessing, good, sedate, old man, who swung the rope so gently to the time of his meditations. I could have blessed the priest or the heritors, or whoever may be concerned with such affairs in France, who had left these sweet old bells to gladden the afternoon, and not held meetings, and made collections, and had their names repeatedly printed in the local paper, to rig up a peal of brand-new, brazen, Birmingham-hearted substitutes, who should bombard their sides to the provocation of a brand-new bell-ringer, and fill the echoes of the valley with terror and riot.

At last the bells ceased, and with their note the sun withdrew. The piece was at an end; shadow and silence possessed the valley of the Oise. We took to the paddle with glad hearts, like people who have sat out a noble performance and returned to work. The river was more dangerous here; it ran swifter, the eddies were more sudden and violent. All the way down we had had our fill of difficulties. Sometimes it was a weir which could be shot, sometimes one so shallow and full of stakes that we must withdraw the boats from the water and carry them round. But the chief sort of obstacle was a consequence of the late high winds. Every two or three hundred yards a tree had fallen across the river, and usually involved more than another in its fall. Often there was free water at the end,

and we could steer round the leafy promontory and hear
the water sucking and bubbling among the twigs. Often,
again, when the tree reached from bank to bank, there was
room, by lying close, to shoot through underneath, canoe
and all. Sometimes it was necessary to get out upon the
trunk itself and pull the boats across; and sometimes, where
the stream was too impetuous for this, there was nothing
for it but to land and 'carry over.' This made a fine series
of accidents in the day's career, and kept us aware of
ourselves.

Shortly after our re-embarkation, while I was leading by
a long way, and still full of a noble, exulting spirit in honour
of the sun, the swift pace, and the church bells, the river
made one of its leonine pounces round a corner, and I was
aware of another fallen tree within a stone-cast. I had my
back-board down in a trice, and aimed for a place where
the trunk seemed high enough above the water, and the
branches not too thick, to let me slip below. When a man
has just vowed eternal brotherhood with the universe he is
not in a temper to take great determinations coolly, and
this, which might have been a very important determination
for me, had not been taken under a happy star. The tree
caught me about the chest, and while I was yet struggling
to make less of myself and get through, the river took the
matter out of my hands and bereaved me of my boat. The
Arethusa swung round broadside on, leaned over, ejected so
much of me as still remained on board, and, thus disen-
cumbered, whipped under the tree, righted, and went merrily away down stream.

I do not know how long it was before I scrambled on to
the tree to which I was left clinging, but it was longer than
I cared about. My thoughts were of a grave and almost
sombre character, but I still clung to my paddle. The stream
ran away with my heels as fast as I could pull up my
shoulders, and I seemed, by the weight, to have all the
water of the Oise in my trousers' pockets. You can never
know, till you try it, what a dead pull a river makes against
a man. Death himself had me by the heels, for this was his
last ambuscade, and he must now join personally in the

fray. And still I held to my paddle. At last I dragged myself on to my stomach on the trunk, and lay there a breathless sop, with a mingled sense of humour and injustice. A poor figure I must have presented to Burns upon the hill-top with his team. But there was the paddle in my hand. On my tomb, if ever I have one, I mean to get these words inscribed: 'He clung to his paddle.'

The *Cigarette* had gone past awhile before; for, as I might have observed, if I had been a little less pleased with the universe at the moment, there was a clear way round the tree-top at the farther side. He had offered his services to haul me out, but, as I was then already on my elbows, I had declined and sent him down stream after the truant *Arethusa*. The stream was too rapid for a man to mount with one canoe, let alone two, upon his hands. So I crawled along the trunk to shore, and proceeded down the meadows by the river-side. I was so cold that my heart was sore. I had now an idea of my own why the reeds so bitterly shivered. I could have given any of them a lesson. The *Cigarette* remarked, facetiously, that he thought I was 'taking exercise' as I drew near, until he made out for certain that I was only twittering with cold. I had a rub-down with a towel, and donned a dry suit from the india-rubber bag. But I was not my own man again for the rest of the voyage. I had a queasy sense that I wore my last dry clothes upon my body. The struggle had tired me; and perhaps, whether I knew it or not, I was a little dashed in spirit. The devouring element in the universe had leaped out against me, in this green valley quickened by a running stream. The bells were all very pretty in their way, but I had heard some of the hollow notes of Pan's music. Would the wicked river drag me down by the heels, indeed? and look so beautiful all the time? Nature's good-humour was only skin deep after all.

There was still a long way to go by the winding course of the stream, and darkness had fallen, and a late bell was ringing in Origny Sainte-Benoîte when we arrived.

ORIGNY SAINTE-BENOÎTE

A BY-DAY

The next day was Sunday, and the church bells had little rest; indeed, I do not think I remember anywhere else so great a choice of services as were here offered to the devout. And while the bells made merry in the sunshine, all the world with his dog was out shooting among the beets and colza.

In the morning a hawker and his wife went down the street at a foot-pace, singing to a very slow, lamentable music, 'O France, mes amours.' It brought everybody to the door; and when our landlady called in the man to buy the words, he had not a copy of them left. She was not the first nor the second who had been taken with the song. There is something very pathetic in the love of the French people, since the war, for dismal patriotic music-making. I have watched a forester from Alsace while some one was singing 'Les malheurs de la France,' at a baptismal party in the neighbourhood of Fontainebleau. He arose from the table and took his son aside, close by where I was standing. 'Listen, listen,' he said, bearing on the boy's shoulder, 'and remember this, my son.' A little after he went out into the garden suddenly, and I could hear him sobbing in the darkness.

The humiliation of their arms and the loss of Alsace and Lorraine made a sore pull on the endurance of this sensitive people; and their hearts are still hot, not so much against Germany as against the Empire. In what other country will you find a patriotic ditty bring all the world into the street? But affliction heightens love; and we shall never know we are Englishmen until we have lost India. Independent America is still the cross of my existence; I cannot think of Farmer George without abhorrence; and I never feel more warmly to my own land than when I see the Stars and Stripes, and remember what our empire might have been.

The hawker's little book, which I purchased, was a curious mixture. Side by side with the flippant, rowdy nonsense of the Paris music-halls there were many pastoral pieces, not without a touch of poetry, I thought, and instinct with the brave independence of the poorer class in France. There you might read how the wood-cutter gloried in his axe, and the gardener scorned to be ashamed of his spade. It was not very well written, this poetry of labour, but the pluck of the sentiment redeemed what was weak or wordy in the expression. The martial and the patriotic pieces, on the other hand, were tearful, womanish productions one and all. The poet had passed under the Caudine Forks;* he sang for an army visiting the tomb of its old renown, with arms reversed; and sang not of victory, but of death. There was a number in the hawker's collection called 'Conscrits Français,' which may rank among the most dissuasive war-lyrics on record. It would not be possible to fight at all in such a spirit. The bravest conscript would turn pale if such a ditty were struck up beside him on the morning of battle; and whole regiments would pile their arms to its tune.

If Fletcher of Saltoun* is in the right about the influence of national songs, you would say France was come to a poor pass. But the thing will work its own cure, and a sound-hearted and courageous people weary at length of snivelling over their disasters. Already Paul Déroulède has written some manly military verses. There is not much of the trumpet note in them, perhaps, to stir a man's heart in his bosom; they lack the lyrical elation, and move slowly; but they are written in a grave, honourable, stoical spirit, which should carry soldiers far in a good cause. One feels as if one would like to trust Déroulède with something. It will be happy if he can so far inoculate his fellow-countrymen that they may be trusted with their own future. And, in the mean time, here is an antidote to 'French Conscripts' and much other doleful versification.

We had left the boats over night in the custody of one whom we shall call Carnival. I did not properly catch his name, and perhaps that was not unfortunate for him, as I am not in a position to hand him down with honour to posterity. To this person's premises we strolled in the course of the day, and found quite a little deputation inspecting the canoes. There was a stout gentleman with a knowledge of the river, which he seemed eager to impart. There was a very elegant young gentleman in a black coat, with a smattering of English, who led the talk at once to the Oxford and Cambridge boat race. And then there were three handsome girls from fifteen to twenty; and an old gentleman in a blouse, with no teeth to speak of, and a strong country accent. Quite the pick of Origny, I should suppose.

The *Cigarette* had some mysteries to perform with his rigging in the coach-house; so I was left to do the parade single-handed. I found myself very much of a hero whether I would or not. The girls were full of little shudderings over the dangers of our journey. And I thought it would be ungallant not to take my cue from the ladies. My mishap of yesterday, told in an off-hand way, produced a deep sensation. It was Othello over again, with no less than three Desdemonas and a sprinkling of sympathetic senators in the background. Never were the canoes more flattered, or flattered more adroitly.

'It is like a violin,' cried one of the girls, in an ecstasy.

'I thank you for the word, mademoiselle,' said I. 'All the more since there are people who call out to me that it is like a coffin.'

'Oh! but it is really like a violin. It is finished like a violin,' she went on.

'And polished like a violin,' added a senator.

'One has only to stretch the cords,' concluded another, 'and then tum-tumty-tum'; he imitated the result with spirit.

Was not this a graceful little ovation? Where this people finds the secret of its pretty speeches I cannot imagine; unless the secret should be no other than a sincere desire to please! But then no disgrace is attached in France to saying a thing neatly; whereas in England, to talk like a book is to give in one's resignation to society.

The old gentleman in the blouse stole into the coach-house, and somewhat irrelevantly informed the *Cigarette* that he was the father of the three girls and four more; quite an exploit for a Frenchman.

'You are very fortunate,' answered the *Cigarette* politely.

And the old gentleman, having apparently gained his point, stole away again.

We all got very friendly together. The girls proposed to start with us on the morrow, if you please! And, jesting apart, every one was anxious to know the hour of our departure. Now, when you are going to crawl into your canoe from a bad launch, a crowd, however friendly, is undesirable, and so we told them not before twelve, and mentally determined to be off by ten at latest.

Towards evening we went abroad again to post some letters. It was cool and pleasant; the long village was quite empty, except for one or two urchins who followed us as they might have followed a menagerie; the hills and the tree-tops looked in from all sides through the clear air, and the bells were chiming for yet another service.

Suddenly we sighted the three girls, standing, with a fourth sister, in front of a shop on the wide selvage of the roadway. We had been very merry with them a little while ago, to be sure. But what was the etiquette of Origny? Had it been a country road, of course we should have spoken to them; but here, under the eyes of all the gossips, ought we to do even as much as bow? I consulted the *Cigarette*.

'Look,' said he.

I looked. There were the four girls on the same spot; but now four backs were turned to us, very upright and conscious. Corporal Modesty had given the word of command, and the well-disciplined picket had gone right-about-face like a single person. They maintained this formation all the while we were in sight; but we heard them tittering among themselves, and the girl whom we had not met laughed with open mouth, and even looked over her shoulder at the enemy. I wonder was it altogether modesty after all, or in part a sort of country provocation?

As we were returning to the inn we beheld something floating in the ample field of golden evening sky, above the chalk cliffs and the trees that grow along their summit. It was too high up, too large, and too steady for a kite; and, as it was dark, it could not be a star. For although a star were as black as ink and as rugged as a walnut, so amply does the sun bathe heaven with radiance that it would sparkle like a point of light for us. The village was dotted with people with their heads in air; and the children were in a bustle all along the street and far up the straight road that climbs the hill, where we could still see them running in loose knots. It was a balloon, we learned, which had left Saint Quentin at half-past five that evening. Mighty composedly the majority of the grown people took it. But we were English, and were soon running up the hill with the best. Being travellers ourselves in a small way, we would fain have seen these other travellers alight.

The spectacle was over by the time we gained the top of the hill. All the gold had withered out of the sky, and the balloon had disappeared. Whither? I ask myself; caught up into the seventh heaven? or come safely to land somewhere in that blue, uneven distance, into which the roadway dipped and melted before our eyes? Probably the aëronauts were already warming themselves at a farm chimney, for they say it is cold in these unhomely regions of the air. The night fell swiftly. Roadside trees and disappointed sightseers, returning through the meadows, stood out in black against a margin of low, red sunset. It was cheerfuller to face the other way, and so down the hill we went, with a full moon, the colour of a melon, swinging high above the wooded valley, and the white cliffs behind us faintly reddened by the fire of the chalk-kilns.

The lamps were lighted, and the salads were being made in Origny Sainte-Benoîte by the river.

ORIGNY SAINTE-BENOÎTE

THE COMPANY AT TABLE

Although we came late for dinner, the company at table treated us to sparkling wine. 'That is how we are in France,' said one. 'Those who sit down with us are our friends.' And the rest applauded.

They were three altogether, and an odd trio to pass the Sunday with.

Two of them were guests like ourselves, both men of the north. One ruddy, and of a full habit of body, with copious black hair and beard, the intrepid hunter of France, who thought nothing so small, not even a lark or a minnow, but he might vindicate his prowess by its capture. For such a great, healthy man, his hair flourishing like Samson's, his arteries running buckets of red blood, to boast of these infinitesimal exploits, produced a feeling of disproportion in the world, as when a steam-hammer is set to cracking nuts. The other was a quiet, subdued person, blond, and lymphatic, and sad, with something the look of a Dane: '*Tristes têtes de Danois!*' as Gaston Lafenestre* used to say.

I must not let that name go by without a word for the best of all good fellows, now gone down into the dust. We shall never again see Gaston in his forest costume,—he was Gaston with all the world, in affection, not in disrespect,— nor hear him wake the echoes of Fontainebleau with the woodland horn. Never again shall his kind smile put peace among all races of artistic men, and make the Englishman at home in France. Never more shall the sheep, who were not more innocent at heart than he, sit all unconsciously for his industrious pencil. He died too early, at the very moment when he was beginning to put forth fresh sprouts and blossom into something worthy of himself; and yet none who knew him will think he lived in vain. I never knew a man so little, for whom yet I had so much affection; and I find it a good test of others, how much they had learned to understand and value him. His was, indeed, a good influence in life while he was still among us; he had a fresh laugh; it did you good to see him; and, however sad he may have been at heart, he always bore a bold and cheerful countenance and took fortune's worst as it were the showers of spring. But now his mother sits alone by the side of Fontainebleau woods, where he gathered mushrooms in his hardy and penurious youth.

Many of his pictures found their way across the Channel; besides those which were stolen, when a dastardly Yankee left him alone in London with two English pence, and, perhaps, twice as many words of English. If anyone who reads these lines should have a scene of sheep, in the manner of Jacques, with this fine creature's signature, let him tell himself that one of the kindest and bravest of men has lent a hand to decorate his lodging. There may be better pictures in the National Gallery; but not a painter among the generations had a better heart. Precious in the sight of the Lord of humanity, the Psalms tell us, is the death of His saints. It had need to be precious; for it is very costly, when, by the stroke, a mother is left desolate, and the peace-maker and *peace-looker* of a whole society is laid in the ground with Cæsar and the Twelve Apostles.

There is something lacking among the oaks of Fontainebleau; and when the dessert comes in at Barbizon, people look to the door for a figure that is gone.

The third of our companions at Origny was no less a person than the landlady's husband; not properly the landlord, since he worked himself in a factory during the day, and came to his own house at evening as a guest; a man worn to skin and bone by perpetual excitement, with baldish head, sharp features, and swift, shining eyes. On Saturday, describing some paltry adventure at a duck hunt, he broke a plate into a score of fragments. Whenever he made a remark, he would look all round the table, with his chin raised and a spark of green light in either eye, seeking approval. His wife appeared now and again in the doorway of the room, where she was superintending dinner, with a 'Henri, you forget yourself,' or a 'Henri, you can surely talk without making such a noise.' Indeed, that was what the honest fellow could not do. On the most trifling matter his eyes kindled, his fist visited the table, and his voice rolled abroad in changeful thunder. I never saw such a petard of a man; I think the devil was in him. He had two favourite expressions: 'It is logical,' or illogical, as the case might be; and this other, thrown out with a certain bravado, as a man might unfurl a banner, at the beginning of many a long and sonorous story: 'I am a proletarian, you see.' Indeed, we saw it very well. God forbid that ever I should find him handling a gun in Paris streets. That will not be a good moment for the general public.

I thought his two phrases very much represented the good and evil of his class, and, to some extent, of his country. It is a strong thing to say what one is, and not be ashamed of it; even although it be in doubtful taste to repeat the statement too often in one evening. I should not admire it in a duke, of course; but as times go the trait is honourable in a workman. On the other hand, it is not at all a strong thing to put one's reliance upon logic; and our own logic particularly, for it is generally wrong. We never know where we are to end if once we begin following words or doctors. There is an upright stock in a man's own heart that is trustier than any syllogism; and the eyes, and the sympathies, and appetites know a thing or two that have never yet been stated in controversy. Reasons are as plentiful as blackberries; and, like fisticuffs, they serve impartially with all sides. Doctrines do not stand or fall by their proofs and are only logical in so far as they are cleverly put. An able controversialist no more than an able general demonstrates the justice of his cause. But France is all gone wandering after one or two big words; it will take some time before they can be satisfied that they are no more than words, however big; and, when once that is done, they will perhaps find logic less diverting.

The conversation opened with details of the day's shooting. When all the sportsmen of a village shoot over the village territory *pro indiviso*, it is plain that many questions of etiquette and priority must arise.

'Here now,' cried the landlord, brandishing a plate, 'here is a field of beet-root. Well. Here am I, then. I advance, do I not? *Eh bien! sacristi* '; and the statement, waxing louder, rolls off into a reverberation of oaths, the speaker glaring about for sympathy, and everybody nodding his head to him in the name of peace.

The ruddy Northman told some tales of his own prowess in keeping order: notably one of a Marquis.

'Marquis,' I said, 'if you take another step I fire upon you. You have committed a dirtiness, Marquis.'

Whereupon, it appeared, the Marquis touched his cap and withdrew.

The landlord applauded noisily. 'It was well done,' he said. 'He did all that he could. He admitted he was wrong.' And then oath upon oath. He was no marquis-lover, either, but he had a sense of justice in him, this proletarian host of ours.

From the matter of hunting, the talk veered into a general comparison of Paris and the country. the proletarian beat the table like a drum in praise in Paris. 'What is Paris? Paris is the cream of France. There are no Parisians; it is you, and I, and everybody who are Parisians. A man has eighty chances per cent. to get on in the world in Paris.' And he drew a vivid sketch of the workman in a den no bigger than a dog-hutch, making articles that were to go all over the world. '*Eh bien, quoi, c'est magnifique, ça!* ' cried he.

The sad Northman interfered in praise of a peasant's life; he thought Paris bad for men and women. 'Centralisation,' said he——

But the landlord was at his throat in a moment. It was all logical, he showed him; and all magnificent. 'What a spectacle! What a glance for an eye!' And the dishes reeled upon the table under a cannonade of blows.

Seeking to make peace, I threw in a word in praise of the liberty of opinion in France. I could hardly have shot more amiss. There was an instant silence and a great wagging of significant heads. They did not fancy the subject, it was plain, but they gave me to understand that the sad Northman was a martyr on account of his views. 'Ask him a bit,' said they. 'Just ask him.'

'Yes, sir,' said he, in his quiet way, answering me, although I had not spoken, 'I am afraid there is less liberty of opinion in France than you may imagine.' And with that he dropped his eyes and seemed to consider the subject at an end.

Our curiosity was mightily excited at this. How, or why, or when was this lymphatic bagman martyred? We concluded at once it was on some religious question, and brushed up our memories of the Inquisition, which were principally drawn from Poe's horrid story, and the sermon in *Tristram Shandy*, I believe.

On the morrow we had an opportunity of going further into the question; for when we rose very early to avoid a sympathising deputation at our departure, we found the hero up before us. He was breaking his fast on white wine and raw onions, in order to keep up the character of martyr, I conclude. We had a long conversation, and made out what we wanted in spite of his reserve. But here was a truly curious circumstance. It seems possible for two Scotsmen and a Frenchman to discuss during a long half-hour, and each nationality have a different idea in view throughout. It was not till the very end that we discovered his heresy had been political, or that he suspected our mistake. The terms and spirit in which he spoke of his political beliefs were, in our eyes, suited to religious beliefs. And *vice versâ*.

Nothing could be more characteristic of the two countries. Politics are the religion of France; as Nanty Ewart* would have said, 'A d——d bad religion;' while we, at home, keep most of our bitterness for little differences about a hymn-book or a Hebrew word which, perhaps, neither of the parties can translate. And perhaps the misconception is typical of many others that may never be cleared up; not only between people of different race, but between those of different sex.

As for our friend's martyrdom, he was a Communist—or perhaps only a Communard, which is a very different thing—and had lost one or more situations in consequence. I think he had also been rejected in marriage; but perhaps he had a sentimental way of considering business which deceived me. He was a mild, gentle creature, any way, and I hope he has got a better situation and married a more suitable wife since then.

DOWN THE OISE

TO MOY

Carnival notoriously cheated us at first. Finding us easy in our ways, he regretted having let us off so cheaply, and, taking me aside, told me a cock-and-bull story, with the moral of another five francs for the narrator. The thing was palpably absurd; but I paid up, and at once dropped all friendliness of manner and kept him in his place as an inferior, with freezing British dignity. He saw in a moment that he had gone too far and killed a willing horse; his face fell; I am sure he would have refunded if he could only have thought of a decent pretext. He wished me to drink with him, but I would none of his drinks. He grew pathetically tender in his professions, but I walked beside him in silence or answered him in stately courtesies, and, when we got to the landing-place, passed the word in English slang to the *Cigarette*.

In spite of the false scent we had thrown out the day before, there must have been fifty people about the bridge. We were as pleasant as we could be with all but Carnival. We said good-by, shaking hands with the old gentleman who knew the river and the young gentleman who had a smattering of English, but never a word for Carnival. Poor Carnival! here was a humiliation. He who had been so much identified with the canoes, who had given orders in our name, who had shown off the boats and even the boatmen like a private exhibition of his own, to be now so publicly shamed by the lions of his caravan! I never saw anybody look more crestfallen than he. He hung in the background, coming timidly forward ever and again as he thought he saw some symptom of a relenting humour, and falling hurriedly back when he encountered a cold stare. Let us hope it will be a lesson to him.

I would not have mentioned Carnival's peccadillo had not the thing been so uncommon in France. This, for instance, was the only case of dishonesty or even sharp practice in our whole voyage. We talk very much about our honesty in England. It is a good‘rule to be on your guard wherever you hear great professions about a very little piece of virtue. If the English could only hear how they are spoken of abroad, they might confine themselves for a while to remedying the fact, and perhaps even when that was done, give us fewer of their airs.

The young ladies, the graces of Origny, were not present at our start; but when we got round to the second bridge, behold, it was black with sight-seers! We were loudly cheered, and for a good way below young lads and lasses ran along the bank, still cheering. What with current and paddling, we were flashing along like swallows. It was no joke to keep up with us upon the woody shore. But the girls picked up their skirts, as if they were sure they had good ankles, and followed until their breath was out. The last to weary were the three graces and a couple of companions; and just as they, too, had had enough, the foremost of the three leaped upon a tree-stump and kissed her hand to the canoeists. Not Diana herself, although this was more of a Venus, after all, could have done a graceful thing more gracefully. 'Come back again!' she cried; and all the others echoed her; and the hills about Origny repeated the words, 'Come back.' But the river had us round an angle in a twinkling, and we were alone with the green trees and running water.

Come back? There is no coming back, young ladies, on the impetuous stream of life.

> The merchant bows unto the seaman's star,
> The ploughman from the sun his season takes.

And we must all set our pocket-watches by the clock of fate. There is a headlong, forthright tide, that bears away man with his fancies like straw, and runs fast in time and space. It is full of curves like this, your winding river of the Oise, and lingers and returns in pleasant pastorals; and yet, rightly thought upon, never returns at all. For though it should revisit the same acre of meadow in the same hour, it will have made an ample sweep between-whiles; many little streams will have fallen in; many exhalations risen towards the sun; and even although it were the same acre, it will not be the same river Oise. And thus, O graces of Origny, although the wandering fortune of my life should carry me back again to where you await death's whistle by the river, that will not be the old I who walks the street; and those wives and mothers, say, will those be you?

There was never any mistake about the Oise, as a matter of fact. In these upper reaches it was still in a prodigious hurry for the sea. It ran so fast and merrily, through all the windings of its channel, that I strained my thumb fighting with the rapids, and had to paddle all the rest of the way with one hand turned up. Sometimes it had to serve mills, and being still a little river, ran very dry and shallow in the meanwhile. We had to put our legs out of the boat, and shove ourselves off the sand of the bottom with our feet. And still it went on its way singing among the poplars, and making a green valley in the world. After a good woman, and a good book, and tobacco, there is nothing so agreeable on earth as a river. I forgave it its attempt on my life; which was, after all, one part owing to the unruly winds of heaven that had blown down the tree, one part to my own mismanagement, and only a third part to the river itself, and that not out of malice, but from its great preoccupation over its own business of getting to the sea. A difficult business, too; for the detours it had to make are not to be counted. The geographers seem to have given up the attempt; for I found no map represent the infinite contortion of its course. A fact will say more than any of them. After we had been some hours—three, if I mistake not—flitting by the trees at this smooth, breakneck gallop, when we came upon a hamlet and asked where we were, we had got no farther than four kilomètres (say two miles and a half) from Origny. If it were not for the honour of the thing (in the Scotch saying), we might almost as well have been standing still.

We lunched on a meadow inside a parallelogram of poplars. The leaves danced and prattled in the wind all round about us. The river hurried on meanwhile, and seemed to chide at our delay. Little we cared. The river knew where it was going; not so we; the less our hurry, where we found good quarters, and a pleasant theatre for a pipe. At that hour stock-brokers were shouting in Paris Bourse for two or three per cent.; but we minded them as little as the sliding stream, and sacrificed a hecatomb of minutes to the gods of tobacco and digestion. Hurry is the resource of the faithless. Where a man can trust his own heart, and those of his friends, to-morrow is as good as to-day. And if he die in the meanwhile, why, then, there he dies, and the question is solved.

We had to take to the canal in the course of the afternoon; because where it crossed the river there was not a bridge, but a siphon. If it had not been for an excited fellow on the bank we should have paddled right into the siphon, and thenceforward not paddled any more. We met a man, a gentleman, on the towpath, who was much interested in our cruise. And I was witness to a strange seizure of lying suffered by the *Cigarette*; who, because his knife came from Norway, narrated all sorts of adventures in that country, where he has never been. He was quite feverish at the end, and pleaded demoniacal possession.

Moy (pronounce Moÿ) was a pleasant little village, gathered round a château in a moat. The air was perfumed with hemp from neighbouring fields. At the Golden Sheep we found excellent entertainment. German shells from the siege of La Fère, Nürnberg figures, goldfish in a bowl, and all manner of knick-knacks, embellished the public room. The landlady was a stout, plain, short-sighted, motherly body, with something not far short of a genius for cookery. She had a guess of her excellence herself. After every dish was sent in, she would come and look on at the dinner for a while, with puckered, blinking eyes. '*C'est bon, n'est-ce pas?*' she would say; and when she had received a proper answer, she disappeared into the kitchen. That common French dish, partridge and cabbages, became a new thing in my eyes at the Golden Sheep; and many subsequent dinners have bitterly disappointed me in consequence. Sweet was our rest in the Golden Sheep at Moy.

LA FÈRE OF CURSED MEMORY

We lingered in Moy a good part of the day, for we were fond of being philosophical, and scorned long journeys and early starts on principle. The place, moreover, invited to repose. People in elaborate shooting costumes sallied from the château with guns and game-bags; and this was a pleasure in itself, to remain behind while these elegant pleasure-seekers took the first of the morning. In this way all the world may be an aristocrat, and play the duke among marquises, and the reigning monarch among dukes, if he will only outvie them in tranquillity. An imperturbable demeanour comes from perfect patience. Quiet minds cannot be perplexed or frightened, but go on in fortune or misfortune at their own private pace, like a clock during a thunderstorm.

We made a very short day of it to La Fère; but the dusk was falling and a small rain had begun before we stowed the boats. La Fère is a fortified town in a plain, and has two belts of rampart. Between the first and the second extends a region of waste land and cultivated patches. Here and there along the wayside were posters forbidding trespass in the name of military engineering. At last a second gateway admitted us to the town itself. Lighted windows looked gladsome, whiffs of comfortable cookery came abroad upon the air. The town was full of the military reserve, out for the French Autumn Manœuvres, and the reservists walked speedily and wore their formidable great-coats. It was a fine night to be within doors over dinner, and hear the rain upon the windows.

The *Cigarette* and I could not sufficiently congratulate each other on the prospect, for we had been told there was a capital inn at La Fère. Such a dinner as we were going to eat! such beds as we were to sleep in! and all the while the rain raining on houseless folk over all the poplared country-side. It made our mouths water. The inn bore the name of some woodland animal, stag, or hart, or hind, I forget which. But I shall never forget how spacious and how eminently habitable it looked as we drew near. The carriage entry was lighted up, not by intention, but from the mere superfluity of fire and candle in the house. A rattle of many dishes came to our ears; we sighted a great field of tablecloth; the kitchen glowed like a forge and smelt like a garden of things to eat.

Into this, the inmost shrine and physiological heart of a hostelry, with all its furnaces in action and all its dressers charged with viands, you are now to suppose us making our triumphal entry, a pair of damp rag-and-bone men, each with a limp india-rubber bag upon his arm. I do not believe I have a sound view of that kitchen; I saw it through a sort of glory, but it seemed to me crowded with the snowy caps of cookmen, who all turned round from their sauce-pans and looked at us with surprise. There was no doubt about the landlady, however; there she was, heading her army, a flushed, angry woman, full of affairs. Her I asked politely—too politely, thinks the *Cigarette*—if we could have beds, she surveying us coldly from head to foot.

'You will find beds in the suburb,' she remarked. 'We are too busy for the like of you.'

If we could make an entrance, change our clothes, and order a bottle of wine, I felt sure we could put things right; so said I, 'If we cannot sleep, we may at least dine,'—and was for depositing my bag.

What a terrible convulsion of nature was that which followed in the landlady's face! She made a run at us and stamped her foot.

'Out with you,—out of the door!' she screeched. '*Sortez! sortez! sortez par la porte!*'

I do not know how it happened, but next moment we were out in the rain and darkness, and I was cursing before the carriage entry like a disappointed mendicant. Where were the boating men of Belgium? where the Judge and his good wines? and where the Graces of Origny? Black, black was the night after the firelit kitchen, but what was that to the blackness in our heart? This was not the first time that I have been refused a lodging. Often and often have I planned what I should do if such a misadventure happened to me again. And nothing is easier to plan. But to put in execution, with the heart boiling at the indignity? Try it; try it only once; and tell me what you did.

It is all very fine to talk about tramps and morality. Six hours of police surveillance (such as I have had) or one brutal rejection from an inn-door change your views upon the subject like a course of lectures. As long as you keep in the upper regions, with all the world bowing to you as you go, social arrangements have a very handsome air; but once get under the wheels and you wish society were at the devil. I will give most respectable men a fortnight of such a life, and then I will offer them twopence for what remains of their morality.

For my part, when I was turned out of the Stag, or the Hind, or whatever it was, I would have set the temple of Diana on fire if it had been handy. There was no crime complete enough to express my disapproval of human institutions. As for the *Cigarette*, I never knew a man so altered. 'We have been taken for pedlars again,' said he. 'Good God, what it must be to be a pedlar in reality!' He particularised a complaint for every joint in the landlady's body. Timon was a philanthropist alongside of him. And then, when he was at the top of his maledictory bent, he would suddenly break away and begin whimperingly to commiserate the poor. 'I hope to God,' he said,—and I trust the prayer was answered,—'that I shall never be uncivil to a pedlar.' Was this the imperturbable *Cigarette?* This, this was he. Oh, change beyond report, thought, or belief !

Meantime the heaven wept upon our heads; and the windows grew brighter as the night increased in darkness. We trudged in and out of La Fère streets; we saw shops, and private houses where people were copiously dining; we saw stables where carters' nags had plenty of fodder and clean straw; we saw no end of reservists, who were very sorry for themselves this wet night, I doubt not, and yearned for their country homes; but had they not each man his place in La Fère barracks? And we, what had we?

There seemed to be no other inn in the whole town. People gave us directions, which we followed as best we could, generally with the effect of bringing us out again upon the scene of our disgrace. We were very sad people indeed, by the time we had gone all over La Fère; and the *Cigarette* had already made up his mind to lie under a poplar and sup off a loaf of bread. But right at the other end, the house next the town-gate was full of light and bustle. '*Bazin, aubergiste, loge à pied*,' was the sign. '*À la Croix de Malte.*'* There were we received.

The room was full of noisy reservists drinking and smoking; and we were very glad indeed when the drums and bugles began to go about the streets, and one and all had to snatch shakoes and be off for the barracks.

Bazin was a tall man, running to fat; soft-spoken, with a delicate, gentle face. We asked him to share our wine; but he excused himself, having pledged reservists all day long. This was a very different type of the workman-innkeeper from the bawling, disputatious fellow at Origny. He also loved Paris, where he had worked as a decorative painter in his youth. There were such opportunities for self-instruction there, he said. And if anyone has read Zola's description of the workman's marriage-party visiting the Louvre* they would do well to have heard Bazin by way of antidote. He had delighted in the museums in his youth. 'One sees there little miracles of work,' he said; 'that is what makes a good workman; it kindles a spark.' We asked him how he managed in La Fère. 'I am married,' he said, 'and I have my pretty children. But frankly, it is no life at all. From morning to night I pledge a pack of good-enough fellows who know nothing.'

It faired as the night went on, and the moon came out of the clouds. We sat in front of the door, talking softly with Bazin. At the guard-house opposite the guard was being forever turned out, as trains of field artillery kept clanking in out of the night or patrols of horsemen trotted by in their cloaks. Madame Bazin came out after a while; she was tired with her day's work, I suppose; and she nestled up to her husband and laid her head upon his breast. He had his arm about her and kept gently patting her on the shoulder. I think Bazin was right, and he was really married. Of how few people can the same be said!

Little did the Bazins know how much they served us. We were charged for candles, for food and drink, and for the beds we slept in. But there was nothing in the bill for the husband's pleasant talk; nor for the pretty spectacle of their married life. And there was yet another item uncharged. For these people's politeness really set us up again in our own esteem. We had a thirst for consideration; the sense of insult was still hot in our spirits; and civil usage seemed to restore us to our position in the world.

How little we pay our way in life! Although we have our purses continually in our hand, the better part of service goes still unrewarded. But I like to fancy that a grateful spirit gives as good as it gets. Perhaps the Bazins knew how much I liked them? perhaps they, also, were healed for some slights by the thanks that I gave them in my manner?

DOWN THE OISE

THROUGH THE GOLDEN VALLEY

Below La Fère the river runs through a piece of open pastoral country; green, opulent, loved by breeders; called the Golden Valley. In wide sweeps, and with a swift and equable gallop, the ceaseless stream of water visits and makes green the fields. Kine, and horses, and little humorous donkeys browse together in the meadows, and come down in troops to the river-side to drink. They make a strange feature in the landscape; above all when startled, and you see them galloping to and fro, with their incongruous forms and faces. It gives a feeling as of great, unfenced pampas, and the herds of wandering nations. There were hills in the distance upon either hand; and on one side the river sometimes bordered on the wooded spurs of Coucy and St Gobain.

The artillery were practising at La Fère; and soon the cannon of heaven joined in that loud play. Two continents of cloud met and exchanged salvos overhead; while all round the horizon we could see sunshine and clear air upon the hills. What with the guns and the thunder, the herds were all frightened in the Golden Valley. We could see them tossing their heads, and running to and from in timorous indecision; and when they had made up their minds, and the donkey followed the horse, and the cow was after the donkey, we could hear their hooves thundering abroad over the meadows. It had a martial sound, like cavalry charges. And altogether, as far as the ears are concerned, we had a very rousing battle-piece performed for our amusement.

At last, the guns and the thunder dropped off; the sun shone on the wet meadows; the air was scented with the breath of rejoicing trees and grass; and the river kept unweariedly carrying us on at its best pace. There was a manufacturing district about Chauny; and after that the banks grew so high that they hid the adjacent country, and we could see nothing but clay sides, and one willow after another. Only, here and there, we passed by a village or a ferry, and some wondering child upon the bank would stare after us until we turned the corner. I daresay we continued to paddle in that child's dreams for many a night after.

Sun and shower alternated like day and night, making the hours longer by their variety. When the showers were heavy I could feel each drop striking through my jersey to my warm skin; and the accumulation of small shocks put me nearly beside myself. I decided I should buy a mackintosh at Noyon. It is nothing to get wet; but the misery of these individual pricks of cold all over my body at the same instant of time made me flail the water with my paddle like a madman. The *Cigarette* was greatly amused by these ebullitions. It gave him something else to look at besides clay banks and willows.

All the time the river stole away like a thief in straight places, or swung round corners with an eddy; the willows nodded and were undermined all day long; the clay banks tumbled in; the Oise, which had been so many centuries making the Golden Valley, seemed to have changed its fancy and be bent upon undoing its performance. What a number of things a river does by simply following Gravity in the innocence of its heart!

NOYON CATHEDRAL

Noyon stands about a mile from the river, in a little plain surrounded by wooded hills, and entirely covers an eminence with its tile roofs, surmounted by a long, straight-backed cathedral with two stiff towers. As we got into the town, the tile roofs seemed to tumble up-hill one upon another, in the oddest disorder; but for all their scrambling they did not attain above the knees of the cathedral, which stood, upright and solemn, over all. As the streets drew near to this presiding genius, through the market-place under the Hôtel de Ville, they grew emptier and more composed. Blank walls and shuttered windows were turned to the great edifice, and grass grew on the white causeway. 'Put off thy shoes from off thy feet, for the place whereon thou standest is holy ground.' The Hôtel du Nord, never-theless, lights its secular tapers within a stone-cast of the church; and we had the superb east end before our eyes all morning from the window of our bedroom. I have seldom looked on the east end of a church with more complete sympathy. As it flanges out in three wide terraces, and settles down broadly on the earth, it looks like the poop of some great old battleship. Hollow-backed buttresses carry vases, which figure for the stern lanterns. There is a roll in the ground, and the towers just appear above the pitch of the roof, as though the good ship were bowing lazily over an Atlantic swell. At any moment it might be a hundred feet away from you, climbing the next billow. At any moment a window might open, and some old admiral thrust forth a cocked hat and proceed to take an observation. The old admirals sail the sea no longer; the old ships of battle are all broken up, and live only in pictures; but this, that was a church before ever they were thought upon, is still a church, and makes as brave an appearance by the Oise. The cathedral and the river are probably the two oldest things for miles around; and certainly they have both a grand old age.

The Sacristan took us to the top of one of the towers, and showed us the five bells hanging in their loft. From above, the town was a tessellated pavement of roofs and gardens; the old line of rampart was plainly traceable; and the Sacristan pointed out to us, far across the plain in a bit of gleaming sky between two clouds, the towers of Château Coucy.

I find I never weary of great churches. It is my favourite kind of mountain scenery. Mankind was never so happily inspired as when it made a cathedral: a thing as single and specious as a statue to the first glance, and yet, on examination, as lively and interesting as a forest in detail. The height of spires cannot be taken by trigonometry; they measure absurdly short, but how tall they are to the admiring eye! And where we have so many elegant proportions, growing one out of the other, and all together into one, it seems as if proportion transcended itself and became something different and more imposing. I could never fathom how a man dares to lift up his voice to preach in a cathedral. What is he to say that will not be an anticlimax? For though I have heard a considerable variety of sermons, I never yet heard one that was so expressive as a cathedral. 'T is the best preacher itself, and preaches day and night; not only telling you of man's art and aspirations in the past, but convicting your own soul of ardent sympathies; or rather, like all good preachers, it sets you preaching to yourself,—and every man is his own doctor of divinity in the last resort.

As I sat outside of the hotel in the course of the afternoon, the sweet, groaning thunder of the organ floated out of the church like a summons. I was not averse, liking the theatre so well, to sit out an act or two of the play, but I could never rightly make out the nature of the service I beheld. Four or five priests and as many choristers were singing *Miserere* before the high altar when I went in. There was no congregation but a few old women on chairs and old men kneeling on the pavement. After a while a long train of young girls, walking two and two, each with a lighted taper in her hand, and all dressed in black with a white veil, came from behind the altar and began to descend the nave; the four first carrying a Virgin and Child upon a table. The priests and choristers arose from their knees and followed after, singing 'Ave Mary' as they went. In this order they made the circuit of the cathedral, passing twice before me where I leaned against a pillar. The priest who seemed of most consequence was a strange, down-looking old man. He kept mumbling prayers with his lips; but, as he looked upon me darkling, it did not seem as if prayer were uppermost in his heart. Two others, who bore the burthen of the chant, were stout, brutal, military-looking men of forty, with bold, over-fed eyes; they sang with some lustiness, and trolled forth 'Ave Mary' like a garrison catch. The little girls were timid and grave. As they footed slowly up the aisle each one took a moment's glance at the Englishman; and the big nun who played marshal fairly stared him out of countenance. As for the choristers, from first to last they misbehaved as only boys can misbehave, and cruelly marred the performance with their antics.

I understood a great deal of the spirit of what went on. Indeed, it would be difficult not to understand the *Miserere*, which I take to be the composition of an atheist. If it ever be a good thing to take such despondency to heart, the *Miserere* is the right music and a cathedral a fit scene. So far I am at one with the Catholics,—an odd name for them, after all! But why, in God's name, these holiday choristers? why these priests who steal wandering looks about the congregation while they feign to be at prayer? why this fat nun, who rudely arranges her procession and shakes delinquent virgins by the elbow? why this spitting, and snuffing, and forgetting of keys, and the thousand and one little misadventures that disturb a frame of mind, laboriously edified with chants and organings? In any play-house reverend fathers may see what can be done with a little art, and how, to move high sentiments, it is necessary to drill the supernumeraries and have every stool in its proper place.

One other circumstance distressed me. I could bear a *Miserere* myself, having had a good deal of open-air exercise of late; but I wished the old people somewhere else. It was neither the right sort of music nor the right sort of divinity for men and women who have come through most accidents by this time, and probably have an opinion of their own upon the tragic element in life. A person up in years can generally do his own *Miserere* for himself; although I notice that such an one often prefers *Jubilate Deo* for his ordinary singing. On the whole, the most religious exercise for the aged is probably to recall their own experience; so many friends dead, so many hopes disappointed, so many slips and stumbles, and withal so many bright days and smiling providences; there is surely the matter of a very eloquent sermon in all this.

On the whole I was greatly solemnised. In the little pictorial map of our whole Inland Voyage, which my fancy still preserves, and sometimes unrolls for the amusement of odd moments, Noyon cathedral figures on a most preposterous scale, and must be nearly as large as the department. I can still see the faces of the priests as if they were at my elbow, and hear *Ave Maria, ora pro nobis* sounding through the church. All Noyon is blotted out for me by these superior memories; and I do not care to say more about the place. It was but a stack of brown roofs at the best, where I believe people live very reputably in a quiet way; but the shadow of the church falls upon it when the sun is low, and the five bells are heard in all quarters, telling that the organ has begun. If ever I join the church of Rome, I shall stipulate to be Bishop of Noyon on the Oise.

DOWN THE OISE

TO COMPIÈGNE

The most patient people grow weary at last with being
continually wetted with rain; except, of course, in the
Scottish Highlands, where there are not enough fine intervals to point the difference. That was like to be our case
the day we left Noyon. I remember nothing of the voyage;
it was nothing but clay banks, and willows, and rain—incessant, pitiless, beating rain—until we stopped to lunch at
a little inn at Pimprez, where the canal ran very near the
river. We were so sadly drenched that the landlady lit a
few sticks in the chimney for our comfort; there we sat in
a steam of vapour, lamenting our concerns. The husband
donned a game-bag and strode out to shoot; the wife sat
in a far corner watching us. I think we were worth looking
at. We grumbled over the misfortune of La Fère; we
forecast other La Fères in the future,—although things went
better with the *Cigarette* for spokesman; he had more aplomb
altogether than I; and a dull, positive way of approaching
a landlady that carried off the india-rubber bags. Talking
of La Fère put us talking of the reservists.

'Reservery,' said he, 'seems a pretty mean way to spend
one's autumn holiday.'

'About as mean,' returned I, dejectedly, 'as canoeing.'

'These gentlemen travel for their pleasure?' asked the
landlady, with unconscious irony.

It was too much. The scales fell from our eyes. Another
wet day, it was determined, and we put the boats into the
train.

The weather took the hint. That was our last wetting.
The afternoon faired up; grand clouds still voyaged in the
sky, but now singly, and with a depth of blue around their
path; and a sunset in the daintiest rose and gold inaugur-
ated a thick night of stars and a month of unbroken
weather. At the same time, the river began to give us a

better outlook into the country. The banks were not so high, the willows disappeared from along the margin, and pleasant hills stood all along its course and marked their profile on the sky.

In a little while the canal, coming to its last lock, began to discharge its water-houses on the Oise; so that we had no lack of company to fear. Here were all our own friends; the *Deo Gratias* of Condé and the *Four Sons of Aymon* journeyed cheerily down the stream along with us; we exchanged waterside pleasantries with the steersman perched among the lumber, or the driver hoarse with bawling to his horses; and the children came and looked over the side as we paddled by. We had never known all this while how much we missed them; but it gave us a fillip to see the smoke from their chimneys.

A little below this junction we made another meeting of yet more account. For there we were joined by the Aisne, already a far-travelled river and fresh out of Champagne. Here ended the adolescence of the Oise; this was his marriage day; thenceforward he had a stately, brimming march, conscious of his own dignity and sundry dams. He became a tranquil feature in the scene. The trees and towns saw themselves in him, as in a mirror. He carried the canoes lightly on his broad breast; there was no need to work hard against an eddy, but idleness became the order of the day, and mere straightforward dipping of the paddle, now on this side, now on that, without intelligence or effort. Truly we were coming into halcyon weather upon all accounts, and were floated towards the sea like gentlemen.

We made Compiègne as the sun was going down: a fine profile of a town above the river. Over the bridge a regiment was parading to the drum. People loitered on the quay, some fishing, some looking idly at the stream. And as the two boats shot in along the water, we could see them pointing them out and speaking one to another. We landed at a floating lavatory, where the washerwomen were still beating the clothes.

AT COMPIÈGNE

We put up at a big, bustling hotel in Compiègne, where nobody observed our presence.

Reservery and general *militarismus* (as the Germans call it) were rampant. A camp of conical white tents without the town looked like a leaf out of a picture Bible; sword-belts decorated the walls of the *cafés*, and the streets kept sounding all day long with military music. It was not possible to be an Englishman and avoid a feeling of elation; for the men who followed the drums were small and walked shabbily. Each man inclined at his own angle, and jolted to his own convenience as he went. There was nothing of the superb gait with which a regiment of tall Highlanders moves behind its music, solemn and inevitable, like a natural phenomenon. Who, that has seen it, can forget the drum-major pacing in front, the drummers' tiger-skins, the pipers' swinging plaids, the strange, elastic rhythm of the whole regiment footing it in time, and the bang of the drum when the brasses cease, and the shrill pipes taking up the martial story in their place?

A girl at school in France began to describe one of our regiments on parade to her French school-mates, and as she went on, she told me, the recollection grew so vivid, she became so proud to be the countrywoman of such soldiers, and so sorry to be in another country, that her voice failed her and she burst into tears. I have never forgotten that girl, and I think she very nearly deserves a statue. To call her a young lady, with all its niminy associations, would be to offer her an insult. She may rest assured of one thing, although she never should marry a heroic general, never see any great or immediate result of her life, she will not have lived in vain for her native land.

But though French soldiers show to ill-advantage on parade, on the march they are gay, alert, and willing, like a troop of fox-hunters. I remember once seeing a company pass through the forest of Fontainebleau, on the Chailly road, between the Bas Bréau and the Reine Blanche. One fellow walked a little before the rest, and sang a loud, audacious marching song. The rest bestirred their feet, and even swung their muskets in time. A young officer on horseback had hard ado to keep his countenance at the words. You never saw anything so cheerful and spontaneous as their gait; schoolboys do not look more eagerly at hare and hounds; and you would have thought it impossible to tire such willing marchers.

My great delight in Compiègne was the town hall. I doted upon the town hall. It is a monument of Gothic insecurity, all turreted, and gargoyled, and slashed, and bedizened with half a score of architectural fancies. Some of the niches are gilt and painted; and in a great square panel in the centre, in black relief on a gilt ground, Louis XII rides upon a pacing horse, with hand on hip, and head thrown back. There is royal arrogance in every line of him, the stirruped foot projects insolently from the frame; the eye is hard and proud; the very horse seems to be treading with gratification over prostrate serfs, and to have the breath of the trumpet in his nostrils. So rides forever, on the front of the town hall, the good king Louis XII, the father of his people.

Over the king's head, in the tall centre turret, appears the dial of a clock; and high above that, three little mechanical figures, each one with a hammer in his hand, whose business it is to chime out the hours, and halves, and quarters for the burgesses of Compiègne. The centre figure has a gilt breast-plate; the two others wear gilt trunk-hose; and they all three have elegant, flapping hats like cavaliers. As the quarter approaches, they turn their heads and look knowingly one to the other; and then, *kling* go the three hammers on three little bells below. The hour follows, deep and sonorous, from the interior of the tower; and the gilded gentlemen rest from their labours with contentment.

I had a great deal of healthy pleasure from their manœuvres, and took good care to miss as few performances as possible; and I found that even the *Cigarette*, while he pretended to despise my enthusiasm, was more or less a devotee himself. There is something highly absurd in the

exposition of such toys to the outrages of winter on a
housetop. They would be more in keeping in a glass case
before a Nürnberg clock. Above all, at night, when the
children are abed, and even grown people are snoring
under quilts, does it not seem impertinent to leave these
ginger-bread figures winking and tinkling to the stars and
the rolling moon? The gargoyles may fitly enough twist
their ape-like heads; fitly enough may the potentate bestride
his charger, like a centurion in an old German print of the
Via Dolorosa; but the toys should be put away in a box
among some cotton, until the sun rises, and the children
are abroad again to be amused.

In Compiègne post-office a great packet of letters awaited
us; and the authorities were, for this occasion only, so polite
as to hand them over upon application.

In some way, our journey may be said to end with this
letter-bag at Compiègne. The spell was broken. We had
partly come home from that moment.

No one should have any correspondence on a journey;
it is bad enough to have to write; but the receipt of letters
is the death of all holiday feeling.

'Out of my country and myself I go.'* I wish to take a
dive among new conditions for a while, as into another
element. I have nothing to do with my friends or my
affections for the time; when I came away, I left my heart
at home in a desk, or sent it forward with my portmanteau
to await me at my destination. After my journey is over, I
shall not fail to read your admirable letters with the attention they deserve. But I have paid all this money, look you,
and paddled all these strokes, for no other purpose than to
be abroad; and yet you keep me at home with your
perpetual communications. You tug the string, and I feel
that I am a tethered bird. You pursue me all over Europe
with the little vexations that I came away to avoid. There
is no discharge in the war of life, I am well aware; but
shall there not be so much as a week's furlough?

We were up by six, the day we were to leave. They had
taken so little note of us that I hardly thought they would
have condescended on a bill. But they did, with some smart

particulars, too; and we paid in a civilised manner to an uninterested clerk, and went out of that hotel, with the india-rubber bags, unremarked. No one cared to know about us. It is not possible to rise before a village; but Compiègne was so grown a town that it took its ease in the morning; and we were up and away while it was still in dressing-gown and slippers. The streets were left to people washing door-steps; nobody was in full dress but the cavaliers upon the town hall; they were all washed with dew, spruce in their gilding, and full of intelligence and a sense of professional responsibility. *Kling* went they on the bells for the half-past six, as we went by. I took it kind of them to make me this parting compliment; they never were in better form, not even at noon upon a Sunday.

There was no one to see us off but the early washer-women,—early and late—who were already beating the linen in their floating lavatory on the river. They were very merry and matutinal in their ways; plunged their arms boldly in, and seemed not to feel the shock. It would be dispiriting to me, this early beginning and first cold dabble of a most dispiriting day's work. But I believe they would have been as unwilling to change days with us as we could be to change with them. They crowded to the door to watch us paddle away into the thin sunny mists upon the river; and shouted heartily after us till we were through the bridge.

CHANGED TIMES

There is a sense in which those mists never rose from off our journey; and from that time forth they lie very densely in my note-book. As long as the Oise was a small, rural river it took us near by people's doors, and we could hold a conversation with natives in the riparian fields. But now that it had grown so wide, the life along shore passed us by at a distance. It was the same difference as between a great public highway and a country by-path that wanders in and out of cottage gardens. We now lay in towns, where nobody troubled us with questions; we had floated into civilised life, where people pass without salutation. In sparsely inhabited places we make all we can of each encounter; but when it comes to a city, we keep to ourselves, and never speak unless we have trodden on a man's toes. In these waters we were no longer strange birds, and nobody supposed we had travelled farther than from the last town. I remember, when we came into L'Isle Adam, for instance, how we met dozens of pleasure-boats outing it for the afternoon, and there was nothing to distinguish the true voyager from the amateur, except, perhaps, the filthy condition of my sail. The company in one boat actually thought they recognised me for a neighbour. Was there ever anything more wounding? All the romance had come down to that. Now, on the upper Oise, where nothing sailed, as a general thing, but fish, a pair of canoeists could not be thus vulgarly explained away; we were strange and picturesque intruders; and out of people's wonder sprang a sort of light and passing intimacy all along our route. There is nothing but tit for tat in this world, though sometimes it be a little difficult to trace: for the scores are older than we ourselves, and there has never yet been a settling-day since things were. You get entertainment pretty much in proportion as you give. As long as we were a sort of odd wanderers, to be stared at and followed like a quack doctor or a caravan, we had no want of amusement in return; but as soon as we sank into commonplace ourselves, all whom we met were similarly disenchanted. And here is one reason of a dozen why the world is dull to dull persons.

In our earlier adventures there was generally something to do, and that quickened us. Even the showers of rain had a revivifying effect, and shook up the brain from torpor. But now, when the river no longer ran in a proper sense, only glided seaward with an even, outright, but imperceptible speed, and when the sky smiled upon us day after day without variety, we began to slip into that golden doze of the mind which follows upon much exercise in the open air. I have stupefied myself in this way more than once: indeed, I dearly love the feeling; but I never had it to the same degree as when paddling down the Oise. It was the apotheosis of stupidity.

We ceased reading entirely. Sometimes, when I found a new paper, I took a particular pleasure in reading a single number of the current novel; but I never could bear more than three instalments; and even the second was a disappointment. As soon as the tale became in any way perspicuous, it lost all merit in my eyes; only a single scene, or, as is the way with these *feuilletons*, half a scene, without antecedent or consequence, like a piece of a dream, had the knack of fixing my interest. The less I saw of the novel, the better I liked it; a pregnant reflection. But for the most part, as I said, we neither of us read anything in the world, and employed the very little while we were awake between bed and dinner in poring upon maps. I have always been fond of maps, and can voyage in an atlas with the greatest enjoyment. The names of places are singularly inviting; the contour of coasts and rivers is enthralling to the eye; and to hit in a map upon some place you have heard of before makes history a new possession. But we thumbed our charts, on those evenings, with the blankest unconcern. We cared not a fraction for this place or that. We started at the sheet as children listen to their rattle, and read the names of towns or villages to forget them again at once. We had no romance in the matter; there was nobody so fancy-free. If you had taken the maps away while we were studying them

most intently, it is a fair bet whether we might not have
continued to study the table with the same delight.

About one thing we were mightily taken up, and that
was eating. I think I made a god of my belly. I remember
dwelling in imagination upon this or that dish till my mouth
watered; and long before we got in for the night my
appetite was a clamant, instant annoyance. Sometimes we
paddled alongside for a while and whetted each other with
gastronomical fancies as we went. Cake and sherry, a
homely refection, but not within reach upon the Oise,
trotted through my head for many a mile; and once, as we
were approaching Verberie, the *Cigarette* brought my heart
into my mouth by the suggestion of oyster-patties and
Sauterne.

I suppose none of us recognise the great part that is
played in life by eating and drinking. The appetite is so
imperious that we can stomach the least interesting viands,
and pass off a dinner hour thankfully enough on bread and
water; just as there are men who must read something, if
it were only *Bradshaw's Guide*. But there is a romance about
the matter, after all. Probably the table has more devotees
than love; and I am sure that food is much more generally
entertaining than scenery. Do you give in, as Walt Whitman
would say, that you are any the less immortal for that? The
true materialism is to be ashamed of what we are. To detect
the flavour of an olive is no less a piece of human perfection
than to find beauty in the colours of the sunset.

Canoeing was easy work. To dip the paddle at the proper
inclination, now right, now left; to keep the head down
stream; to empty the little pool that gathered in the lap of
the apron; to screw up the eyes against the glittering
sparkles of sun upon the water; or now and again to pass
below the whistling tow-rope of the *Deo Gratias* of Condé,
or the *Four Sons of Aymon*—there was not much art in that;
certainly silly muscles managed it between sleep and waking; and meanwhile the brain had a whole holiday, and
went to sleep. We took in, at a glance, the larger features
of the scene, and beheld, with half an eye, bloused fishers
and dabbling washerwomen on the bank. Now and again

we might be half wakened by some church spire, by a leaping fish, or by a trail of river grass that clung about the paddle and had to be plucked off and thrown away. But these luminous intervals were only partially luminous. A little more of us was called into action, but never the whole. The central bureau of nerves, what in some moods we call Ourselves, enjoyed its holiday without disturbance, like a Government Office. The great wheels of intelligence turned idly in the head, like fly-wheels, grinding no grist. I have gone on for half an hour at a time, counting my strokes and forgetting the hundreds. I flatter myself the beasts that perish could not underbid that, as a low form of consciousness. And what a pleasure it was! What a hearty, tolerant temper did it bring about! There is nothing captious about a man who has attained to this, the one possible apotheosis in life, the Apotheosis of Stupidity; and he begins to feel dignified and longævous like a tree.

There was one odd piece of practical metaphysics which accompanied what I may call the depth, if I must not call it the intensity, of my abstraction. What philosophers call *me* and *not-me, ego* and *non ego*, preoccupied me whether I would or no. There was less *me* and more *not-me* than I was accustomed to expect. I looked on upon somebody else, who managed the paddling; I was aware of somebody's else feet against the stretcher; my own body seemed to have no more intimate relation to me than the canoe, or the river, or the river banks. Nor this alone: something inside my mind, a part of my brain, a province of my proper being, had thrown off allegiance and set up for itself, or perhaps for the somebody else who did the paddling. I had dwindled into quite a little thing in a corner of myself. I was isolated in my own skull. Thoughts presented themselves unbidden; they were not my thoughts, they were plainly some one else's; and I considered them like a part of the landscape. I take it, in short, that I was about as near Nirvana as would be convenient in practical life; and, if this be so, I make the Buddhists my sincere compliments; 't is an agreeable state, not very consistent with mental brilliancy, not exactly profitable in a money point of view, but very calm, golden, and incurious, and one that sets a man superior to alarms. It may be best figured by supposing yourself to get dead drunk, and yet keep sober to enjoy it. I have a notion that open-air labourers must spend a large portion of their days in this ecstatic stupor, which explains their high composure and endurance. A pity to go to the expense of laudanum when here is a better paradise for nothing!

This frame of mind was the great exploit of our voyage, take it all in all. It was the farthest piece of travel accomplished. Indeed, it lies so far from the beaten paths of language that I despair of getting the reader into sympathy with the smiling, complacent idiocy of my condition; when ideas came and went like motes in a sunbeam; when trees and church spires along the bank surged up from time to time into my notice, like solid objects through a rolling cloudland; when the rhythmical swish of boat and paddle in the water became a cradle-song to lull my thoughts asleep; when a piece of mud on the deck was sometimes an intolerable eyesore, and sometimes quite a companion for me, and the object of pleased consideration; and all the time, with the river running and the shores changing upon either hand, I kept counting my strokes and forgetting the hundreds, the happiest animal in France.

DOWN THE OISE

CHURCH INTERIORS

We made our first stage below Compiègne to Pont Sainte Maxence. I was abroad a little after six the next morning. The air was biting and smelt of frost. In an open place a score of women wrangled together over the day's market; and the noise of their negotiation sounded thin and querulous, like that of sparrows on a winter's morning. The rare passengers blew into their hands, and shuffled in their wooden shoes to set the blood agog. The streets were full of icy shadow, although the chimneys were smoking overhead in golden sunshine. If you wake early enough at this season of the year, you may get up in December to break your fast in June.

I found my way to the church, for there is always something to see about a church, whether living worshippers or dead men's tombs; you find there the deadliest earnest, and the hollowest deceit; and even where it is not a piece of history, it will be certain to leak out some contemporary gossip. It was scarcely so cold in the church as it was without, but it looked colder. The white nave was positively arctic to the eye; and the tawdriness of a continental altar looked more forlorn than usual in the solitude and the bleak air. Two priests sat in the chancel reading and waiting penitents; and out in the nave one very old woman was engaged in her devotions. It was a wonder how she was able to pass her beads when healthy young people were breathing in their palms and slapping their chests; but though this concerned me, I was yet more dispirited by the nature of her exercises. She went from chair to chair, from altar to altar, circumnavigating the church. To each shrine she dedicated an equal number of beads and an equal length of time. Like a prudent capitalist with a somewhat cynical view of the commercial prospect, she desired to place her supplications in a great variety of heavenly securities. She would risk nothing on the credit of any single intercessor. Out of the whole company of saints and angels, not one but was to suppose himself her champion elect against the Great Assizes! I could only think of it as a dull, transparent jugglery, based upon unconscious unbelief.

She was as dead an old woman as ever I saw; no more than bone and parchment, curiously put together. Her eyes, with which she interrogated mine, were vacant of sense. It depends on what you call seeing, whether you might not call her blind. Perhaps she had known love: perhaps borne children, suckled them, and given them pet names. But now that was all gone by, and had left her neither happier nor wiser; and the best she could do with her mornings was to come up here into the cold church and juggle for a slice of heaven. It was not without a gulp that I escaped into the streets and the keen morning air. Morning? why, how tired of it she would be before night! and if she did not sleep, how then? It is fortunate that not many of us are brought up publicly to justify our lives at the bar of threescore years and ten; fortunate that such a number are knocked opportunely on the head in what they call the flower of their years, and go away to suffer for their follies in private somewhere else. Otherwise, between sick children and discontented old folk, we might be put out of all conceit of life.

I had need of all my cerebral hygiene during that day's paddle: the old devotee stuck in my throat sorely. But I was soon in the seventh heaven of stupidity; and knew nothing but that somebody was paddling a canoe, while I was counting his strokes and forgetting the hundreds. I used sometimes to be afraid I should remember the hundreds, which would have made a toil of a pleasure; but the terror was chimerical, they went out of my mind by enchantment, and I knew no more than the man in the moon about my only occupation.

At Creil, where we stopped to lunch, we left the canoes in another floating lavatory, which, as it was high noon, was packed with washerwomen, red-handed and loud-voiced; and they and their broad jokes are about all I remember of the place. I could look up my history books, if you were very anxious, and tell you a date or two; for it figured rather largely in the English wars. But I prefer to mention a girls' boarding-school, which had an interest for us because it was a girls' boarding-school, and because we imagined we had rather an interest for it. At least—there were the girls about the garden; and here were we on the river; and there was more than one handkerchief waved as we went by. It caused quite a stir in my heart; and yet how we should have wearied and despised each other, these girls and I, if we had been introduced at a croquet-party! But this is a fashion I love: to kiss the hand or wave a handkerchief to people I shall never see again, to play with possibility, and knock in a peg for fancy to hang upon. It gives the traveller a jog, reminds him that he is not a traveller everywhere, and that his journey is no more than a siesta by the way on the real march of life.

The church at Creil was a nondescript place in the inside, splashed with gaudy lights from the windows, and picked out with medallions of the Dolorous Way. But there was one oddity, in the way of an *ex voto*, which pleased me hugely: a faithful model of a canal boat, swung from the vault, with a written aspiration that God should conduct the *Saint Nicolas* of Creil to a good haven. The thing was neatly executed, and would have made the delight of a party of boys on the waterside. But what tickled me was the gravity of the peril to be conjured. You might hang up the model of a sea-going ship, and welcome: one that is to plough a furrow round the world, and visit the tropic or the frosty poles, runs dangers that are well worth a candle and a mass. But the *Saint Nicolas* of Creil, which was to be tugged for some ten years by patient draught-horses, in a weedy canal, with the poplars chattering overhead, and the skipper whistling at the tiller; which was to do all its errands in green inland places, and never got out of sight of a village belfry in all its cruising; why, you would have thought if anything could be done without the intervention of Providence, it would be that! But perhaps the skipper was a humorist: or perhaps a prophet, reminding people of the seriousness of life by this preposterous token.

At Creil, as at Noyon, Saint Joseph seemed a favourite saint on the score of punctuality. Day and hour can be specified; and grateful people do not fail to specify them on a votive tablet, when prayers have been punctually and neatly answered. Whenever time is a consideration, Saint Joseph is the proper intermediary. I took a sort of pleasure in observing the vogue he had in France, for the good man plays a very small part in my religion at home. Yet I could not help fearing that, where the saint is so much commended for exactitude, he will be expected to be very grateful for his tablet.

This is foolishness to us Protestants; and not of great importance anyway. Whether people's gratitude for the good gifts that come to them be wisely conceived or dutifully expressed is a secondary matter, after all, so long as they feel gratitude. The true ignorance is when a man does not know that he has received a good gift, or begins to imagine that he has got it for himself. The self-made man is the funniest wind-bag after all! There is a marked difference between decreeing light in chaos, and lighting the gas in a metropolitan back-parlour with a box of patent matches; and, do what we will, there is always something made to our hand, if it were only our fingers.

But there was something worse than foolishness placarded in Creil Church. The Association of the Living Rosary (of which I had never previously heard) is responsible for that. This association was founded, according to the printed advertisement, by a brief of Pope Gregory Sixteenth, on the 17th of January, 1832: according to a coloured bas-relief, it seems to have been founded, some time or other, by the Virgin giving one rosary to Saint Dominic, and the Infant Saviour giving another to Saint Catharine of Siena. Pope Gregory is not so imposing, but he is nearer hand. I could not distinctly make out whether the association was entirely devotional, or had an eye to good works; at least it is highly organised: the names of fourteen matrons and misses were filled in for each week of the month as associates, with one other, generally a married woman, at the top for *zélatrice,** the leader of the band. Indulgences, plenary and partial, follow on the performance of the duties of the association. 'The partial indulgences are attached to the recitation of the rosary.' On 'the recitation of the required *dizaine*,'* a partial indulgence promptly follows. When people serve the kingdom of heaven with a pass-book in their hands, I should always be afraid lest they should carry the same commercial spirit into their dealings with their fellow-men, which would make a sad and sordid business of this life.

There is one more article, however, of happier import. 'All these indulgences,' it appeared, 'are applicable to souls in purgatory.' For God's sake, ye ladies of Creil, apply them all to the souls in purgatory without delay! Burns would take no hire for his last songs preferring to serve his country out of unmixed love. Suppose you were to imitate the exciseman, mesdames, and even if the souls in purgatory were not greatly bettered, some souls in Creil upon the Oise would find themselves none the worse either here or hereafter.

I cannot help wondering, as I transcribe these notes, whether a Protestant born and bred is in a fit state to understand these signs, and do them what justice they deserve; and I cannot help answering that he is not. They cannot look so merely ugly and mean to the faithful as they do to me. I see that as clearly as a proposition in Euclid. For these believers are neither weak nor wicked. They can put up their tablet commending Saint Joseph for his despatch as if he were still a village carpenter; they can 'recite the required *dizaine*,' and metaphorically pocket the indulgence as if they had done a job for heaven; and then they can go out and look down unabashed upon this wonderful river flowing by, and up without confusion at the pin-point stars, which are themselves great worlds full of flowing rivers greater than the Oise. I see it as plainly, I say, as a proposition in Euclid, that my Protestant mind has missed the point, and that there goes with these deformities some higher and more religious spirit and I dream.

I wonder if other people would make the same allowances for me? Like the ladies of Creil, having recited my rosary of toleration, I look for my indulgence on the spot.

PRÉCY AND THE MARIONETTES

We made Précy about sundown. The plain is rich with tufts of poplar. In a wide, luminous curve the Oise lay under the hillside. A faint mist began to rise and confound the different distances together. There was not a sound audible but that of the sheep-bells in some meadows by the river, and the creaking of a cart down the long road that descends the hill. The villas in their gardens, the shops along the street, all seemed to have been deserted the day before, and I felt inclined to walk discreetly as one feels in a silent forest. All of a sudden we came round a corner, and there, in a little green round the church, was a bevy of girls in Parisian costumes playing croquet. Their laughter and the hollow sound of ball and mallet made a cheery stir in the neighbourhood; and the look of these slim figures, all corseted and ribboned, produced an answerable disturbance in our hearts. We were within sniff of Paris, it seemed. And here were females of our own species playing croquet, just as if Précy had been a place in real life instead of a stage in the fairyland of travel. For, to be frank, the peasant woman is scarcely to be counted as a woman at all, and after having passed by such a succession of people in petticoats digging, and hoeing, and making dinner, this company of coquettes under arms made quite a surprising feature in the landscape, and convinced us at once of being fallible males.

The inn at Précy is the worst inn in France. Not even in Scotland have I found worse fare. It was kept by a brother and sister, neither of whom was out of their teens. The sister, so to speak, prepared a meal for us; and the brother, who had been tippling, came in and brought with him a tipsy butcher, to entertain us as we ate. We found pieces of loo-warm pork among the salad, and pieces of unknown yielding substance in the *ragoût*. The butcher entertained us with pictures of Parisian life, with which he professed himself well acquainted; the brother sitting the while on the edge of the billiard table, toppling precariously, and sucking the stump of a cigar. In the midst of these diversions bang went a drum past the house, and a hoarse voice began issuing a proclamation. It was a man with marionettes announcing a performance for that evening.

He had set up his caravan and lighted his candles on another part of the girls' croquet-green, under one of those open sheds which are so common in France to shelter markets; and he and his wife, by the time we strolled up there, were trying to keep order with the audience.

It was the most absurd contention. The show-people had set out a certain number of benches; and all who sat upon them were to pay a couple of *sous* for the accommodation. They were always quite full—a bumper house—as long as nothing was going forward; but let the show-woman appear with an eye to a collection, and at the first rattle of the tambourine the audience slipped off the seats and stood round on the outside, with their hands in their pockets. It certainly would have tried an angel's temper. The showman roared from the proscenium; he had been all over France, and nowhere, nowhere, 'not even on the borders of Germany,' had he met with such misconduct. Such thieves, and rogues, and rascals as he called them! And now and again the wife issued on another round, and added her shrill quota to the tirade. I remarked here, as elsewhere, how far more copious is the female mind in the material of insult. The audience laughed in high good-humour over the man's declamations; but they bridled and cried aloud under the woman's pungent sallies. She picked out the sore points. She had the honour of the village at her mercy. Voices answered her angrily out of the crowd, and received a smarting retort for their trouble. A couple of old ladies beside me, who had duly paid for their seats, waxed very red and indignant, and discoursed to each other audibly about the impudence of these mountebanks; but as soon as the show-woman caught a whisper of this she was down upon them with a swoop; if mesdames could persuade their neighbours to act with common honesty, the mountebanks, she assured them, would be polite enough; mesdames had probably had their bowl of soup, and perhaps a glass of wine that evening; the mountebanks, also, had a taste for soup, and did not choose to have their little earnings stolen from them before their eyes. Once, things came as far as a brief personal encounter between the showman and some lads, in which the former went down as readily as one of his own marionettes to a peal of jeering laughter.

I was a good deal astonished at this scene, because I am pretty well acquainted with the ways of French strollers, more or less artistic, and have always found them singularly pleasing. Any stroller must be dear to the right-thinking heart; if it were only as a living protest against offices and the mercantile spirit, and as something to remind us that life is not by necessity the kind of thing we generally make it. Even a German band, if you see it leaving town in the early morning for a campaign in country places, among trees and meadows, has a romantic flavour for the imagination. There is nobody under thirty so dead but his heart will stir a little at sight of a gypsies' camp. 'We are not cotton-spinners all'—or, at least, not all through. There is some life in humanity yet; and youth will now and again find a brave word to say in dispraise of riches, and throw up a situation to go strolling with a knapsack.

An Englishman has always special facilities for intercourse with French gymnasts; for England is the natural home of gymnasts. This or that fellow, in his tights and spangles, is sure to know a word or two of English, to have drunk English *aff-'n-aff* * and, perhaps, performed in an English music-hall. He is a countryman of mine by profession. He leaps like the Belgian boating-men to the notion that I must be an athlete myself.

But the gymnast is not my favourite; he has little or no tincture of the artist in his composition; his soul is small and pedestrian, for the most part, since his profession makes no call upon it, and does not accustom him to high ideas. But if a man is only so much of an actor that he can stumble through a farce, he is made free of a new order of thoughts. He has something else to think about beside the money-box. He has a pride of his own, and, what is of far more importance, he has an aim before him that he can never quite attain. He has gone upon a pilgrimage that will last him his life long, because there is no end to it short of perfection. He will better himself a little day by day; or, even if he has given up the attempt, he will always remember that once upon a time he had conceived this high ideal, that once upon a time he had fallen in love with a star. ''Tis better to have loved and lost.' Although the moon should have nothing to say to Endymion, although he should settle down with Audrey and feed pigs, do you not think he would move with a better grace and cherish higher thoughts to the end? The louts he meets at church never had a fancy above Audrey's snood; but there is a reminiscence in Endymion's heart that, like a spice, keeps it fresh and haughty.

To be even one of the outskirters of art leaves a fine stamp on a man's countenance. I remember once dining with a party in the inn at Château Landon. Most of them were unmistakable bagmen; others well-to-do peasantry; but there was one young fellow in a blouse, whose face stood out from among the rest surprisingly. It looked more finished; more of the spirit looked out through it; it had a living, expressive air, and you could see that his eyes took things in. My companion and I wondered greatly who and what he could be. It was fair time in Château Landon, and when we went along to the booths we had our question answered; for there was our friend busily fiddling for the peasants to caper to. He was a wandering violinist.

A troop of strollers once came to the inn where I was staying, in the department of Siene et Marne. There were a father and mother; two daughters, brazen, blowsy hussies, who sang and acted, without an idea of how to set about either; and a dark young man, like a tutor, a recalcitrant house-painter, who sang and acted not amiss. The mother was the genius of the party, so far as genius can be spoken of with regard to such a pack of incompetent humbugs; and her husband could not find words to express his admiration for her comic countryman. 'You should see my old woman,' said he, and nodded his beery countenance. One night they performed in the stable-yard, with flaring lamps—a wretched exhibition, coldly looked upon by a village audience. Next night, as soon as the lamps were lighted, there came a plump of rain, and they had to sweep away their baggage as fast as possible, and make off to the barn, where they harboured, cold, wet, and supperless. In the morning a dear friend of mine, who has as warm a heart for strollers as I have myself, made a little collection, and sent it by my hands to comfort them for their disappointment. I gave it to the father; he thanked me cordially, and we drank a cup together in the kitchen, talking of roads and audiences, and hard times.

When I was going, up got my old stroller, and off with his hat. 'I am afraid,' said he, 'that Monsieur will think me altogether a beggar; but I have another demand to make upon him.' I began to hate him on the spot. 'We play again to-night,' he went on. 'Of course I shall refuse to accept any more money from Monsieur and his friends, who have been already so liberal. But our programme of to-night is something truly creditable; and I cling to the idea that Monsieur will honour us with his presence.' And then, with a shrug and a smile: 'Monsieur understands,—the vanity of an artist!' Save the mark! The vanity of an artist! That is the kind of thing that reconciles me to life: a ragged, tippling, incompetent old rogue, with the manners of a gentleman and the vanity of an artist, to keep up his self-respect!

But the man after my own heart is M. de Vauversin. It is nearly two years since I saw him first, and indeed I hope I may see him often again. Here is his first programme, as I found it on the breakfast-table, and have kept it ever since as a relic of bright days:

'*Mesdames et Messieurs,*

'*Mademoiselle Ferrario et M. de Vauversin auront l'honneur de chanter ce soir les morceaux suivants*:

'*Mademoiselle Ferrario chantera—Mignon—Oiseaux Légers— France—Des Français dorment là—Le château bleu—Où voulez- vous aller?*

'M. de Vauversin—Madame Fontaine et M. Robinet—Les plongeurs à cheval—Le Mari Mécontent—Tais-toi, gamin—Mon voisin l'original—Heureux comme ça—Comme on est trompé.'

They made a stage at one end of the *salle-à-manger*. And what a sight it was to see M. de Vauversin, with a cigarette in his mouth, twanging a guitar, and following Mademoiselle Ferrario's eyes with the obedient, kindly look of a dog! The entertainment wound up with a tombola, or auction of lottery tickets: an admirable amusement, with all the excitement of gambling, and no hope of gain to make you ashamed of your eagerness; for there, all is loss; you make haste to be out of pocket; it is a competition who shall lose most money for the benefit of M. de Vauversin and Mademoiselle Ferrario.

M. de Vauversin is a small man, with a great head of black hair, a vivacious and engaging air, and a smile that would be delightful if he had better teeth. He was once an actor in the Châtelet; but he contracted a nervous affection from the heat and glare of the foot-lights, which unfitted him for the stage. At this crisis Mademoiselle Ferrario, otherwise Mademoiselle Rita of the Alcazar,* agreed to share his wandering fortunes. 'I could never forget the generosity of that lady,' said he. He wears trousers so tight that it has long been a problem to all who knew him how he manages to get in and out of them. He sketches a little in water-colours; he writes verses; he is the most patient of fishermen, and spent long days at the bottom of the inn garden fruitlessly dabbling a line in the clear river.

You should hear him recounting his experiences over a bottle of wine; such a pleasant vein of talk as he has, with a ready smile at his own mishaps, and every now and then a sudden gravity, like a man who should hear the surf roar while he was telling the perils of the deep. For it was no longer ago than last night, perhaps, that the receipts only amounted to a franc and a half to cover three francs of railway fare and two of board and lodging. The Maire, a man worth a million of money, sat in the front seat, repeatedly applauding Mlle Ferrario, and yet gave no more than three sous the whole evening. Local authorities look with such an evil eye upon the strolling artist. Alas! I know it well, who have been myself taken for one, and pitilessly incarcerated on the strength of the misapprehension. Once, M. de Vauversin visited a commissary of police for permission to sing. The commissary, who was smoking at his ease, politely doffed his hat upon the singer's entrance. 'Mr Commissary,' he began, 'I am an artist.' And on went the commissary's hat again. No courtesy for the companions of Apollo! 'They are as degraded as that,' said M. de Vauversin, with a sweep of his cigarette.

But what pleased me most was one outbreak of his, when we had been talking all the evening of the rubs, indignities, and pinchings of his wandering life. Some one said it would be better to have a million of money down, and Mlle Ferrario admitted that she would prefer that mightily. '*Eh bien, moi non*;—not I,' cried De Vauversin, striking the table with his hand. 'If anyone is a failure in the world, is it not I? I had an art, in which I have done things well,—as well as some—better, perhaps, than others; and now it is closed against me. I must go about the country gathering coppers and singing nonsense. Do you think I regret my life? Do you think I would rather be a fat burgess, like a calf? Not I! I have had moments when I have been applauded on the boards: I think nothing of that; but I have known in my own mind sometimes, when I had not a clap from the whole house, that I had found a true intonation, or an exact and speaking gesture; and then, messieurs, I have known what pleasure was, what it was to do a thing well, what it was to be an artist. And to know what art is, is to have an interest forever, such as no burgess can find in his petty concerns. *Tenez, messuieurs, je vais vous le dire*,*—it is like a religion.'

Such, making some allowance for the tricks of memory and the inaccuracies of translation, was the profession of faith of M. de Vauversin. I have given him his own name, lest any other wanderer should come across him, with his guitar and cigarette, and Mademoiselle Ferrario; for should not all the world delight to honour this unfortunate and loyal follower of the Muses? May Apollo send him rhymes hitherto undreamed of; may the river be no longer scanty of her silver fishes to his lure; may the cold not pinch him on long winter rides, nor the village jack-in-office affront him with unseemly manners; and may he never miss Mademoiselle Ferrario from his side, to follow with his dutiful eyes and accompany on the guitar!

The marionettes made a very dismal entertainment. They performed a piece called *Pyramus and Thisbe*, in five mortal acts, and all written in Alexandrines fully as long as the performers. One marionette was the king; another the wicked counsellor; a third, credited with exceptional beauty, represented Thisbe; and then there were guards, and obdurate fathers, and walking gentlemen. Nothing particular took place during the two or three acts that I sat out; but you will be pleased to learn that the unities were properly respected, and the whole piece, with one exception, moved in harmony with classical rules. That exception was the comic countryman, a lean marionette in wooden shoes, who spoke in prose and in a broad *patois* much appreciated by the audience. He took unconstitutional liberties with the person of his sovereign; kicked his fellow-marionettes in the mouth with his wooden shoes, and whenever none of the versifying suitors were about, made love to Thisbe on his own account in comic prose.

This fellow's evolutions, and the little prologue, in which the showman made a humorous eulogium of his troop, praising their indifference to applause and hisses, and their single devotion to their art, were the only circumstances in the whole affair that you could fancy would so much as raise a smile. But the villagers of Précy seemed delighted. Indeed, so long as a thing is an exhibition, and you pay to see it, it is nearly certain to amuse. If we were charged so much a head for sunsets, or if God sent round a drum before the hawthorns came in flower, what work should we not make about their beauty! But these things, like good companions, stupid people early cease to observe; and the Abstract Bagman tittups past in his spring gig, and is positively not aware of the flowers along the lane, or the scenery of the weather overhead.

BACK TO THE WORLD

Of the next two days' sail little remains in my mind, and nothing whatever in my note-book. The river streamed on steadily through pleasant river-side landscapes. Washerwomen in blue dresses, fishers in blue blouses, diversified the green banks; and the relation of the two colours was like that of the flower and the leaf in the forget-me-not. A symphony in forget-me-not; I think Théophile Gautier might thus have characterised that two days' panorama. The sky was blue and cloudless, and the sliding surface of the river held up, in smooth places, a mirror to the heaven and the shores. The washerwomen hailed us laughingly; and the noise of trees and water made an accompaniment to our dozing thoughts, as we fleeted down the stream.

The great volume, the indefatigable purpose of the river, held the mind in chain. It seemed now so sure of its end, so strong and easy in its gait, like a grown man full of determination. The surf was roaring for it on the sands of Havre.

For my own part, slipping along this moving thoroughfare in my fiddle-case of a canoe, I also was beginning to grow aweary for my ocean. To the civilised man there must come, sooner or later, a desire for civilisation. I was weary of dipping the paddle; I was weary of living on the skirts of life; I wished to be in the thick of it once more; I wished to get to work; I wished to meet people who understood my own speech, and could meet with me on equal terms, as a man, and no longer as a curiosity.

And so a letter at Pontoise decided us, and we drew up our keels for the last time out of that river of Oise that had faithfully piloted them, through rain and sunshine, for so long. For so many miles had this fleet and footless beast of burthen charioted our fortunes that we turned our back upon it with a sense of separation. We had made a long détour out of the world, but now we were back in the familiar places, where life itself makes all the running, and we are carried to meet adventure without a stroke of the paddle. Now we were to return, like the voyager in the play, and see what rearrangements fortune had perfected the while in our surroundings; what surprises stood ready made for us at home; and whither and how far the world had voyaged in our absence. You may paddle all day long; but it is when you come back at nightfall, and look in at the familiar room, that you find Love or Death awaiting you beside the stove; and the most beautiful adventures are not those we go to seek.

EPILOGUE*

The country where they journeyed, that green, breezy valley of the Loing, is one very attractive to cheerful and solitary people. The weather was superb; all night it thundered and lightened, and the rain fell in sheets; by day, the heavens were cloudless, the sun fervent, the air vigorous and pure. They walked separate: the *Cigarette* plodding behind with some philosophy, the lean *Arethusa* posting on ahead. Thus each enjoyed his own reflections by the way; each had perhaps time to tire of them before he met his comrade at the designated inn; and the pleasures of society and solitude combined to fill the day. The *Arethusa* carried in his knapsack the works of Charles of Orleans, and employed some of the hours of travel in the concoction of English roundels. In this path, he must thus have preceded Mr Lang, Mr Dobson, Mr Henley, and all contemporary roundeleers; but for good reasons, he will be the last to publish the result. The *Cigarette* walked burthened with a volume of Michelet. And both these books, it will be seen, played a part in the subsequent adventure.

The *Arethusa* was unwisely dressed. He is no precisian in attire; but by all accounts, he was never so ill-inspired as on that tramp; having set forth indeed, upon a moment's notice, from the most unfashionable spot in Europe, Barbizon. On his head, he wore a smoking-cap of Indian work, the gold lace pitifully frayed and tarnished. A flannel shirt of an agreeable dark hue, which the satirical called black; a light tweed coat made by a good English tailor; ready-made cheap linen trousers and leathern gaiters completed his array. In person, he is exceptionally lean; and his face is not like those of happier mortals, a certificate. For years he could not pass a frontier or visit a bank without suspicion; the police, everywhere but in his native city, looked askance upon him; and (though I am sure it will not be credited) he is actually denied admittance to the casino of Monte Carlo. If you will imagine him, dressed as above, stooping under his knapsack, walking nearly five miles an hour with the folds of the ready-made trousers fluttering about his spindle shanks, and still looking eagerly round him as if in terror of pursuit—the figure, when realised, is far from reassuring. When Villon journeyed (perhaps by the same pleasant valley) to his exile at Roussillon, I wonder if he had not something of the same appearance. Something of the same preoccupation he had beyond a doubt, for he too must have tinkered verses as he walked, with more success than his successor. And if he had anything like the same inspiring weather, the same nights of uproar, men in armour rolling and resounding down the stairs of heaven, the rain hissing on the village streets, the wild bull's-eye of the storm flashing all night long into the bare inn-chamber—the same sweet return of day, the same unfathomable blue of noon, the same high-coloured, halcyon eyes—and, above all, if he had anything like as good a comrade, anything like as keen a relish for what he saw, and what he ate, and the rivers that he bathed in, and the rubbish that he wrote, I would exchange estates to-day with the poor exile, and count myself a gainer.

But there was another point of similarity between the two journeys, for which the *Arethusa* was to pay dear: both were gone upon in days of incomplete security. It was not long after the Franco-Prussian war. Swiftly as men forget, that country-side was still alive with tales of uhlans, and outlying sentries, and hairbreadth 'scapes from the ignominious cord, and pleasant momentary friendships between invader and invaded. A year, at the most two years later, you might have tramped all that country over and not heard one anecdote. And a year or two later, you would—if you were a rather ill-looking young man in nondescript array—have gone your rounds in greater safety; for along with more interesting matter, the Prussian spy would have somewhat faded from men's imaginations.

For all that, our voyager had got beyond Château Renard before he was conscious of arousing wonder. On the road between that place and Châtillon-sur-Loing, however, he encountered a rural postman; they fell together in talk, and spoke of a variety of subjects; but through one and all, the postman was still visibly preoccupied, and his eyes were faithful to the *Arethusa's* knapsack. At last, with mysterious roguishness, he inquired what it contained, and on being answered, shook his head with kindly incredulity. '*Non,*' said he, '*non, vous avez des portraits.*'* And then with a languishing appeal, '*Voyons,* show me the portraits!' It was some little while before the *Arethusa,* with a shout of laughter, recognised his drift. By portraits he meant indecent photographs; and in the *Arethusa,* an austere and rising author, he thought to have identified a pornographic *colporteur.** When countryfolk in France have made up their minds as to a person's calling, argument is fruitless. Along all the rest of the way, the postman piped and fluted meltingly to get a sight of the collection; now he would upbraid, now he would reason—'*Voyons,* I will tell nobody'; then he tried corruption, and insisted on paying for a glass of wine; and, at last, when their ways separated—'*Non,*' said he, '*ce n'est pas bien de votre part. O non, ce n'est pas bien.*'* And shaking his head with quite a sentimental sense of injury, he departed unrefreshed.

On certain little difficulties encountered by the *Arethusa* at Châtillon-sur-Loing, I have not space to dwell; another Châtillon, of grislier memory, looms too near at hand. But the next day, in a certain hamlet called La Jussière, he stopped to drink a glass of syrup in a very poor, bare drinking-shop. The hostess, a comely woman, suckling a child, examined the traveller with kindly and pitying eyes. 'You are not of this Department?' she asked. The *Arethusa* told her he was English. 'Ah!' she said, surprised. 'We have no English. We have many Italians, however, and they do very well; they do not complain of the people of hereabouts. An Englishman may do very well also; it will be something new.' Here was a dark saying, over which the *Arethusa* pondered as he drank his grenadine; but when he rose and asked what was to pay, the light came upon him in a flash. '*Oh, pour vous,*' replied the landlady, 'a halfpenny!' *Pour vous?* By heaven, she took him for a beggar! He paid his halfpenny, feeling that it were ungracious to correct her. But when he was forth again upon the road, he became vexed in spirit. The conscience is no gentleman, he is a rabbinical fellow; and his conscience told him he had stolen the syrup.

That night the travellers slept in Gien; the next day they passed the river and set forth (severally, as their custom was) on a short stage through the green plain upon the Berry side, to Châtillon-sur-Loire. It was the first day of the shooting; and the air rang with the report of fire-arms and the admiring cries of sportsmen. Overhead the birds were in consternation, wheeling in clouds, settling and re-arising. And yet with all this bustle on either hand, the road itself lay solitary. The *Arethusa* smoked a pipe beside a mile-stone, and I remember he laid down very exactly all he was to do at Châtillon: how he was to enjoy a cold plunge, to change his shirt, and to await the *Cigarette's* arrival, in sublime inaction, by the margin of the Loire. Fired by these ideas, he pushed the more rapidly forward, and came, early in the afternoon and in a breathing heat, to the entering-in of that ill-fated town. Childe Roland to the dark tower came.

A polite gendarme threw his shadow on the path.

'*Monsieur est voyageur?*' he asked.

And the *Arethusa*, strong in his innocence, forgetful of his vile attire, replied—I had almost said with gaiety: 'So it would appear.'

'His papers are in order?' said the gendarme. And when the *Arethusa* with a slight change of voice, admitted he had none, he was informed (politely enough) that he must appear before the Commissary.

The Commissary sat at a table in his bedroom, stripped to the shirt and trousers, but still copiously perspiring; and when he turned upon the prisoner a large meaningless countenance, that was (like Bardolph's) 'all whelks and bubukles,' the dullest might have been prepared for grief. Here was a stupid man, sleepy with the heat and fretful at the interruption, whom neither appeal nor argument could reach.

THE COMMISSARY. You have no papers?

The ARETHUSA. Not here.

THE COMMISSARY. Why?

THE ARETHUSA. I have left them behind in my valise.

THE COMMISSARY. You know, however, that it is forbidden to circulate without papers?

THE ARETHUSA. Pardon me: I am convinced of the contrary. I am here on my rights as an English subject by international treaty.

THE COMMISSARY (*with scorn*). You call yourself an Englishman?

THE ARETHUSA. I do.

THE COMMISSARY. Humph.—What is your trade?

THE ARETHUSA. I am a Scottish Advocate.

THE COMMISSARY (*with singular annoyance*). A Scottish advocate! Do you then pretend to support yourself by that in this Department?

The *Arethusa* modestly disclaimed the pretension. The Commissary had scored a point.

THE COMMISSARY. Why, then, do you travel?

THE ARETHUSA. I travel for pleasure.

THE COMMISSARY (*pointing to the knapsack, and with sublime incredulity*). Avec ça? Voyez-vous, je suis un homme intelligent! (With that? Look here, I am a person of intelligence!)

The culprit remaining silent under this home thrust, the Commissary relished his triumph for awhile, and then demanded (like the postman, but with what different expectations!) to see the contents of the knapsack. And here the *Arethusa*, not yet sufficiently awake to his position, fell into a grave mistake. There was little or no furniture in the room except the Commissary's chair and table; and to facilitate matters, the *Arethusa* (with all the innocence on earth) leant the knapsack on a corner of the bed. The Commissary fairly bounded from his seat; his face and neck flushed past purple, almost into blue; and he screamed to lay the desecrating object on the floor.

The knapsack proved to contain a change of shirts, of shoes, of socks, and of linen trousers, a small dressing-case, a piece of soap in one of the shoes, two volumes of the *Collection Jannet* lettered *Poésies de Charles d'Orléans*, a map, and a version book containing divers notes in prose and the remarkable English roundels of the voyager, still to this day unpublished: the Commissary of Châtillon is the only living man who has clapped an eye on these artistic trifles. He turned the assortment over with a contumelious finger; it was plain from his daintiness that he regarded the *Arethusa* and all his belongings as the very temple of infection. Still there was nothing suspicious about the map, nothing really criminal except the roundels; as for Charles of Orleans, to the ignorant mind of the prisoner, he seemed as good as a certificate; and it was supposed the farce was nearly over.

The inquisitor resumed his seat.

THE COMMISSARY (*after a pause*). *Eh bien, je vais vous dire ce que vous êtes. Vous êtes allemand et vous venez chanter à la foire.* (Well, then, I will tell you what you are. You are a German and have come to sing at the fair.)

THE ARETHUSA. Would you like to hear me sing? I believe I could convince you of the contrary.

THE COMMISSARY. *Pas de plaisanterie, monsieur!*

THE ARETHUSA. Well, sir, oblige me at least by looking at this book. Here, I open it with my eyes shut. Read one of these songs—read this one—and tell me, you who are a man of intelligence, if it would be possible to sing it at a fair?

THE COMMISSARY. (*critically*). *Mais oui. Très bien.*

THE ARETHUSA. *Comment, monsieur!* What! But you do not observe it is antique. It is difficult to understand, even for you and me; but for the audience at a fair, it would be meaningless.

THE COMMISSARY (*taking a pen*). *Enfin, il faut en finir.* What is your name?

THE ARETHUSA. (*speaking with the swallowing vivacity of the English*). Robert-Louis-Stev'ns'n.

THE COMMISSARY (*aghast*). *Hé! Quoi?*

THE ARETHUSA (*perceiving and improving his advantage*). Rob'rt-Lou's-Stev'ns'n.

THE COMMISSARY (*after several conflicts with his pen*). *Eh bien, il faut se passer du nom. Ça ne s'écrit pas.* (Well, we must do without the name: it is unspellable.)

The above is a rough summary of this momentous conversation, in which I have been chiefly careful to preserve the plums of the Commissary; but the remainder of the scene, perhaps because of his rising anger, has left but little definite in the memory of the *Arethusa*. The Commissary was not, I think, a practised literary man; no sooner, at least, had he taken pen in hand and embarked on the composition of the *procès-verbal*,* than he became distinctly more uncivil and began to show a predilection for that simplest of all forms of repartee: 'You lie!' Several times the *Arethusa* let it pass, and then suddenly flared up, refused to accept more insults or to answer further questions, defied the Commissary to do his worst, and promised him, if he did, that he should bitterly repent it. Perhaps if he had worn his proud front from the first, instead of beginning with a sense of entertainment and then going on to argue, the thing might have turned otherwise; for even at this eleventh hour the Commissary was visibly staggered. But it was too late; he had been challenged; the *procès-verbal* was begun; and he again squared his elbows over his writing, and the *Arethusa* was led forth a prisoner.

A step or two down the hot road stood the gendarmerie. Thither was our unfortunate conducted, and there he was bidden to empty forth the contents of his pockets. A handkerchief, a pen, a pencil, a pipe and tobacco, matches, and some ten francs of change: that was all. Not a file, not a cipher, not a scrap of writing whether to identify or to condemn. The very gendarme was appalled before such destitution.

'I regret,' he said, 'that I arrested you, for I see that you are no *voyou*.' And he promised him every indulgence.

The *Arethusa*, thus encouraged, asked for his pipe. That he was told was impossible, but if he chewed, he might have some tobacco. He did not chew, however, and asked instead to have his handkerchief.

'*Non*,' said the gendarme. '*Nous avons eu des histoires de gens qui se sont pendus.*' (No, we have had histories of people who hanged themselves.)

'What,' cried the *Arethusa*. 'And is it for that you refuse me my handkerchief? But see how much more easily I could hang myself in my trousers!'

The man was struck by the novelty of the idea; but he stuck to his colours, and only continued to repeat vague offers of service.

'At least,' said the *Arethusa*, 'be sure that you arrest my comrade; he will follow me ere long on the same road, and you can tell him by the sack upon his shoulders.'

This promised, the prisoner was led round into the back court of the building, a cellar door was opened, he was motioned down the stair, and bolts grated and chains clanged behind his descending person.

The philosophic and still more the imaginative mind is apt to suppose itself prepared for any mortal accident. Prison, among other ills, was one that had been often faced by the undaunted *Arethusa*. Even as he went down the stairs, he was telling himself that here was a famous occasion for a roundel, and that like the committed linnets of the tuneful cavalier, he too would make his prison musical. I will tell the truth at once: the roundel was never written, or it should be printed in this place, to raise a smile. Two reasons interfered: the first moral, the second physical.

It is one of the curiosities of human nature, that although all men are liars, they can none of them bear to be told so of themselves. To get and take the lie with equanimity is a stretch beyond the stoic; and the *Arethusa*, who had been surfeited upon that insult, was blazing inwardly with a white heat of smothered wrath. But the physical had also its part. The cellar in which he was confined was some feet underground, and it was only lighted by an unglazed, narrow aperture high up in the wall and smothered in the leaves of a green vine. The walls were of naked masonry, the floor of bare earth; by way of furniture there was an earthenware basin, a water-jug, and a wooden bedstead with a blue-grey cloak for bedding. To be taken from the hot air of a summer's afternoon, the reverberation of the road and the stir of rapid exercise, and plunged into the gloom and damp of this receptacle for vagabonds,

struck an instant chill upon the *Arethusa's* blood. Now see
in how small a matter a hardship may consist: the floor
was exceedingly uneven underfoot, with the very spade-
marks, I suppose, of the labourers who dug the foundations
of the barrack; and what with the poor twilight and the
irregular surface, walking was impossible. The caged author
resisted for a good while; but the chill of the place struck
deeper and deeper; and at length, with such reluctance as
you may fancy, he was driven to climb upon the bed and
wrap himself in the public covering. There, then, he lay
upon the verge of shivering, plunged in semi-darkness,
wound in a garment whose touch he dreaded like the
plague, and (in a spirit far removed from resignation) telling
the roll of the insults he had just received. These are not
circumstances favourable to the Muse.

Meantime (to look at the upper surface where the sun
was still shining and the guns of sportsmen were still noisy
through the tufted plain) the *Cigarette* was drawing near at
his more philosophic pace. In those days of liberty and
health he was the constant partner of the *Arethusa*, and had
ample opportunity to share in that gentleman's disfavour
with the police. Many a bitter bowl had he partaken of
with that disastrous comrade. He was himself a man born
to float easily through life, his face and manner artfully
recommending him to all. There was but one suspicious
circumstance he could not carry off, and that was his
companion. He will not readily forget the Commissary in
what is ironically called the free town of Frankfort-on-the-
Main; nor the Franco-Belgian frontier; nor the inn at La
Fère; last, but not least, he is pretty certain to remember
Châtillon-sur-Loire.

At the town entry, the gendarme culled him like a
wayside flower; and a moment later, two persons, in a high
state of surprise, were confronted in the Commissary's
office. For if the *Cigarette* was surprised to be arrested, the
Commissary was no less taken aback by the appearance
and appointments of his captive. Here was a man about
whom there could be no mistake: a man of an unquestion-
able and unassailable manner, in apple-pie order, dressed

not with neatness merely but elegance, ready with his passport, at a word, and well supplied with money: a man the Commissary would have doffed his hat to on chance upon the highway; and this *beau cavalier* unblushingly claimed the *Arethusa* for his comrade! The conclusion of the interview was foregone; of its humours, I remember only one. 'Baronet?' demanded the magistrate, glancing up from the passport. '*Alors, monsieur, vous êtes le fils d'un baron?*' And when the *Cigarette* (his one mistake throughout the interview) denied the soft impeachment, '*Alors,*' from the Commissary, '*ce n'est pas votre passeport!*' But these were ineffectual thunders; he never dreamed of laying hands upon the *Cigarette*; presently he fell into a mood of unrestrained admiration, gloating over the contents of the knapsack, commending our friend's tailor. Ah, what an honoured guest was the Commissary entertaining! what suitable clothes he wore for the warm weather! what beautiful maps, what an attractive work of history he carried in his knapsack! You are to understand there was now but one point of difference between them: what was to be done with the *Arethusa?* the *Cigarette* demanding his release, the Commissary still claiming him as the dungeon's own. Now it chanced that the *Cigarette* had passed some years of his life in Egypt, where he had made acquaintance with two very bad things, cholera morbus and pashas; and in the eye of the Commissary, as he fingered the volume of Michelet, it seemed to our traveller there was something Turkish. I pass over this lightly; it is highly possible there was some misunderstanding, highly possible that the Commissary (charmed with his visitor) supposed the attraction to be mutual and took for an act of growing friendship what the *Cigarette* himself regarded as a bribe. And at any rate, was there ever a bribe more singular than an odd volume of Michelet's history? The work was promised him for the morrow, before our departure; and presently after, either because he had his price, or to show that he was not the man to be behind in friendly offices—'*Eh bien,*' he said, '*je suppose qu'il faut lâcher votre camarade.*'* And he tore up that feast of humour, the unfinished *procès-verbal*. Ah, if he had only torn up instead the *Arethusa's* roundels! There were many works burnt at Alexandria, there are many treasured in the British Museum, that I could better spare than the *procès-verbal* of Châtillon. Poor bubukled Commissary! I begin to be sorry that he never had his Michelet: perceiving in him fine human traits, a broad-based stupidity, a gusto in his magisterial functions, a taste for letters, a ready admiration for the admirable. And if he did not admire the *Arethusa*, he was not alone in that.

To the imprisoned one, shivering under the public covering, there came suddenly a noise of bolts and chains. He sprang to his feet, ready to welcome a companion in calamity; and instead of that, the door was flung wide, the friendly gendarme appeared above in the strong daylight, and with a magnificent gesture (being probably a student of the drama)—'*Vous êtes libre!*'* he said. None too soon for the *Arethusa*. I doubt if he had been half an hour imprisoned; but by the watch in a man's brain (which was the only watch he carried) he should have been eight times longer; and he passed forth with ecstasy up the cellar stairs into the healing warmth of the afternoon sun; and the breath of the earth came as sweet as a cow's into his nostril; and he heard again (and could have laughed for pleasure) the concord of delicate noises that we call the hum of life.

And here it might be thought that my history ended; but not so, this was an act-drop and not the curtain. Upon what followed in front of the barrack, since there was a lady in the case, I scruple to expatiate. The wife of the Maréchal-des-logis was a handsome woman, and yet the *Arethusa* was not sorry to be gone from her society. Something of her image, cool as a peach on that hot afternoon, still lingers in his memory: yet more of her conversation. 'You have there a very fine parlour,' said the poor gentleman.—'Ah,' said Madame la Maréchale (des-logis), 'You are very well acquainted with such parlours!' And you should have seen with what a hard and scornful eye she measured the vagabond before her! I do not think he ever hated the Commissary; but before that interview was at an end, he hated Madame la Maréchale. His passion (as I am led to understand by one who was present) stood confessed in a burning eye, a pale cheek, and a trembling utterance; Madame meanwhile, tasting the joys of the matador, goading him with barbed words and staring him coldly down.

It was certainly good to be away from this lady, and better still to sit down to an excellent dinner in the inn. Here, too, the despised travellers scraped acquaintance with their next neighbour, a gentleman of these parts, returned from the day's sport, who had the good taste to find pleasure in their society. The dinner at an end, the gentleman proposed the acquaintance should be ripened in the *café*.

The *café* was crowded with sportsmen conclamantly explaining to each other and the world the smallness of their bags. About the centre of the room, the *Cigarette* and the *Arethusa* sat with their new acquaintance; a trio very well pleased, for the travellers (after their late experience) were greedy of consideration, and their sportsman rejoiced in a pair of patient listeners. Suddenly the glass door flew open with a crash; the Maréchal-des-logis appeared in the interval, gorgeously belted and befrogged, entered without salutation, strode up the room with a clang of spurs and weapons, and disappeared through a door at the far end. Close at his heels followed the *Arethusa's* gendarme of the afternoon, imitating, with a nice shade of difference, the imperial bearing of his chief; only, as he passed, he struck lightly with his open hand on the shoulder of his late captive, and with that ringing, dramatic utterance of which he had the secret—'*Suivez!*' said he.

The arrest of the members, the oath of the Tennis Court, the signing of the Declaration of Independence, Mark Antony's oration, all the brave scenes of history, I conceive as having been not unlike that evening in the *café* at Châtillon. Terror breathed upon the assembly. A moment later, when the *Arethusa* had followed his recaptors into the farther part of the house, the *Cigarette* found himself alone with his coffee in a ring of empty chairs and tables, all the lusty sportsmen huddled into corners, all their clamorous voices hushed in whispering, all their eyes shooting at him furtively as at a leper.

And the *Arethusa?* Well, he had a long, sometimes a trying, interview in the back kitchen. The Maréchal-des-logis, who was a very handsome man, and I believe both intelligent and honest, had no clear opinion on the case. He thought the Commissary had done wrong, but he did not wish to get his subordinates into trouble; and he proposed this, that, and the other, to all of which the *Arethusa* (with a growing sense of his position) demurred.

'In short,' suggested the *Arethusa*, 'you want to wash your hands of further responsibility? Well, then, let me go to Paris.'

The Maréchal-des-logis looked at his watch.

'You may leave,' said he, 'by the ten o'clock train for Paris.'

And at noon the next day the travellers were telling their misadventure in the dining-room at Siron's.

TRAVELS WITH A DONKEY
IN THE CEVENNES

DEDICATION

My dear Sidney Colvin,

The journey which this little book is to describe was very agreeable and fortunate for me. After an uncouth beginning, I had the best of luck to the end. But we are all travellers in which John Bunyan calls the wilderness of this world—all, too, travellers with a donkey; and the best that we find in our travels is an honest friend. He is a fortunate voyager who finds many. We travel, indeed, to find them. They are the end and the reward of life. They keep us worthy of ourselves; and, when we are alone, we are only nearer to the absent.

Every book is, in an intimate sense, a circular letter to the friends of him who writes it. They alone take his meaning; they find private messages, assurances of love, and expressions of gratitude dropped for them in every corner. The public is but a generous patron who defrays the postage. Yet though the letter is directed to all, we have an old and kindly custom of addressing it on the outside to one. Of what shall a man be proud, if he is not proud of his friends? And so, my dear Sidney Colvin, it is with pride that I sign myself

Affectionately yours,

R.L.S.

A MOUNTAIN TOWN IN FRANCE*

Le Monastier is the chief place of a hilly canton in Haute Loire, the ancient Velay. As the name betokens, the town is of monastic origin; and it still contains a towered bulk of monastery and a church of some architectural pretensions, the seat of an archpriest and several vicars. It stands on the side of a hill above the river Gazeille, about fifteen miles from Le Puy, up a steep road where the wolves sometimes pursue the diligence in winter. The road, which is bound for Vivarais, passes through the town from end to end in a single narrow street; there you may see the fountain where women fill their pitchers; there also some old houses with carved doors and pediments and ornamental work in iron.

For Monastier, like Maybole in Ayrshire, was a sort of country capital, where the local aristocracy had their town mansions for the winter; and there is a certain baron still alive and, I am told, extremely penitent, who found means to ruin himself by high living in this village on the hills. He certainly has claims to be considered the most remarkable spendthrift on record. How he set about it, in a place where there are no luxuries for sale, and where the board at the best inn comes to little more than a shilling a day, is a problem for the wise. His son, ruined as the family was, went as far as Paris to sow his wild oats; and so the cases of father and son mark an epoch in the history of centralisation in France. Not until the latter had got into the train was the work of Richelieu complete.

It is a people of lace-makers. The women sit in the streets by groups of five or six; and the noise of the bobbins is audible from one group to another. Now and then you will hear one woman clattering off prayers for the edification of the others at their work. They wear gaudy shawls, white caps with a gay ribbon about the head, and sometimes a black felt brigand hat above the cap; and so they give the street colour and brightness and a foreign air. A while ago, when England largely supplied herself from this district with the lace called *torchon*, it was not unusual to earn five francs a day; and five francs in Monastier is worth a pound in London. Now, from a change in the market, it takes a clever and industrious workwoman to earn from three to four in the week, or less than an eighth of what she made easily a few years ago. The tide of prosperity came and went, as with our northern pitmen, and left nobody the richer. The women bravely squandered their gains, kept the men in idleness, and gave themselves up, as I was told, to sweet-hearting and a merry life. From week's end to week's end it was one continuous gala in Monastier; people spent the day in the wine-shops, and the drum or the bagpipes led on the *bourrées** up to ten at night. Now these dancing days are over. '*Il n'y a plus de jeunesse*,'* said Victor the garçon. I hear of no great advance in what are thought the essentials of morality; but the *bourrée*, with its rambling, sweet, interminable music, and alert and rustic figures, has fallen into disuse, and is mostly remembered as a custom of the past. Only on the occasion of the fair shall you hear a drum discreetly rattling in a wine-shop or perhaps one of the company singing the measure while the others dance. I am sorry at the change, and marvel once more at the complicated scheme of things upon this earth, and how a turn of fashion in England can silence so much mountain merriment in France. The lace-makers themselves have not entirely forgiven our countrywomen; and I think they take a special pleasure in the legend of the northern quarter of the town, called L'Anglade, because there the English free-lances were arrested and driven back by the potency of a little Virgin Mary on the wall.

From time to time a market is held, and the town has a season of revival; cattle and pigs are stabled in the streets; and pickpockets have been known to come all the way from Lyons for the occasion. Every Sunday the countryfolk throng in with daylight to buy apples, to attend mass, and to visit one of the wine-shops, of which there are no fewer than fifty in this little town. Sunday wear for the men is a green tailcoat of some coarse sort of drugget, and usually a complete suit to match. I have never set eyes on such degrading raiment. Here it clings, there bulges; and the human body, with its agreeable and lively lines, is turned into a mockery and laughing-stock. Another piece of Sunday business with the peasants is to take their ailments to the chemist for advice. It is as much a matter for Sunday as church-going. I have seen a woman who had been unable to speak since the Monday before, wheezing, catching her breath, endlessly and painfully coughing; and yet she had waited upwards of a hundred hours before coming to seek help, and had the week been twice as long, she would have waited still. There was a canonical day for consultation; such was the ancestral habit, to which a respectable lady must study to conform.

Two conveyances go daily to Le Puy, but they rival each other in polite concessions rather than in speed. Each will wait an hour or two hours cheerfully while an old lady does her marketing or a gentleman finishes the papers in a *café*. The *Courrier* (such is the name of one) should leave Le Puy by two in the afternoon on the return voyage, and arrive at Monastier in good time for a six o'clock dinner. But the driver dares not disoblige his customers. He will postpone his departure again and again, hour after hour; and I have known the sun to go down on his delay. These purely personal favours, this consideration of men's fancies, rather than the hands of a mechanical clock, as marking the advance of the abstraction, time, makes a more humorous business of stage-coaching than we are used to see it.

As far as the eye can reach, one swelling line of hill-top rises and falls behind another; and if you climb an eminence, it is only to see new and farther ranges behind these. Many little rivers run from all sides in cliffy valleys; and one of them, a few miles from Monastier, bears the great name of Loire. The mean level of the country is a little more than three thousand feet above the sea, which makes the atmosphere proportionally brisk and wholesome. There is little timber except pines, and the greater part of the country lies in moorland pasture. The country is wild and tumbled rather than commanding; an upland rather

than a mountain district; and the most striking as well as
the most agreeable scenery lies low beside the rivers. There,
indeed, you will find many corners that take the fancy; such
as made the English noble choose his grave by a Swiss
streamlet, where nature is at her freshest, and looks as
young as on the seventh morning. Such a place is the course
of the Gazeille, where it waters the common of Monastier
and thence downwards till it joins the Loire; a place to
hear birds singing; a place for lovers to frequent. The name
of the river was perhaps suggested by the sound of its
passage over the stones; for it is a great warbler, and at
night, after I was in bed at Monastier, I could hear it go
singing down the valley till I fell asleep.

On the whole, this is a Scottish landscape, although not
so noble as the best in Scotland; and by an odd coincidence,
the population is, in its way, as Scottish as the country.
They have abrupt, uncouth, Fifeshire manners, and accost
you, as if you were trespassing, with an '*Où'st-ce que vous
allez?*' only translatable into the Lowland 'Whau'r ye gaun?'
They keep the Scottish Sabbath. There is no labour done
on that day but to drive in and out the various pigs and
sheep and cattle that make so pleasant a tinkling in the
meadows. The lace-makers have disappeared from the
street. Not to attend mass would involve social degradation;
and you may find people reading Sunday books, in particular a sort of Catholic *Monthly Visitor* on the doings of
Our Lady of Lourdes. I remember one Sunday, when I was
walking in the country, that I fell on a hamlet and found
all the inhabitants, from the patriarch to the baby, gathered
in the shadow of a gable at prayer. One strapping lass stood
with her back to the wall and did the solo part, the rest
chiming in devoutly. Not far off, a lad lay flat on his face
asleep among some straw, to represent the worldly element.

Again, this people is eager to proselytise; and the postmaster's daughter used to argue with me by the half-hour
about my heresy, until she grew quite flushed. I have heard
the reverse process going on between a Scotswoman and a
French girl; and the arguments in the two cases were
identical. Each apostle based her claim on the superior

virtue and attainments of her clergy, and clenched the business with a threat of hell-fire. '*Pas bong prêtres ici,*' said the Presbyterian, '*bong prêtres en Écosse.*'* And the postmaster's daughter, taking up the same weapon, plied me, so to speak, with the butt of it instead of the bayonet. We are a hopeful race, it seems, and easily persuaded for our good. One cheerful circumstance I note in these guerilla missions, that each side relies on hell, and Protestant and Catholic alike address themselves to a supposed misgiving in their adversary's heart. And I call it cheerful, for faith is a more supporting quality than imagination.

Here, as in Scotland, many peasant families boast a son in holy orders. And here also, the young men have a tendency to emigrate. It is certainly not poverty that drives them to the great cities or across the seas, for many peasant families, I was told, have a fortune of at least 40,000 francs. The lads go forth pricked with the spirit of adventure and the desire to rise in life, and leave their homespun elders grumbling and wondering over the event. Once, at a village called Laussonne, I met one of these disappointed parents: a drake who had fathered a wild swan and seen it take wing and disappear. The wild swan in question was now an apothecary in Brazil. He had flown by way of Bordeaux, and first landed in America, bareheaded and barefoot, and with a single halfpenny in his pocket. And now he was an apothecary! Such a wonderful thing is an adventurous life! I thought he might as well have stayed at home; but you never can tell wherein a man's life consists, nor in what he sets his pleasure: one to drink, another to marry, a third to write scurrilous articles and be repeatedly caned in public, and now this fourth, perhaps, to be an apothecary in Brazil. As for his old father, he could conceive no reason for the lad's behaviour. 'I had always bread for him,' he said; 'he ran away to annoy me. He loved to annoy me. He had no gratitude.' But at heart he was swelling with pride over his travelled offspring; and he produced a letter out of his pocket, where, as he said, it was rotting, a mere lump of paper rags, and waved it gloriously in the air. 'This comes from America,' he cried, 'six thousand leagues away!'

And the wine-shop audience looked upon it with a certain
thrill.

I soon became a popular figure, and was known for miles
in the country. *Où'st-ce que vous allez?** was changed for me
into *Quoi, vous rentrez au Monastier ce soir?** and in the town
itself every urchin seemed to know my name, although no
living creature could pronounce it. There was one particular group of lace-makers who brought out a chair for me
whenever I went by, and detained me from my walk to
gossip. They were filled with curiosity about England, its
language, its religion, the dress of the women, and were
never weary of seeing the Queen's head on English post-
age-stamps or seeking for French words in English journals.
The language, in particular, filled them with surprise.

'Do they speak *patois** in England?' I was once asked; and
when I told them not, 'Ah, then, French?' said they.

'No, no,' I said, 'not French.'

'Then,' they concluded, 'they speak *patois*.'

You must obviously either speak French or *patois*. Talk of
the force of logic—here it was in all its weakness. I gave
up the point, but proceeding to give illustrations of my
native jargon, I was met with a new mortification. Of all
patois they declared that mine was the most preposterous
and the most jocose in sound. At each new word there was
a new explosion of laughter, and some of the younger ones
were glad to rise from their chairs and stamp about the
street in ecstasy; and I looked on upon their mirth in a
faint and slightly disagreeable bewilderment. 'Bread,' which
sounds a commonplace, plain-sailing monosyllable in England, was the word that most delighted these good ladies
of Monastier; it seemed to them frolicsome and racy, like
a page of *Pickwick*; and they all got it carefully by heart, as
a stand-by, I presume, for winter evenings. I have tried it
since then with every sort of accent and inflection, but I
seem to lack the sense of humour.

They were of all ages: children at their first web of lace,
a stripling girl with a bashful but encouraging play of eyes,
solid married women, and grandmothers, some on the top
of their age and some falling towards decrepitude. One and

all were pleasant and natural, ready to laugh and ready with a certain quiet solemnity when that was called for by the subject of our talk. Life, since the fall in wages, had begun to appear to them with a more serious air. The stripling girl would sometimes laugh at me in a provocative and not unadmiring manner, if I judge aright; and one of the grandmothers, who was my great friend of the party, gave me many a sharp word of judgment on my sketches, my heresy, or even my arguments, and gave them with a wry mouth and a humorous twinkle in her eye that were eminently Scottish. But the rest used me with a certain reverence, as something come from afar and not entirely human. Nothing would put them at their ease but the irresistible gaiety of my native tongue. Between the old lady and myself I think there was a real attachment. She was never weary of sitting to me for her portrait, in her best cap and brigand hat, and with all her wrinkles tidily composed, and though she never failed to repudiate the result, she would always insist upon another trial. It was as good as a play to see her sitting in judgment over the last. 'No, no,' she would say, 'that is not it. I am old, to be sure, but I am better-looking than that. We must try again.' When I was about to leave she bade me good-bye for this life in a somewhat touching manner. We should not meet again, she said; it was a long farewell, and she was sorry. But life is so full of crooks, old lady, that who knows? I have said good-bye to people for greater distances and times, and, please God, I mean to see them yet again.

One thing was notable about these women, from the youngest to the oldest, and with hardly an exception. In spite of their piety, they could twang off an oath with Sir Toby Belch in person. There was nothing so high or so low, in heaven or earth or in the human body, but a woman of this neighbourhood would whip out the name of it, fair and square, by way of conversational adornment. My land-lady, who was pretty and young, dressed like a lady and avoided *patois* like a weakness, commonly addressed her child in the language of a drunken bully. And of all the swearers that I have ever heard, commend me to an old lady in Goudet, a village of the Loire. I was making a sketch, and her curse was not yet ended when I had finished it and took my departure. It is true she had a right to be angry; for here was her son, a hulking fellow, visibly the worse for drink before the day was well begun. But it was strange to hear her unwearying flow of oaths and obscenities, endless like a river, and now and then rising to a passionate shrillness, in the clear and silent air of the morning. In city slums, the thing might have passed unnoticed; but in a country valley, and from a plain and honest countrywoman, this beastliness of speech surprised the ear.

The *Conductor*, as he is called, of *Roads and Bridges* was my principal companion. He was generally intelligent, and could have spoken more or less falsetto on any of the trite topics; but it was his speciality to have a generous taste in eating. This was what was most indigenous in the man; it was here he was an artist; and I found in his company what I had long suspected, that enthusiasm and special knowledge are the great social qualities, and what they are about, whether white sauce or Shakespeare's plays, an altogether secondary question.

I used to accompany the *Conductor* on his professional rounds, and grew to believe myself an expert in the business. I thought I could make an entry in a stone-breaker's time-book, or order manure off the wayside with any living engineer in France. Goudet was one of the places we visited together; and Laussonne, where I met the apothecary's father, was another. There, at Laussonne, George Sand spent a day while she was gathering materials for the *Marquis de Villemer*; and I have spoken with an old man, who was then a child running about the inn kitchen, and who still remembers her with a sort of reverence. It appears that he spoke French imperfectly; for this reason George Sand chose him for companion, and whenever he let slip a broad and picturesque phrase in *patois*, she would make him repeat it again and again till it was graven in her memory. The word for a frog particularly pleased her fancy; and it would be curious to know if she afterwards employed it in her works. The peasants, who knew nothing of letters and had never so much as heard of local colour, could not explain her chattering with this backward child; and to them she seemed a very homely lady and far from beautiful; the most famous man-killer of the age appealed so little to Velaisian swineherds!

On my first engineering excursion, which lay up by Crouzials towards Mount Mézenc and the borders of Ardèche, I began an improving acquaintance with the foreman road-mender. He was in great glee at having me with him, passed me off among his subalterns as the supervising engineer, and insisted on what he called 'the gallantry' of paying for my breakfast in a roadside wine-shop. On the whole, he was a man of great weather-wisdom, some spirits, and a social temper. But I am afraid he was superstitious. When he was nine years old, he had seen one night a company of *bourgeois et dames qui faisaient la manège avec des chaises*,* and concluded that he was in the presence of a witches' Sabbath. I suppose, but venture with timidity on the suggestion, that this may have been a romantic and nocturnal picnic party. Again, coming from Pradelles with his brother, they saw a great empty cart drawn by six enormous horses before them on the road. The driver cried aloud and filled the mountains with the cracking of his whip. He never seemed to go faster than a walk, yet it was impossible to overtake him; and at length, at the corner of a hill, the whole equipage disappeared bodily into the night. At the time, people said it was the devil *qui s'amusait à faire ça.**

I suggested there was nothing more likely, as he must have some amusement.

The foreman said it was odd, but there was less of that sort of thing than formerly. '*C'est difficile*,' he added, '*à expliquer.*'*

When we were well up on the moors and the *Conductor* was trying some road-metal with the gauge—

'Hark!' said the foreman, 'do you hear nothing?'

We listened, and the wind, which was blowing chilly out of the east, brought a faint, tangled jangling to our ears.

'It is the flocks of Vivarais,' said he.

For every summer, the flocks of all Ardèche are brought up to pasture on these grassy plateaux.

Here and there a little private flock was being tended by a girl, one spinning with a distaff, another seated on a wall and intently making lace. This last, when we addressed her, leaped up in a panic and put out her arms, like a person swimming, to keep us at a distance, and it was some seconds before we could persuade her of the honesty of our intentions.

The *Conductor* told me of another herdswoman from whom he had once asked his road while he was yet new to the country, and who fled from him, driving her beasts before her, until he had given up the information in despair. A tale of old lawlessness may yet be read in these uncouth timidities.

The winter in these uplands is a dangerous and melancholy time. Houses are snowed up, and wayfarers lost in a flurry within hail of their own fireside. No man ventures abroad without meat and a bottle of wine, which he replenishes at every wine-shop; and even thus equipped he takes the road with terror. All day the family sits about the fire in a foul and airless hovel, and equally without work or diversion. The father may carve a rude piece of furniture, but that is all that will be done until the spring sets in again, and along with it the labours of the field. It is not for nothing that you find a clock in the meanest of these mountain habitations. A clock and an almanack, you would fancy, were indispensable in such a life. . .

VELAY

'Many are the mighty things, and nought is more
mighty than man. . . . He masters by his devices the
tenant of the fields.'

SOPHOCLES

'Who hath loosed the bands of the wild ass?'

JOB

THE DONKEY, THE PACK, AND THE
PACK-SADDLE

In a little place called Le Monastier, in a pleasant highland
valley fifteen miles from Le Puy, I spent about a month of
fine days. Monastier is notable for the making of lace, for
drunkenness, for freedom of language, and for unparelleled
political dissension. There are adherents of each of the four
French parties—Legitimists, Orleanists, Imperialists, and
Republicans*—in this little mountain-town; and they all
hate, loathe, decry, and calumniate each other. Except for
business purposes, or to give each other the lie in a tavern
brawl, they have laid aside even the civility of speech. 'Tis
a mere mountain Poland. In the midst of this Babylon I
found myself a rallying-point; every one was anxious to be
kind and helpful to the stranger. This was not merely from
the natural hospitality of mountain people, nor even from
the surprise with which I was regarded as a man living of
his own free will in Le Monastier, when he might just as
well have lived anywhere else in this big world; it arose a
good deal from my projected excursion southward through
the Cevennes. A traveller of my sort was a thing hitherto
unheard-of in that district. I was looked upon with contempt,
like a man who should project a journey to the moon, but
yet with a respectful interest, like one setting forth for the
inclement Pole. All were ready to help in my preparations; a
crowd of sympathisers supported me at the critical moment

of a bargain; not a step was taken but was heralded by glasses round and celebrated by a dinner or a breakfast.

It was already hard upon October before I was ready to set forth, and at the high altitudes over which my road lay there was no Indian summer to be looked for. I was determined, if not to camp out, at least to have the means of camping out in my possession; for there is nothing more harassing to an easy mind than the necessity of reaching shelter by dusk, and the hospitality of a village inn is not always to be reckoned sure by those who trudge on foot. A tent, above all for a solitary traveller, is troublesome to pitch, and troublesome to strike again; and even on the march it forms a conspicuous feature in your baggage. A sleeping-sack, on the other hand, is always ready—you have only to get into it; it serves a double purpose—a bed by night, a portmanteau by day; and it does not advertise your intention of camping out to every curious passer-by. This is a huge point. If the camp is not secret, it is but a troubled resting-place; you become a public character; the convivial rustic visits your bedside after an early supper; and you must sleep with one eye open, and be up before the day. I decided on a sleeping-sack; and after repeated visits to Le Puy, and a deal of high living for myself and my advisers, a sleeping-sack was designed, constructed, and triumphantly brought home.

This child of my invention was nearly six feet square, exclusive of two triangular flaps to serve as a pillow by night and as the top and bottom of the sack by day. I call it 'the sack,' but it was never a sack by more than courtesy: only a sort of long roll or sausage, green waterproof cart cloth without and blue sheep's fur within. It was commodious as a valise, warm and dry for a bed. There was luxurious turning room for one; and at a pinch the thing might serve for two. I could bury myself in it up to the neck; for my head I trusted to a fur cap, with a hood to fold down over my ears and a band to pass under my nose like a respirator; and in case of heavy rain I proposed to make myself a little tent, or tentlet, with my waterproof coat, three stones, and a bent branch.

It will readily be conceived that I could not carry this huge package on my own, merely human, shoulders. It remained to choose a beast of burden. Now, a horse is a fine lady among animals, flighty, timid, delicate in eating, of tender health; he is too valuable and too restive to be left alone, so that you are chained to your brute as to a fellow galley-slave; a dangerous road puts him out of his wits; in short, he's an uncertain and exacting ally, and adds thirtyfold to the troubles of the voyager. What I required was something cheap and small and hardy, and of a stolid and peaceful temper; and all these requisites pointed to a donkey.

There dwelt an old man in Monastier, of rather unsound intellect according to some, much followed by street-boys, and known to fame as Father Adam. Father Adam had a cart, and to draw the cart a diminutive she-ass, not much bigger than a dog, the colour of a mouse, with a kindly eye and a determined under-jaw. There was something neat and high-bred, a quakerish elegance, about the rogue that hit my fancy on the spot. Our first interview was in Monastier market-place. To prove her good temper, one child after another was set upon her back to ride, and one after another went head over heels into the air; until a want of confidence began to reign in youthful bosoms, and the experiment was discontinued from a dearth of subjects. I was already backed by a deputation of my friends; but as if this were not enough, all the buyers and sellers came round and helped me in the bargain; and the ass and I and Father Adam were the centre of a hubbub for near half an hour. At length she passed into my service for the consideration of sixty-five francs and a glass of brandy. The sack had already cost eighty francs and two glasses of beer; so that Modestine, as I instantly baptised her, was upon all accounts the cheaper article. Indeed, that was as it should be; for she was only an appurtenance of my mattress, or self-acting bedstead on four castors.

I had a last interview with Father Adam in a billiard-room at the witching hour of dawn, when I administered the brandy. He professed himself greatly touched by the

separation, and declared he had often bought white bread
for the donkey when he had been content with black bread
for himself; but this, according to the best authorities, must
have been a flight of fancy. He had a name in the village
for brutally misusing the ass; yet it is certain that he shed
a tear, and the tear made a clean mark down one cheek.

By the advice of a fallacious local saddler, a leather pad
was made for me with rings to fasten on my bundle; and
I thoughtfully completed my kit and arranged my toilette.
By way of armoury and utensils, I took a revolver, a little
spirit-lamp and pan, a lantern and some halfpenny candles,
a jack-knife and a large leather flask. The main cargo
consisted of two entire changes of warm clothing—besides
my travelling wear of country velveteen, pilot-coat, and
knitted spencer—some books, and my railway-rug, which,
being also in the form of a bag, made me a double castle
for cold nights. The permanent larder was represented by
cakes of chocolate and tins of Bologna sausage. All this,
except what I carried about my person, was easily stowed
into the sheepskin bag; and by good fortune I threw in my
empty knapsack, rather for convenience of carriage than
from any thought that I should want it on my journey. For
more immediate needs, I took a leg of cold mutton, a bottle
of Beaujolais, an empty bottle to carry milk, an egg-beater,
and a considerable quantity of black bread and white, like
Father Adam, for myself and donkey, only in my scheme
of things the destinations were reversed.

Monastrians, of all shades of thought in politics, had
agreed in threatening me with many ludicrous misadventures, and with sudden death in many surprising forms.
Cold, wolves, robbers, above all the nocturnal practical
joker, were daily and eloquently forced on my attention.
Yet in these vaticinations, the true, patent danger was left
out. Like Christian, it was from my pack I suffered by the
way. Before telling my own mishaps, let me, in two words,
relate the lesson of my experience. If the pack is well
strapped at the ends, and hung at full length—not doubled,
for your life—across the pack-saddle, the traveller is safe.
The saddle will certainly not fit, such is the imperfection

of our transitory life; it will assuredly topple and tend to overset; but there are stones on every roadside, and a man soon learns the art of correcting any tendency to overbalance with a well-adjusted stone.

On the day of my departure I was up a little after five; by six, we began to load the donkey; and ten minutes after, my hopes were in the dust. The pad would not stay on Modestine's back for half a moment. I returned it to its maker, with whom I had so contumelious a passage that the street outside was crowded from wall to wall with gossips looking on and listening. The pad changed hands with much vivacity; perhaps it would be more descriptive to say that we threw it at each other's heads; and, any rate, we were very warm and unfriendly, and spoke with a deal of freedom.

I had a common donkey pack-saddle—a *barde*, as they call it—fitted upon Modestine; and once more loaded her with my effects. The doubled sack, my pilot-coat (for it was warm, and I was to walk in my waistcoat), a great bar of black bread, and an open basket containing the white bread, the mutton, and the bottles, were all corded together in a very elaborate system of knots, and I looked on the result with fatuous content. In such a monstrous deck-cargo, all poised above the donkey's shoulders, with nothing below to balance, on a brand-new pack-saddle that had not yet been worn to fit the animal, and fastened with brand-new girths that might be expected to stretch and slacken by the way, even a very careless traveller should have seen disaster brewing. That elaborate system of knots, again, was the work of too many sympathisers to be very artfully designed. It is true they tightened the cords with a will; as many as three at a time would have a foot against Modestine's quarters, and be hauling with clenched teeth; but I learned afterwards that one thoughtful person, without any exercise of force, can make a more solid job than half a dozen heated and enthusiastic grooms. I was then but a novice; even after the misadventure of the pad nothing could disturb my security, and I went forth from the stable-door as an ox goeth to the slaughter.

THE GREEN DONKEY-DRIVER

The bell of Monastier was just striking nine as I got quit of these preliminary troubles and descended the hill through the common. As long as I was within sight of the windows, a secret shame and the fear of some laughable defeat withheld me from tampering with Modestine. She tripped along upon her four small hoofs with a sober daintiness of gait; from time to time she shook her ears or her tail; and she looked so small under the bundle that my mind misgave me. We got across the ford without difficulty—there was no doubt about the matter, she was docility itself—and once on the other bank, where the road begins to mount through pine-woods, I took in my right hand the unhallowed staff, and with a quaking spirit applied it to the donkey. Modestine brisked up her pace for perhaps three steps, and then relapsed into her former minuet. Another application had the same effect, and so with the third. I am worthy the name of an Englishman, and it goes against my conscience to lay my hand rudely on a female. I desisted, and looked her all over from head to foot; the poor brute's knees were trembling and her breathing was distressed; it was plain that she could go no faster on a hill. God forbid, thought I, that I should brutalise this innocent creature; let her go at her own pace, and let me patiently follow.

What that pace was, there is no word mean enough to describe; it was something as much slower than a walk as a walk is slower then a run; it kept me hanging on each foot for an incredible length of time; in five minutes it exhausted the spirit and set up a fever in all the muscles of the leg. And yet I had to keep close at hand and measure my advance exactly upon hers; for if I dropped a few yards into the rear, or went on a few yards ahead, Modestine came instantly to a halt and began to browse. The thought that this was to last from here to Alais nearly broke my heart. Of all conceivable journeys, this promised to be the most tedious. I tried to tell myself it was a lovely day; I tried to charm my foreboding spirit with tobacco; but I had a vision ever present to me of the long, long roads, up hill and down dale, and a pair of figures ever infinitesimally moving, foot by foot, a yard to the minute, and, like things enchanted in a nightmare, approaching no nearer to the goal.

In the meantime there came up behind us a tall peasant, perhaps forty years of age, of an ironical snuffy countenance, and arrayed in the green tail-coat of the country. He overtook us hand over hand, and stopped to consider our pitiful advance.

'Your donkey,' says he, 'is very old?'

I told him, I believed not.

Then, he supposed, we had come far.

I told him, we had but newly left Monastier.

'*Et vous marchez comme ça!* '* cried he; and, throwing back his head, he laughed long and heartily. I watched him, half prepared to feel offended, until he had satisfied his mirth; and then, 'You must have no pity on these animals,' said he; and, plucking a switch out of a thicket, he began to lace Modestine about the stern-works, uttering a cry. The rogue pricked up her ears and broke into a good round pace, which she kept up without flagging, and without exhibiting the least symptom of distress, as long as the peasant kept beside us. Her former panting and shaking had been, I regret to say, a piece of comedy.

My *deus ex machina*, before he left me, supplied some excellent, if inhumane, advice; presented me with the switch, which he declared she would feel more tenderly than my cane; and finally taught me the true cry or masonic word of donkey-drivers, 'Proot!' All the time, he regarded me with a comical incredulous air, which was embarrassing to confront; and smiled over my donkey-driving, as I might have smiled over his orthography, or his green tail-coat. But it was not my turn for the moment.

I was proud of my new lore, and thought I had learned the art to perfection. And certainly Modestine did wonders for the rest of the forenoon, and I had a breathing space to look about me. It was Sabbath; the mountain-fields were all vacant in the sunshine; and as we came down through St. Martin de Frugères, the church was crowded to the door, there were people kneeling without upon the steps, and the sound of the priest's chanting came forth out of the dim interior. It gave me a home feeling on the spot; for I am a countryman of the Sabbath, so to speak, and all Sabbath observances, like a Scottish accent, strike in me mixed feelings, grateful and the reverse. It is only a traveller, hurrying by like a person from another planet, who can rightly enjoy the peace and beauty of the great ascetic feast. The sight of the resting country does his spirit good. There is something better than music in the wide unusual silence; and it disposes him to amiable thoughts, like the sound of a little river or the warmth of sunlight.

In this pleasant humour I came down the hill to where Goudet stands in the green end of a valley, with Château Beaufort opposite upon a rocky steep, and the stream, as clear as crystal, lying in a deep pool between them. Above and below, you may hear it wimpling over the stones, an amiable stripling of a river, which it seems absurd to call the Loire. On all sides, Goudet is shut in by mountains; rocky footpaths, practicable at best for donkeys, join it to the outer world of France; and the men and women drink and swear, in their green corner, or look up at the snow-clad peaks in winter from the threshold of their homes, in an isolation, you would think, like that of Homer's Cyclops. But it is not so; the postman reaches Goudet with the letter-bag; the aspiring youth of Goudet are within a day's walk of the railway at Le Puy; and here in the inn you may find an engraved portrait of the host's nephew, Régis Senac, 'Professor of Fencing and Champion of the two Americas,' a distinction gained by him, along with the sum of five hundred dollars, at Tammany Hall, New York, on the 10th April, 1876.

I hurried over my midday meal, and was early forth again. But, alas, as we climbed the interminable hill upon the other side, 'Proot!' seemed to have lost its virtue. I prooted like a lion, I prooted mellifluously like a sucking-dove; but Modestine would be neither softened nor intimidated. She held doggedly to her pace; nothing but a blow would move her, and that only for a second. I must follow at her heels, incessantly belabouring. A moment's pause in this ignoble toil, and she relapsed into her own private gait. I think I never heard of anyone in as mean a situation. I must reach the lake of Bouchet, where I meant to camp, before sundown, and, to have even a hope of this, I must instantly maltreat this uncomplaining animal. The sound of my own blows sickened me. Once, when I looked at her, she had a faint resemblance to a lady of my acquaintance who formerly loaded me with kindness; and this increased my horror of my cruelty.

To make matters worse, we encountered another donkey, ranging at will upon the roadside; and this other donkey chanced to be a gentleman. He and Modestine met nickering for joy, and I had to separate the pair and beat down their young romance with a renewed and feverish bastinado. If the other donkey had had the heart of a male under his hide, he would have fallen upon me tooth and hoof; and this was a kind of consolation—he was plainly unworthy of Modestine's affection. But the incident saddened me, as did everything that spoke of my donkey's sex.

It was blazing hot up the valley, windless, with vehement sun upon my shoulders; and I had to labour so consistently with my stick that the sweat ran into my eyes. Every five minutes, too, the pack, the basket, and the pilot-coat would take an ugly slew to one side or the other; and I had to stop Modestine, just when I had got her to a tolerable pace of about two miles an hour, to tug, push, shoulder, and readjust the load. And at last, in the village of Ussel, saddle and all, the whole hypothec turned round and grovelled in the dust below the donkey's belly. She, none better pleased, incontinently drew up and seemed to smile; and a party of one man, two women, and two children came up, and, standing round me in a half-circle, encouraged her by their example.

I had the devil's own trouble to get the thing righted; and the instant I had done so, without hesitation, it toppled and fell down upon the other side. Judge if I was hot! And yet not a hand was offered to assist me. The man, indeed, told me I ought to have a package of a different shape. I suggested, if he knew nothing better to the point in my predicament, he might hold his tongue. And the good-natured dog agreed with me smilingly. It was the most despicable fix. I must plainly content myself with the pack for Modestine, and take the following items for my own share of the portage: a cane, a quart flask, a pilot-jacket heavily weighted in the pockets, two pounds of black bread, and an open basket full of meats and bottles. I believe I may say I am not devoid of greatness of soul; for I did not recoil from this infamous burden. I disposed it, Heaven knows how, so as to be mildly portable, and then proceeded to steer Modestine through the village. She tried, as was indeed her invariable habit, to enter every house and every courtyard in the whole length; and, encumbered as I was, without a hand to help myself, no words can render an idea of my difficulties. A priest, with six or seven others, was examining a church in process of repair, and he and his acolytes laughed loudly as they saw my plight. I remembered having laughed myself when I had seen good men struggling with adversity in the person of a jackass, and the recollection filled me with penitence. That was in my old light days, before this trouble came upon me. God knows at least that I shall never laugh again, thought I. But oh, what a cruel thing is a farce to those engaged in it!

A little out of the village, Modestine, filled with the demon, set her heart upon a by-road, and positively refused to leave it. I dropped all my bundles, and, I am ashamed to say, struck the poor sinner twice across the face. It was pitiful to see her lift up her head with shut eyes, as if waiting for another blow. I came very near crying; but I did a wiser thing than that, and sat squarely down by the roadside to consider my situation under the cheerful influence of to-bacco and a nip of brandy. Modestine, in the meanwhile, munched some black bread with a contrite, hypocritical air. It was plain that I must make a sacrifice to the gods of shipwreck. I threw away the empty bottle destined to carry milk; I threw away my own white bread, and, disdaining to act by general average, kept the black bread for Modestine; lastly, I threw away the cold leg of mutton and the egg-whisk, although this last was dear to my heart. Thus I found room for everything in the basket, and even stowed the boating-coat on the top. By means of an end of cord I slung it under one arm; and although the cord cut my shoulder, and the jacket hung almost to the ground, it was with a heart greatly lightened that I set forth again.

I had now an arm free to thrash Modestine, and cruelly I chastised her. If I were to reach the lakeside before dark she must bestir her little shanks to some tune. Already the sun had gone down into a windy-looking mist; and although there were still a few streaks of gold far off to the east on the hills and the black fir-woods, all was cold and grey about our onward path. An infinity of little country by-roads led hither and thither among the fields. It was the most pointless labyrinth. I could see my destination over-head, or rather the peak that dominates it, but choose as I pleased, the roads always ended by turning away from it, and sneaking back towards the valley, or northward along the margin of the hills. The failing light, the waning colour, the naked, unhomely, stony country through which I was travelling, threw me into some despondency. I promise you, the stick was not idle; I think every decent step that Modestine took must have cost me at least two emphatic blows. There was not another sound in the neighbourhood but that of my unwearying bastinado.

Suddenly, in the midst of my toils, the load once more bit the dust, and, as by enchantment, all the cords were simultaneously loosened, and the road scattered with my dear possessions. The packing was to begin again from the beginning; and as I had to invent a new and better system, I do not doubt but I lost half an hour. It began to be dusk in earnest as I reached a wilderness of turf and stones. It had the air of being a road which should lead everywhere at the same time; and I was falling into something not unlike despair when I saw two figures stalking towards me over the stones. They walked one behind the other like tramps, but their pace was remarkable. The son led the way, a tall, ill-made, sombre Scotch-looking man; the mother followed, all in her Sunday's best, with an elegantly embroidered ribbon to her cap, and a new felt hat atop, and proffering, as she strode along with kilted petticoats, a string of obscene and blasphemous oaths.

I hailed the son and asked him my direction. He pointed loosely west and north-west, muttered an inaudible comment, and, without slackening his pace for an instant, stalked on, as he was going, right athwart my path. The mother followed without so much as raising her head. I shouted and shouted after them, but they continued to scale the hillside, and turned a deaf ear to my outcries. At last, leaving Modestine by herself, I was constrained to run after them, hailing the while. They stopped as I drew near, the mother still cursing; and I could see she was a handsome, motherly, respectable-looking woman. The son once more answered me roughly and inaudibly, and was for setting out again. But this time I simply collared the mother, who was nearest me, and, apologising for my violence, declared that I could not let them go until they had put me on my road. They were neither of them offended—rather mollified than otherwise; told me I had only to follow them; and then the mother asked me what I wanted by the lake at such an hour. I replied, in the Scotch manner, by inquiring if she had far to go herself. She told me, with another oath, that she had an hour and a half's road before her. And then, without salutation, the pair strode forward again up the hillside in the gathering dusk.

I returned for Modestine, pushed her briskly forward, and, after a sharp ascent of twenty minutes, reached the edge of a plateau. The view, looking back on my day's journey, was both wild and sad. Mount Mézenc and the peaks beyond St. Julien stood out in trenchant gloom against a cold glitter in the east; and the intervening field of hills had fallen together into one broad wash of shadow, except here and there the outline of a wooded sugar-loaf in black, here and there a white irregular patch to represent a cultivated farm, and here and there a blot where the Loire, the Gazeille, or the Lausonne wandered in a gorge.

Soon we were on a highroad, and surprise seized on my mind as I beheld a village of some magnitude close at hand; for I had been told that the neighbourhood of the lake was uninhabited except by trout. The road smoked in the twilight with children driving home cattle from the fields; and a pair of mounted stride-legged women, hat and cap and all, dashed past me at a hammering trot from the canton where they had been to church and market. I asked one of the children where I was. At Bouchet St. Nicolas, he told me. Thither, about a mile south of my destination, and on the other side of a respectable summit, had these confused roads and treacherous peasantry conducted me. My shoulder was cut, so that it hurt sharply; my arm ached like toothache from perpetual beating; I gave up the lake and my design to camp, and asked for the *auberge*.

I HAVE A GOAD

The *auberge* of Bouchet St. Nicholas was among the least pretentious I have ever visited; but I saw many more of the like upon my journey. Indeed, it was typical of these French highlands. Imagine a cottage of two stories, with a bench before the door; the stable and kitchen in a suite, so that Modestine and I could hear each other dining; furniture of the plainest, earthen floors, a single bed-chamber for travellers, and that without any convenience but beds. In the kitchen cooking and eating go forward side by side, and the family sleep at night. Anyone who has a fancy to wash must do so in public at the common table. The food is sometimes spare; hard fish and omelette have been my portion more than once; the wine is of the smallest, the brandy abominable to man; and the visit of a fat sow, grouting under the table and rubbing against your legs, is no impossible accompaniment to dinner.

But the people of the inn, in nine cases out of ten, show themselves friendly and considerate. As soon as you cross the doors you cease to be a stranger; and although this peasantry are rude and forbidding on the highway, they show a tincture of kind breeding when you share their hearth. At Bouchet, for instance, I uncorked my bottle of Beaujolais, and asked the host to join me. He would take but little.

'I am an amateur of such wine, do you see?' he said, 'and I am capable of leaving you not enough.'

In these hedge-inns the traveller is expected to eat with his own knife; unless he ask, no other will be supplied: with a glass, a whang of bread, and an iron fork, the table is completely laid. My knife was cordially admired by the landlord of Bouchet, and the spring filled him with wonder.

'I should never have guessed that,' he said. 'I would bet,' he added, weighing it in his hand, 'that this cost you not less than five francs.'

When I told him it had cost me twenty, his jaw dropped.

He was a mild, handsome, sensible, friendly old man, astonishingly ignorant. His wife, who was not so pleasant in her manners, knew how to read, although I do not suppose she ever did so. She had a share of brains and spoke with a cutting emphasis, like one who ruled the roost.

'My man knows nothing,' she said, with an angry nod; 'he is like the beasts.'

And the old gentleman signified acquiescence with his head. There was no contempt on her part, and no shame on his; the facts were accepted loyally, and no more about the matter.

I was tightly cross-examined about my journey; and the lady understood in a moment, and sketched out what I should put into my book when I got home. 'Whether people harvest or not in such or such a place; if there were forests; studies of manners; what, for example, I and the master of the house say to you; the beauties of Nature, and all that.' And she interrogated me with a look.

'It is just that,' said I.

'You see,' she added to her husband, 'I understood that.'

They were both much interested by the story of my misadventures.

'In the morning,' said the husband, 'I will make you something better than your cane. Such a beast as that feels nothing; it is in the proverb—*dur comme un âne*;* you might beat her insensible with a cudgel, and yet you would arrive nowhere.'

Something better! I little knew what he was offering.

The sleeping-room was furnished with two beds. I had one; and I will own I was a little abashed to find a young man and his wife and child in the act of mounting into the other. This was my first experience of the sort; and if I am always to feel equally silly and extraneous, I pray God it be my last as well. I kept my eyes to myself, and know nothing of the woman except that she had beautiful arms, and seemed no whit abashed by my appearance. As a matter of fact, the situation was more trying to me than to the pair. A pair keep each other in countenance; it is the single gentleman who has to blush. But I could not help

attributing my sentiments to the husband, and sought to
conciliate his tolerance with a cup of brandy from my flask.
He told me that he was a cooper of Alais travelling to St
Etienne in search of work, and that in his spare moments
he followed the fatal calling of a maker of matches. Me he
readily enough divined to be a brandy merchant.

I was up first in the morning (Monday, September 23rd),
and hastened my toilette guiltily, so as to leave a clear field
for madam, the cooper's wife. I drank a bowl of milk, and
set off to explore the neighbourhood of Bouchet. It was
perishing cold, a grey, windy, wintry morning; misty clouds
flew fast and low; the wind piped over the naked platform;
and the only speck of colour was away behind Mount
Mézenc and the eastern hills, where the sky still wore the
orange of the dawn.

It was five in the morning, and four thousand feet above
the sea; and I had to bury my hands in my pockets and
trot. People were trooping out to the labours of the field
by twos and threes, and all turned round to stare upon the
stranger. I had seen them coming back last night, I saw
them going afield again; and there was the life of Bouchet
in a nutshell.

When I came back to the inn for a bit of breakfast, the
landlady was in the kitchen, combing out her daughter's
hair; and I made her my compliments upon its beauty.

'Oh, no,' said the mother; 'it is not so beautiful as it
ought to be. Look, it is too fine.'

Thus does a wise peasantry console itself under adverse
physical circumstances, and, by a startling democratic process, the defects of the majority decide the type of beauty.

'And where,' said I, 'is monsieur?'

'The master of the house is upstairs,' she answered,
'making you a goad.'

Blessed be the man who invented goads! Blessed the
innkeeper of Bouchet St Nicolas, who introduced me to
their use! This plain wand, with an eighth of an inch of
pin, was indeed a sceptre when he put it in my hands.
Thenceforward Modestine was my slave. A prick, and she
passed the most inviting stable-door. A prick, and she broke

forth into a gallant little trotlet that devoured the miles. It
was not a remarkable speed, when all was said; and we
took four hours to cover ten miles at the best of it. But
what a heavenly change since yesterday! No more wielding
of the ugly cudgel; no more flailing with an aching arm;
no more broadsword exercise, but a discreet and gentle-
manly fence. And what although now and then a drop of
blood should appear on Modestine's mouse-coloured
wedge-like rump? I should have preferred it otherwise,
indeed; but yesterday's exploits had purged my heart of all
humanity. The perverse little devil, since she would not be
taken with kindness, must even go with pricking.

It was bleak and bitter cold, and, except a cavalcade of
stride-legged ladies and a pair of post-runners, the road was
dead solitary all the way to Pradelles. I scarce remember
an incident but one. A handsome foal with a bell about his
neck came charging up to us upon a stretch of common,
sniffed the air martially as one about to do great deeds,
and, suddenly thinking otherwise in his green young heart,
put about and galloped off as he had come, the bell tinkling
in the wind. For a long while afterwards I saw his noble
attitude as he drew up, and heard the note of his bell; and
when I struck the highroad, the song of the telegraph-wires
seemed to continue the same music.

Pradelles stands on a hillside, high above the Allier,
surrounded by rich meadows. They were cutting aftermath
on all sides, which gave the neighbourhood, this gusty
autumn morning, an untimely smell of hay. On the opposite
bank of the Allier the land kept mounting for miles to the
horizon, a tanned and sallow autumn landscape, with black
blots of fir-wood and white roads wandering through the
hills. Over all this the clouds shed a uniform and purplish
shadow, sad and somewhat menacing, exaggerating height
and distance, and throwing into still higher relief the twisted
ribbons of the high way. It was a cheerless prospect, but
one stimulating to a traveller. For I was now upon the limit
of Velay, and all that I beheld lay in another county—wild
Gévaudan, mountainous, uncultivated, and but recently
disforested from terror of the wolves.

Wolves, alas, like bandits, seem to flee the traveller's advance; and you may trudge through all our comfortable Europe, and not meet with an adventure worth the name. But here, if anywhere, a man was on the frontiers of hope. For this was the land of the ever-memorable BEAST, the Napoleon Bonaparte of wolves.* What a career was his! He lived ten months at free quarters in Gévaudan and Vivarais; he ate women and children and 'shepherdesses celebrated for their beauty'; he pursued armed horsemen; he has been seen at broad noonday chasing a post-chaise and outrider along the king's highroad, and chaise and outrider fleeing before him at the gallop. He was placarded like a political offender, and ten thousand francs were offered for his head. And yet, when he was shot and sent to Versailles, behold! a common wolf, and even small for that. 'Though I could reach from pole to pole,' sang Alexander Pope; the little corporal shook Europe; and if all wolves had been as this wolf, they would have changed the history of man. M. Élie Berthet* has made him the hero of a novel, which I have read, and do not wish to read again.

I hurried over my lunch and was proof against the landlady's desire that I should visit our Lady of Pradelles, 'who performed many miracles, although she was of wood'; and before three quarters of an hour I was goading Modestine down the steep descent that leads to Langogne on the Allier. On both sides of the road, in big dusty fields, farmers were preparing for next spring. Every fifty yards a yoke of great-necked stolid oxen were patiently haling at the plough. I saw one of these mild, formidable servants of the glebe, who took a sudden interest in Modestine and me. The furrow down which he was journeying lay at an angle to the road, and his head was solidly fixed to the yoke like those of caryatides below a ponderous cornice; but he screwed round his big honest eyes and followed us with a ruminating look, until his master bade him turn the plough and proceed to reascend the field. From all these furrowing ploughshares, from the feet of oxen, from a labourer here and there who was breaking the dry clods with a hoe, the wind carried away a thin dust like so much smoke. It was a fine, busy, breathing, rustic landscape; and as I continued to descend, the highlands of Gévaudan kept mounting in front of me against the sky.

I had crossed the Loire the day before; now I was to cross the Allier; so near are these two confluents in their youth. Just at the bridge of Langogne, as the long-promised rain was beginning to fall, a lassie of some seven or eight addressed me in the sacramental phrase, '*D'où'st-ce-que vous venez?*'* She did it with so high an air that she set me laughing, and this cut her to the quick. She was evidently one who reckoned on respect, and stood looking after me in silent dudgeon, as I crossed the bridge and entered the county of Gévaudan.

UPPER GÉVAUDAN

'The way also here was very wearisome through dirt
and slabbiness: nor was there on all this ground so
much as one inn or victualling-house wherein to
refresh the feebler sort.'

PILGRIM'S PROGRESS.

A CAMP IN THE DARK

The next day (Tuesday, September 24th), it was two o'clock
in the afternoon before I got my journal written up and
my knapsack repaired, for I was determined to carry my
knapsack in the future and have no more ado with baskets;
and half an hour afterwards I set out for Le Cheylard
l'Évêque, a place on the borders of the forest of Mercoire.
A man, I was told, should walk there in an hour and a
half; and I thought it scarce too ambitious to suppose that
a man encumbered with a donkey might cover the same
distance in four hours.

All the way up the long hill from Langogne it rained and
hailed alternately; the wind kept freshening steadily, although slowly; plentiful hurrying clouds—some dragging
veils of straight rain-shower, others massed and luminous,
as though promising snow—careered out of the north and
followed me along my way. I was soon out of the cultivated
basin of the Allier, and away from the ploughing oxen, and
such-like sights of the country. Moor, heathery marsh, tracts
of rock and pines, woods of birch all jewelled with the
autumn yellow, here and there a few naked cottages and
bleak fields,—these were the characters of the country. Hill
and valley followed valley and hill; the little green and stony
cattle-tracks wandered in and out of one another, split into
three or four, died away in marshy hollows, and began
again sporadically on hillsides or at the borders of a wood.

There was no direct road to Cheylard, and it was no
easy affair to make a passage in this uneven country and

through this intermittent labyrinth of tracks. It must have been about four when I struck Sagnerousse, and went on my way rejoicing in a sure point of departure. Two hours, afterwards, the dusk rapidly falling, in a lull of the wind, I issued from a fir-wood where I had long been wandering and found, not the looked-for village, but another marish bottom among rough-and-tumble hills. For some time past I had heard the ringing of cattle-bells ahead; and now, as I came out of the skirts of the wood, I saw near upon a dozen cows and perhaps as many more black figures, which I conjectured to be children, although the mist had almost unrecognizably exaggerated their forms. These were all silently following each other round and round in a circle, now taking hands, now breaking up with chains and reverences. A dance of children appeals to very innocent and lively thoughts; but, at nightfall on the marshes, the thing was eerie and fantastic to behold. Even I, who am well enough read in Herbert Spencer,* felt a sort of silence fall for an instant on my mind. The next, I was pricking Modestine forward, and guiding her like an unruly ship through the open. In a path, she went doggedly ahead of her own accord, as before a fair wind; but once on the turf or among heather, and the brute became demented. The tendency of lost travellers to go round in a circle was developed in her to the degree of passion, and it took all the steering I had in me to keep even a decently straight course through a single field.

While I was thus desperately tacking through the bog, children and cattle began to disperse, until only a pair of girls remained behind. From these I sought direction on my path. The peasantry in general were but little disposed to counsel a wayfarer. One old devil simply retired into his house, and barricaded the door on my approach; and I might beat and shout myself hoarse, he turned a deaf ear. Another, having given me a direction which, as I found afterwards, I had misunderstood, complacently watched me going wrong without adding a sign. He did not care a stalk of parsley if I wandered all night upon the hills! As for these two girls, they were a pair of impudent sly sluts, with not a thought but mischief. One put out her tongue at me, the other bade me follow the cows; and they both giggled and jogged each other's elbows. The Beast of Gévaudan ate about a hundred children of this district; I began to think of him with sympathy.

Leaving the girls, I pushed on through the bog, and got into another wood and upon a well-marked road. It grew darker and darker. Modestine, suddenly beginning to smell mischief, bettered the pace of her own accord, and from that time forward gave me no trouble. It was the first sign of intelligence I had occasion to remark in her. At the same time, the wind freshened into half a gale, and another heavy discharge of rain came flying up out of the north. At the other side of the wood I sighted some red windows in the dusk. This was the hamlet of Fouzilhic; three houses on a hillside, near a wood of birches. Here I found a delightful old man, who came a little way with me in the rain to put me safely on the road for Cheylard. He would hear of no reward; but shook his hands above his head almost as if in menace, and refused volubly and shrilly, in unmitigated *patois*.

All seemed right at last. My thoughts began to turn upon dinner and a fireside, and my heart was agreeably softened in my bosom. Alas, and I was on the brink of new and greater miseries! Suddenly, at a single swoop, the night fell. I have been abroad in many a black night, but never in a blacker. A glimmer of rocks, a glimmer of the track where it was well beaten, a certain fleecy density, or night within night, for a tree,—this was all that I could discriminate. The sky was simply darkness overhead; even the flying clouds pursued their way invisibly to human eyesight. I could not distinguish my hand at arm's length from the track, nor my goad, at the same distance, from the meadows or the sky.

Soon the road that I was following split, after the fashion of the country, into three or four in a piece of rocky meadow. Since Modestine had shown such a fancy for beaten roads, I tried her instinct in this predicament. But the instinct of an ass is what might be expected from the name; in half a minute she was clambering round and round among some boulders, as lost a donkey as you would wish to see. I should have camped long before had I been properly provided; but as this was to be so short a stage, I had brought no wine, no bread for myself, and little over a pound for my lady-friend. Add to this, that I and Modestine were both handsomely wetted by the showers. But now, if I could have found some water, I should have camped at once in spite of all. Water, however, being entirely absent, except in the form of rain, I determined to return to Fouzilhic, and ask a guide a little farther on my way—'a little farther lend thy guiding hand.'*

The thing was easy to decide, hard to accomplish. In this sensible roaring blackness I was sure of nothing but the direction of the wind. To this I set my face; the road had disappeared, and I went across country, now in marshy opens, now baffled by walls unscalable to Modestine, until I came once more in sight of some red windows. This time they were differently disposed. It was not Fouzilhic, but Fouzilhac, a hamlet little distant from the other in space, but worlds away in the spirit of its inhabitants. I tied Modestine to a gate, and groped forward, stumbling among rocks, plunging midleg in bog, until I gained the entrance of the village. In the first lighted house there was a woman who would not open to me. She could do nothing, she cried to me through the door, being alone and lame; but if I would apply at the next house, there was a man who could help me if he had a mind.

They came to the next door in force, a man, two women, and a girl, and brought a pair of lanterns to examine the wayfarer. The man was not ill-looking, but had a shifty smile. He leaned against the door-post, and heard me state my case. All I asked was a guide as far as Cheylard.

'*C'est que, voyez-vous, il fait noir,*'* said he.

I told him that was just my reason for requiring help.

'I understand that,' said he, looking uncomfortable; '*mais—c'est—de la peine.*'*

I was willing to pay, I said. He shook his head. I rose as high as ten francs; but he continued to shake his head. 'Name your own price, then,' said I.

'*Ce n'est pas ça,*' he said at length, and with evident difficulty; 'but I am not going to cross the door—*mais je ne sortirai pas de la porte.*'*

I grew a little warm, and asked him what he proposed that I should do.

'Where are you going beyond Cheylard?' he asked by way of answer.

'That is no affair of yours,' I returned, for I was not going to indulge his bestial curiosity; 'it changes nothing in my present predicament.'

'*C'est vrai, ça,*' he acknowledged, with a laugh; '*oui, c'est vrai. Et d'où venez-vous?*'*

A better man than I might have felt nettled.

'Oh,' said I, 'I am not going to answer any of your questions, so you may spare yourself the trouble of putting them. I am late enough already; I want help. If you will not guide me yourself, at least help me to find some one else who will.'

'Hold on,' he cried suddenly. 'Was it not you who passed in the meadow while it was still day?'

'Yes, yes,' said the girl, whom I had not hitherto recognised; 'it was monsieur; I told him to follow the cow.'

'As for you, mademoiselle,' said I, 'you are a *farceuse.*'*

'And,' added the man, 'what the devil have you done to be still here?'

What the devil, indeed! But there I was.

'The great thing,' said I, 'is to make an end of it'; and once more proposed that he should help me to find a guide.

'*C'est que,*' he said again, '*c'est que—il fait noir.*'

'Very well,' said I; 'take one of your lanterns.'

'No,' he cried, drawing a thought backward, and again intrenching himself behind one of his former phrases; 'I will not cross the door.'

I looked at him. I saw unaffected terror struggling on his face with unaffected shame; he was smiling pitifully and wetting his lip with his tongue, like a detected schoolboy. I drew a brief picture of my state, and asked him what I was to do.

'I don't know,' he said; 'I will not cross the door.'

Here was the Beast of Gévaudan, and no mistake.

'Sir,' said I, with my most commanding manners, 'you are a coward.'

And with that I turned my back upon the family party, who hastened to retire within their fortifications; and the famous door was closed again, but not till I had overheard the sound of laughter. *Filia barbara pater barbarior.** Let me say it in the plural: the Beasts of Gévaudan.

The lanterns had somewhat dazzled me, and I ploughed distressfully among stones and rubbish-heaps. All the other houses in the village were both dark and silent; and though I knocked at here and there a door, my knocking was unanswered. It was a bad business; I gave up Fouzilhac with my curses. The rain had stopped, and the wind, which still kept rising, began to dry my coat and trousers. 'Very well,' thought I, 'water or no water, I must camp.' But the first thing was to return to Modestine. I am pretty sure I was twenty minutes groping for my lady in the dark; and if it had not been for the unkindly services of the bog, into which I once more stumbled, I might have still been groping for her at the dawn. My next business was to gain the shelter of a wood, for the wind was cold as well as boisterous. How, in this well-wooded district, I should have been so long in finding one, is another of the insoluble mysteries of this day's adventures; but I will take my oath that I put near an hour to the discovery.

At last black trees began to show upon my left, and, suddenly crossing the road, made a cave of unmitigated blackness right in front. I call it a cave without exaggeration; to pass below that arch of leaves was like entering a dungeon. I felt about until my hand encountered a stout branch, and to this I tied Modestine, a haggard, drenched, desponding donkey. Then I lowered my pack, laid it along the wall on the margin of the road, and unbuckled the straps. I knew well enough where the lantern was; but where were the candles? I groped and groped among the tumbled articles, and, while I was thus groping, suddenly I touched the spirit-lamp. Salvation! This would serve my turn as well. The wind roared unwearyingly among the trees; I could hear the boughs tossing and the leaves churning through half a mile of forest; yet the scene of my encampment was not only as black as the pit, but admirably sheltered. At the second match the wick caught flame. The light was both livid and shifting; but it cut me off from the universe, and doubled the darkness of the surrounding night.

I tied Modestine more conveniently for herself, and broke up half the black bread for her supper, reserving the other half against the morning. Then I gathered what I should want within reach, took off my wet boots and gaiters, which I wrapped in my waterproof, arranged my knapsack for a pillow under the flap of my sleeping-bag, insinuated my limbs into the interior, and buckled myself in like a *bambino*. I opened a tin of Bologna sausage and broke a cake of chocolate, and that was all I had to eat. It may sound offensive, but I ate them together, bite by bite, by way of bread and meat. All I had to wash down this revolting mixture was neat brandy: a revolting beverage in itself. But I was rare and hungry; ate well, and smoked one of the best cigarettes in my experience. Then I put a stone in my straw hat, pulled the flap of my fur cap over my neck and eyes, put my revolver ready to my hand, and snuggled well down among the sheepskins.

I questioned at first if I were sleepy, for I felt my heart beating faster than usual, as if with an agreeable excitement to which my mind remained a stranger. But as soon as my eyelids touched, that subtle glue leaped between them, and they would no more come separate.

The wind among the trees was my lullaby. Sometimes it sounded for minutes together with a steady even rush, not rising nor abating; and again it would swell and burst like a great crashing breaker, and the trees would patter me all over with big drops from the rain of the afternoon. Night after night, in my own bedroom in the country, I have given ear to this perturbing concert of the wind among the woods; but whether it was a difference in the trees, or the lie of the ground, or because I was myself outside and in the midst of it, the fact remains that the wind sang to a different tune among these woods of Gévaudan. I hearkened and hearkened; and meanwhile sleep took gradual possession of my body and subdued my thoughts and senses; but still my last waking effort was to listen and distinguish, and my last conscious state was one of wonder at the foreign clamour in my ears.

Twice in the course of the dark hours—once when a stone galled me underneath the sack, and again when the poor patient Modestine, growing angry, pawed and stamped upon the road—I was recalled for a brief while to consciousness, and saw a star or two overhead, and the lace-like edge of the foliage against the sky. When I awoke for the third time (Wednesday, September 25th), the world was flooded with a blue light, the mother of the dawn. I saw the leaves labouring in the wind and the ribbon of the road; and, on turning my head, there was Modestine tied to a beech, and standing half across the path in an attitude of inimitable patience. I closed my eyes again, and set to thinking over the experience of the night. I was surprised to find how easy and pleasant it had been, even in this tempestuous weather. The stone which annoyed me would not have been there, had I not been forced to camp blindfold in the opaque night; and I had felt no other inconvenience, except when my feet encountered the lantern or the second volume of Peyrat's *Pastors of the Desert** among the mixed contents of my sleeping-bag; nay, more, I had felt not a touch of cold, and awakened with unusually lightsome and clear sensations.

With that, I shook myself, got once more into my boots and gaiters, and, breaking up the rest of the bread for Modestine, strolled about to see in what part of the world I had awakened. Ulysses, left on Ithaca, and with a mind unsettled by the goddess, was not more pleasantly astray. I have been after an adventure all my life, a pure dispassionate adventure, such as befell early and heroic voyagers; and thus to be found by morning in a random woodside nook in Gévaudan—not knowing north from south, as strange to my surroundings as the first man upon the earth, an inland castaway—was to find a fraction of my daydreams realised.

I was on the skirts of a little wood of birch, sprinkled with a few beeches; behind, it adjoined another wood of fir; and in front, it broke up and went down in open order into a shallow and meadowy dale. All around there were bare hill-tops, some near, some far away, as the perspective closed or opened, but none apparently much higher than the rest. The wind huddled the trees. The golden specks of autumn in the birches tossed shiveringly. Overhead the sky was full of strings and shreds of vapour, flying, vanishing, reappearing, and turning about an axis like tumblers, as the wind hounded them through heaven. It was wild weather and famishing cold. I ate some chocolate, swallowed a mouthful of brandy, and smoked a cigarette before the cold should have time to disable my fingers. And by the time I had got all this done, and had made my pack and bound it on the pack-saddle, the day was tiptoe on the threshold of the east. We had not gone many steps along the lane, before the sun, still invisible to me, sent a glow of gold over some cloud mountains that lay ranged along the eastern sky.

The wind had us on the stern, and hurried us bitingly forward. I buttoned myself into my coat, and walked on in a pleasant frame of mind with all men, when suddenly, at a corner, there was Fouzilhic once more in front of me. Nor only that, but there was the old gentleman who had escorted me so far the night before, running out of his house at sight of me, with hands upraised in horror.

'My poor boy!' he cried, 'what does this mean?'

I told him what had happened. He beat his old hands like clappers in a mill, to think how lightly he had let me go; but when he heard of the man of Fouzilhac, anger and depression seized upon his mind.

'This time, at least,' said he, 'there shall be no mistake.'

And he limped along, for he was very rheumatic, for about half a mile, and until I was almost within sight of Cheylard, the destination I had hunted for so long.

CHEYLARD AND LUC

Candidly, it seemed little worthy of all this searching. A few broken ends of village, with no particular street, but a succession of open places heaped with logs and fagots; a couple of tilted crosses, a shrine to our Lady of all Graces on the summit of a little hill; and all this, upon a rattling highland river, in the corner of a naked valley. What went ye out for to see? thought I to myself. But the place had a life of its own. I found a board commemorating the liberalities of Cheylard for the past year, hung up, like a banner, in the diminutive and tottering church. In 1877, it appeared, the inhabitants subscribed forty-eight francs ten centimes for the 'Work of the Propagation of the Faith.' Some of this, I could not help hoping, would be applied to my native land. Cheylard scrapes together halfpence for the darkened souls in Edinburgh; while Balquhidder and Dunrossness* bemoan the ignorance of Rome. Thus, to the high entertainment of the angels, do we pelt each other with evangelists, like schoolboys bickering in the snow.

The inn was again singularly unpretentious. The whole furniture of a not ill-to-do family was in the kitchen: the beds, the cradle, the clothes, the plate-rack, the meal-chest, and the photograph of the parish priest. There were five children, one of whom was set to its morning prayers at the stair-foot soon after my arrival, and a sixth would ere long be forthcoming. I was kindly received by these good folk. They were much interested in my misadventure. The wood in which I had slept belonged to them, the man of Fouzilhac they thought a monster of iniquity, and counselled me warmly to summon him at law—'because I might have died.' The good wife was horror-stricken to see me drink over a pint of uncreamed milk.

'You will do yourself an evil,' she said. 'Permit me to boil it for you.'

After I had begun the morning on this delightful liquor, she having an infinity of things to arrange, I was permitted, nay requested, to make a bowl of chocolate for myself. My boots and gaiters were hung up to dry, and, seeing me trying to write my journal on my knee, the eldest daughter let down a hinged table in the chimney-corner for my convenience. Here I wrote, drank my chocolate, and finally ate an omelette before I left. The table was thick with dust; for, as they explained, it was not used except in winter weather. I had a clear look up the vent, through brown agglomerations of soot and blue vapour, to the sky; and whenever a handful of twigs was thrown on to the fire, my legs were scorched by the blaze.

The husband had begun life as a muleteer, and when I came to charge Modestine showed himself full of the prudence of his art. 'You will have to change this package,' said he; 'it ought to be in two parts, and then you might have double the weight.'

I explained that I wanted no more weight; and for no donkey hitherto created would I cut my sleeping-bag in two.

'It fatigues her, however,' said the innkeeper; 'it fatigues her greatly on the march. Look.'

Alas, there were her two forelegs no better than raw beef on the inside, and blood was running from under her tail. They told me when I started, and I was ready to believe it, that before a few days I should come to love Modestine like a dog. Three days had passed, we had shared some misadventures, and my heart was still as cold as a potato towards my beast of burden. She was pretty enough to look at; but then she had given proof of dead stupidity, redeemed indeed by patience, but aggravated by flashes of sorry and ill-judged light-heartedness. And I own this new discovery seemed another point against her. What the devil was the good of a she-ass if she could not carry a sleeping-bag and a few necessaries? I saw the end of the fable rapidly approaching, when I should have to carry Modestine. Æsop was the man to know the world! I assure you I set out with heavy thoughts upon my short day's march.

It was not only heavy thoughts about Modestine that weighted me upon the way; it was a leaden business altogether. For first, the wind blew so rudely that I had to hold on the pack with one hand from Cheylard to Luc; and second, my road lay through one of the most beggarly countries in the world. It was like the worst of the Scottish Highlands, only worse; cold, naked, and ignoble, scant of wood, scant of heather, scant of life. A road and some fences broke the unvarying waste, and the line of the road was marked by upright pillars, to serve in time of snow.

Why anyone should desire to visit either Luc or Cheylard is more than my much-inventing spirit can suppose. For my part, I travel not to go anywhere, but to go. I travel for travel's sake. The great affair is to move; to feel the needs and hitches of our life more nearly; to come down off this feather-bed of civilisation, and find the globe granite underfoot and strewn with cutting flints. Alas, as we get up in life, and are more preoccupied with our affairs, even a holiday is a thing that must be worked for. To hold a pack upon a pack-saddle against a gale out of the freezing north is no high industry, but it is one that serves to occupy and compose the mind. And when the present is so exacting, who can annoy himself about the future?

I came out at length above the Allier. A more unsightly prospect at this season of the year it would be hard to fancy. Shelving hills rose round it on all sides, here dabbled with wood and fields, there rising to peaks alternately naked and hairy with pines. The colour throughout was black or ashen, and came to a point in the ruins of the castle of Luc, which pricked up impudently from below my feet, carrying on a pinnacle a tall white statue of Our Lady, which, I heard with interest, weighed fifty quintals, and was to be dedicated on the 6th of October. Through this sorry landscape trickled the Allier and a tributary of nearly equal size, which came down to join it through a broad nude valley in Vivarais. The weather had somewhat lightened, and the clouds massed in squadron; but the fierce wind still hunted them through heaven, and cast great ungainly splashes of shadow and sunlight over the scene.

Luc itself was a straggling double file of houses wedged between hill and river. It had no beauty, nor was there any

notable feature, save the old castle overhead with its fifty
quintals of brand-new Madonna. But the inn was clean and
large. The kitchen, with its two box-beds hung with clean
check curtains, with its wide stone chimney, its chimney-
shelf four yards long and garnished with lanterns and
religious statuettes, its array of chests and pair of ticking
clocks, was the very model of what a kitchen ought to be;
a melodrama kitchen, suitable for bandits or noblemen in
disguise. Nor was the scene disgraced by the landlady, a
handsome, silent, dark old woman, clothed and hooded in
black like a nun. Even the public bedroom had a character
of its own, with the long deal tables and benches, where
fifty might have dined, set out as for a harvest-home, and
the three box-beds along the wall. In one of these, lying
on straw and covered with a pair of table-napkins, did I
do penance all night long in goose-flesh and chattering
teeth, and sigh from time to time as I awakened for my
sheepskin sack and the lee of some great wood.

OUR LADY OF THE SNOWS

'I behold
The House, the Brotherhood austere —
And what am I, that I am here?'

MATTHEW ARNOLD

FATHER APOLLINARIS

Next morning (Thursday, 26th September) I took the road in a new order. The sack was no longer doubled, but hung at full length across the saddle, a green sausage six feet long with a tuft of blue wool hanging out of either end. It was more picturesque, it spared the donkey, and, as I began to see, it would insure stability, blow high, blow low. But it was not without a pang that I had so decided. For although I had purchased a new cord, and made all as fast as I was able, I was yet jealously uneasy lest the flaps should tumble out and scatter my effects along the line of march.

My way lay up the bald valley of the river, along the march of Vivarais and Gévaudan. The hills of Gévaudan on the right were a little more naked, if anything, than those of Vivarais upon the left, and the former had a monopoly of a low dotty underwood that grew thickly in the gorges and died out in solitary burrs upon the shoulders and the summits. Black bricks of fir-wood were plastered here and there upon both sides, and here and there were cultivated fields. A railway ran beside the river; the only bit of railway in Gévaudan, although there are many proposals afoot and surveys being made, and even, as they tell me, a station standing ready-built in Mende. A year or two hence and this may be another world. The desert is beleaguered. Now may some Languedocian Wordsworth turn the sonnet into *patois:* 'Mountains and vales and floods, heard YE that whistle?'*

At a place called La Bastide I was directed to leave the river, and follow a road that mounted on the left among the hills of Vivarais, the modern Ardèche; for I was now come within a little way of my strange destination, the Trappist monastery of Our Lady of the Snows. The sun came out as I left the shelter of a pine wood, and I beheld suddenly a fine wild landscape to the south. High rocky hills, as blue as sapphire, closed the view, and between these lay ridge upon ridge, heathery, craggy, the sun glittering on veins of rock, the underwood clambering in the hollows, as rude as God made them at the first. There was not a sign of man's hand in all the prospect; and indeed not a trace of his passage, save where generation after generation had walked in twisted footpaths, in and out among the beeches, and up and down upon the channelled slopes. The mists, which had hitherto beset me, were now broken into clouds, and fled swiftly and shone brightly in the sun. I drew a long breath. It was grateful to come, after so long, upon a scene of some attraction for the human heart. I own I like definite form in what my eyes are to rest upon; and if landscapes were sold, like the sheets of characters of my boyhood, one penny plain and twopence coloured, I should go the length of twopence every day of my life.*

But if things had grown better to the south, it was still desolate and inclement near at hand. A spidery cross on every hill-top marked the neighbourhood of a religious house; and a quarter of a mile beyond, the outlook southward opening out and growing bolder with every step, a white statue of the Virgin at the corner of a young plantation directed the traveller to Our Lady of the Snows. Here, then, I struck leftward, and pursued my way, driving my secular donkey before me, and creaking in my secular boots and gaiters, towards the asylum of silence.

I had not gone very far ere the wind brought to me the clanging of a bell, and somehow, I can scarce tell why, my heart sank within me at the sound. I have rarely approached anything with more unaffected terror than the monastery of Our Lady of the Snows. This it is to have had a Protestant education. And suddenly, on turning a corner, fear took hold on me from head to foot—slavish, superstitious fear; and though I did not stop in my advance, yet I went on slowly, like a man who should have passed a bourne unnoticed, and strayed into the country of the dead. For there upon the narrow new-made road, between the stripling pines, was a mediæval friar, fighting with a barrowful of turfs. Every Sunday of my childhood I used to study the *Hermits* of Marco Sadeler*—enchanting prints, full of wood and field and mediæval landscapes, as large as a country, for the imagination to go a-travelling in; and here, sure enough, was one of Marco Sadeler's heroes. He was robed in white like any spectre, and the hood falling back, in the instancy of his contention with the barrow, disclosed a pate as bald and yellow as a skull. He might have been buried any time these thousand years, and all the lively parts of him resolved into earth and broken up with the farmer's harrow.

I was troubled besides in my mind as to etiquette. Durst I address a person who was under a vow of silence? Clearly not. But drawing near, I doffed my cap to him with a far-away superstitious reverence. He nodded back, and cheerfully addressed me. Was I going to the monastery? Who was I? An Englishman? Ah, an Irishman, then?

'No,' I said, 'a Scotsman.'

A Scotsman? Ah, he had never seen a Scotsman before. And he looked me all over, his good, honest, brawny countenance shining with interest, as a boy might look upon a lion or an alligator. From him I learned with disgust that I could not be received at Our Lady of the Snows; I might get a meal, perhaps, but that was all. And then, as our talk ran on, and it turned out that I was not a pedlar, but a literary man, who drew landscapes and was going to write a book, he changed his manner of thinking as to my reception (for I fear they respect persons even in a Trappist monastery), and told me I must be sure to ask for the Father Prior, and state my case to him in full. On second thoughts he determined to go down with me himself; he thought he could manage for me better. Might he say that I was a geographer?

No; I thought, in the interests of truth, he positively might not.

'Very well, then' (with disappointment), 'an author.'

It appeared he had been in a seminary with six young Irishmen, all priests, long since, who had received newspapers and kept him informed of the state of ecclesiastical affairs in England. And he asked me eagerly after Dr. Pusey, for whose conversion the good man had continued ever since to pray night and morning.

'I thought he was very near the truth,' he said; 'and he will reach it yet; there is so much virtue in prayer.'

He must be a stiff, ungodly Protestant who can take anything but pleasure in this kind and hopeful story. While he was thus near the subject, the good father asked me if I were a Christian; and when he found I was not, or not after his way, he glossed it over with great goodwill.

The road which we were following, and which this stalwart father had made with his own two hands within the space of a year, came to a corner, and showed us some white buildings, a little farther on beyond the wood. At the same time, the bell once more sounded abroad. We were hard upon the monastery. Father Apollinaris (for that was my companion's name) stopped me.

'I must not speak to you down there,' he said. 'Ask for the Brother Porter, and all will be well. But try to see me as you go out again through the wood, where I may speak to you. I am charmed to have made your acquaintance.'

And then suddenly raising his arms, flapping his fingers, and crying out twice, 'I must not speak! I must not speak!' he ran away in front of me, and disappeared into the monastery door.

I own this somewhat ghastly eccentricity went a good way to revive my terrors. But where one was so good and simple, why should not all be alike? I took heart of grace, and went forward to the gate as fast as Modestine, who seemed to have a disaffection for monasteries, would permit. It was the first door, in my acquaintance of her, which she had not shown an indecent haste to enter. I summoned the place in form, though with a quaking heart. Father Michael, the Father Hospitaller, and a pair of brown-robed brothers came to the gate and spoke with me a while. I

think my sack was the great attraction; it had already
beguiled the heart of poor Apollinaris, who had charged
me on my life to show it to the Father Prior. But whether
it was my address, or the sack, or the idea speedily published among that part of the brotherhood who attend on
strangers that I was not a pedlar after all, I found no
difficulty as to my reception. Modestine was led away by
a layman to the stables, and I and my pack were received
into Our Lady of the Snows.

THE MONKS

Father Michael, a pleasant, fresh-faced, smiling man, perhaps of thirty-five, took me to the pantry, and gave me a glass of liqueur to stay me until dinner. We had some talk, or rather I should say he listened to my prattle indulgently enough, but with an abstracted air, like a spirit with a thing of clay. And truly when I remember that I descanted principally on my appetite, and that it must have been by that time more than eighteen hours since Father Michael had so much as broken bread, I can well understand that he would find an earthly savour in my conversation. But his manner, though superior, was exquisitely gracious; and I find I have a lurking curiosity as to Father Michael's past.

The whet administered, I was left alone for a little in the monastery garden. This is no more than the main court, laid out in sandy paths and beds of parti-coloured dahlias, and with a fountain and a black statue of the Virgin in the centre. The buildings stand around it four-square, bleak, as yet unseasoned by the years and weather, and with no other features than a belfry and a pair of slated gables. Brothers in white, brothers in brown, passed silently along the sanded alleys; and when I first came out, three hooded monks were kneeling on the terrace at their prayers. A naked hill commands the monastery upon one side, and the wood commands it on the other. It lies exposed to wind; the snow falls off and on from October to May, and sometimes lies six weeks on end; but if they stood in Eden, with a climate like heaven's, the buildings themselves would offer the same wintry and cheerless aspect; and for my part, on this wild September day, before I was called to dinner, I felt chilly in and out.

When I had eaten well and heartily, Brother Ambrose, a hearty conversable Frenchman (for all those who wait on strangers have the liberty to speak), led me to a little room in that part of the building which is set apart for *MM les retraitants*.* It was clean and whitewashed, and furnished

with strict necessaries, a crucifix, a bust of the late Pope,
the *Imitation* in French, a book of religious meditations, and
the *Life of Elizabeth Seton**—evangelist, it would appear, of
North America and of New England in particular. As far
as my experience goes, there is a fair field for some more
evangelisation in these quarters; but think of Cotton
Mather!* I should like to give him a reading of this little
work in heaven, where I hope he dwells; but perhaps he
knows all that already, and much more; and perhaps he
and Mrs. Seton are the dearest friends, and gladly unite
their voices in the everlasting psalm. Over the table, to
conclude the inventory of the room, hung a set of regula-
tions for *MM les retraitants:* what services they should attend,
when they were to tell their beads or meditate, and when
they were to rise and go to rest. At the foot was a notable
NB: '*Le temps libre est employé à l'examen de conscience, à la
confession, à faire de bonnes résolutions,*' etc. To make good
resolutions, indeed! You might talk as fruitfully of making
the hair grow on your head.

I had scarce explored my niche when Brother Ambrose
returned. An English boarder, it appeared, would like to
speak with me. I professed my willingness, and the friar
ushered in a fresh, young, little Irishman of fifty, a deacon
of the Church, arrayed in strict canonicals, and wearing on
his head what, in default of knowledge, I can only call the
ecclesiastical shako.* He had lived seven years in retreat at
a convent of nuns in Belgium, and now five at Our Lady
of the Snows; he never saw an English newspaper; he spoke
French imperfectly, and had he spoken it like a native,
there was not much chance of conversation where he dwelt.
With this, he was a man eminently sociable, greedy of
news, and simple-minded like a child. If I was pleased
to have a guide about the monastery, he was no less delighted to see an English face and hear an English tongue.

He showed me his own room, where he passed his time
among breviaries, Hebrew Bibles, and the Waverley novels.
Thence he led me to the cloisters, into the chapter-house,
through the vestry, where the brothers' gowns and broad
straw hats were hanging up, each with his religious name

upon a board,—names full of legendary suavity and interest, such as Basil, Hilarion, Raphael, or Pacifique;* into the
library where were all the works of Veuillot and Chateaubriand,* and the *Odes et Ballades*, if you please, and even
Molière to say nothing of innumerable fathers and a great
variety of local and general historians. Thence my good
Irishman took me round the workshops, where brothers
bake bread, and make cartwheels, and take photographs;
where one superintends a collection of curiosities, and
another a gallery of rabbits. For in a Trappist monastery
each monk has an occupation of his own choice, apart from
his religious duties and the general labours of the house.
Each must sing in the choir, if he has a voice and ear, and
join in the haymaking if he has a hand to stir; but in his
private hours, although he must be occupied, he may be
occupied on what he likes. Thus I was told that one brother
was engaged with literature; while Father Apollinaris busies
himself in making roads, and the Abbot employs himself in
binding books. It is not so long since this Abbot was
consecrated, by the way; and on that occasion, by a special
grace, his mother was permitted to enter the chapel and
witness the ceremony of consecration. A proud day for her
to have a son a mitred abbot; it makes you glad to think
they let her in.

In all these journeyings to and fro, many silent fathers
and brethren fell in our way. Usually they paid no more
regard to our passage than if we had been a cloud; but
sometimes the good deacon had a permission to ask of
them, and it was granted by a peculiar movement of the
hands, almost like that of a dog's paws in swimming, or
refused by the usual negative signs, and in either case with
lowered eyelids and a certain air of contrition, as of a man
who was steering very close to evil.

The monks, by special grace of their Abbot, were still
taking two meals a day; but it was already time for their
grand fast, which begins somewhere in September and lasts
till Easter, and during which they eat but once in the
twenty-four hours, and that at two in the afternoon, twelve
hours after they have begun the toil and vigil of the day.

Their meals are scanty, but even of these they eat sparingly; and though each is allowed a small carafe of wine, many refrain from this indulgence. Without doubt, the most of mankind grossly over-eat themselves; our meals serve not only for support, but as a hearty and natural diversion from the labour of life. Although excess may be hurtful, I should have thought this Trappist regimen defective. And I am astonished, as I look back, at the freshness of face and cheerfulness of manner of all whom I beheld. A happier nor a healthier company I should scarce suppose that I have ever seen. As a matter of fact, on this bleak upland, and with the incessant occupation of the monks, life is of an uncertain tenure, and death no infrequent visitor, at Our Lady of the Snows. This, at least, was what was told me. But if they die easily, they must live healthily in the meantime, for they seemed all firm of flesh and high in colour; and the only morbid sign that I could observe, an unusual brilliancy of eye, was one that served rather to increase the general impression of vivacity and strength.

Those with whom I spoke were singularly sweet-tempered, with what I can only call a holy cheerfulness in air and conversation. There is a note, in the direction to visitors, telling them not to be offended at the curt speech of those who wait upon them, since it is proper to monks to speak little. The note might have been spared; to a man the hospitallers were all brimming with innocent talk, and, in my experience of the monastery, it was easier to begin than to break off a conversation. With the exception of Father Michael, who was a man of the world, they showed themselves full of kind and healthy interest in all sorts of subjects—in politics, in voyages, in my sleeping-sack—and not without a certain pleasure in the sound of their own voices.

As for those who are restricted to silence, I can only wonder how they bear their solemn and cheerless isolation. And yet, apart from any view of mortification, I can see a certain policy, not only in the exclusion of women, but in this vow of silence. I have had some experience of lay phalansteries,* of an artistic, not to say a bacchanalian,

character; and seen more than one association easily formed
and yet more easily dispersed. With a Cistercian rule,
perhaps they might have lasted longer. In the neighbourhood of women it is but a touch-and-go association that
can be formed among defenceless men; the stronger elec-
tricity is sure to triumph; the dreams of boyhood, the
schemes of youth, are abandoned after an interview of ten
minutes, and the arts and sciences, and professional male
jollity, deserted at once for two sweet eyes and a caressing
accent. And next after this, the tongue is the great divider.

I am almost ashamed to pursue this worldly criticism of
a religious rule; but there is yet another point in which the
Trappist order appeals to me as a model of wisdom. By
two in the morning the clapper goes upon the bell, and so
on, hour by hour, and sometimes quarter by quarter, till
eight, the hour of rest; so infinitesimally is the day divided
among different occupations. The man who keeps rabbits,
for example, hurries from his hutches to the chapel, the
chapter-room, or the refectory, all day long: every hour he
has an office to sing, a duty to perform; from two, when
he rises in the dark, till eight, when he returns to receive
the comfortable gift of sleep, he is upon his feet and
occupied with manifold and changing business. I know
many persons, worth several thousands in the year, who
are not so fortunate in the disposal of their lives. Into how
many houses would not the note of the monastery bell,
dividing the day into manageable portions, bring peace of
mind and healthful activity of body? We speak of hardships,
but the true hardship is to be a dull fool, and permitted to
mismanage life in our own dull and foolish manner.

From this point of view, we may perhaps better understand the monk's existence. A long novitiate, and every
proof of constancy of mind and strength of body is required
before admission to the order; but I could not find that
many were discouraged. In the photographer's studio,
which figures so strangely among the outbuildings, my eye
was attracted by the portrait of a young fellow in the
uniform of a private of foot. This was one of the novices,
who came of age for service, and marched and drilled and

mounted guard for the proper time among the garrison of Algiers. Here was a man who had surely seen both sides of life before deciding; yet as soon as he was set free from service he returned to finish his novitiate.

This austere rule entitles a man to heaven as by right. When the Trappist sickens, he quits not his habit; he lies in the bed of death as he has prayed and laboured in his frugal and silent existence; and when the Liberator comes, at the very moment, even before they have carried him in his robe to lie his little last in the chapel among continual chantings, joy-bells break forth, as if for a marriage, from the slated belfry, and proclaim throughout the neighbourhood that another soul has gone to God.

At night, under the conduct of my kind Irishman, I took my place in the gallery to hear compline and *Salve Regina*, with which the Cistercians bring every day to a conclusion. There were none of those circumstances which strike the Protestant as childish or as tawdry in the public offices of Rome. A stern simplicity, heightened by the romance of the surroundings, spoke directly to the heart. I recall the whitewashed chapel, the hooded figures in the choir, the lights alternately occluded and revealed, the strong manly singing, the silence that ensued, the sight of cowled heads bowed in prayer, and then the clear trenchant beating of the bell, breaking in to show that the last office was over and the hour of sleep had come; and when I remember, I am not surprised that I made my escape into the court with somewhat whirling fancies, and stood like a man bewildered in the windy starry night.

But I was weary; and when I had quieted my spirits with Elizabeth Seton's memoirs—a dull work—the cold and the raving of the wind among the pines (for my room was on that side of the monastery which adjoins the woods) disposed me readily to slumber. I was wakened at black midnight, as it seemed, though it was really two in the morning, by the first stroke upon the bell. All the brothers were then hurrying to the chapel; the dead in life, at this untimely hour, were already beginning the uncomforted labours of their day. The dead in life—there was a chill reflection. And the words of a French song came back into my memory, telling of the best of our mixed existence:

> 'Que t'as de belles filles,
>> Giroflé!
>> Girofla!
> Que t'as de belles filles,
> *L'Amour les comptera!'* *

And I blessed God that I was free to wander, free to hope, and free to love.

THE BOARDERS

But there was another side to my residence at Our Lady of the Snows. At this late season there were not many boarders; and yet I was not alone in the public part of the monastery. This itself is hard by the gate, with a small dining-room on the ground-floor, and a whole corridor of cells similar to mine upstairs. I have stupidly forgotten the board for a regular *retraitant;* but it was somewhere between three and five francs a day, and I think most probably the first. Chance visitors like myself might give what they chose as a free-will offering, but nothing was demanded. I may mention that when I was going away Father Michael refused twenty francs as excessive. I explained the reasoning which led me to offer him so much; but even then, from a curious point of honour, he would not accept it with his own hand. 'I have no right to refuse for the monastery,' he explained, 'but I should prefer if you would give it to one of the brothers.'

I had dined alone, because I arrived late; but at supper I found two other guests. One was a country parish priest, who had walked over that morning from the seat of his cure near Mende to enjoy four days of solitude and prayer. He was a grenadier in person, with the hale colour and circular wrinkles of a peasant; and as he complained much of how he had been impeded by his skirts upon the march, I have a vivid fancy portrait of him, striding along, upright, big-boned, with kilted cassock, through the bleak hills of Gévaudan. The other was a short, grizzling, thick-set man, from forty-five to fifty, dressed in tweed with a knitted spencer, and the red ribbon of a decoration in his button-hole. This last was a hard person to classify. He was an old soldier, who had seen service and risen to the rank of commandant; and he retained some of the brisk decisive manners of the camp. On the other hand, as soon as his resignation was accepted, he had come to Our Lady of the Snows as a boarder, and after a brief experience of its ways, had decided to remain as a novice. Already the new life was beginning to modify his appearance; already he had acquired somewhat of the quiet and smiling air of the brethren; and he was yet neither an officer nor a Trappist, but partook of the character of each. And certainly here was a man in an interesting nick of life. Out of the noise of cannon and trumpets, he was in the act of passing into this still country bordering on the grave, where men sleep nightly in their grave-clothes, and, like phantoms, communicate by signs.

At supper we talked politics. I make it my business, when I am in France, to preach political good-will and moderation, and to dwell on the example of Poland, much as some alarmists in England dwell on the example of Carthage. The priest and the commandant assured me of their sympathy with all I said, and made a heavy sighing over the bitterness of contemporary feeling.

'Why, you cannot say anything to a man with which he does not absolutely agree,' said I, 'but he flies up at you in a temper.'

They both declared that such a state of things was antichristian.

While we were thus agreeing, what should my tongue stumble upon but a word in praise of Gambetta's moderation.* The old soldier's countenance was instantly suffused with blood; with the palms of his hands he beat the table like a naughty child.

'*Comment, monsieur?*' he shouted. '*Comment?* Gambetta moderate? Will you dare to justify these words?'

But the priest had not forgotten the tenor of our talk. And suddenly, in the height of his fury, the old soldier found a warning look directed on his face; the absurdity of his behaviour was brought home to him in a flash; and the storm came to an abrupt end, without another word.

It was only in the morning, over our coffee (Friday, September 27th), that this couple found out I was a heretic. I suppose I had misled them by some admiring expressions as to the monastic life around us; and it was only by a point-blank question that the truth came out. I had been tolerantly used, both by simple Father Apollinaris and astute Father Michael; and the good Irish deacon, when he heard of my religious weakness, had only patted me upon the shoulder and said, 'You must be a Catholic and come to heaven.' But I was now among a different sect of orthodox. These two men were bitter and upright and narrow, like the worst of Scotsmen, and indeed, upon my heart, I fancy they were worse. The priest snorted aloud like a battle-horse.

'*Et vous prétendez mourir dans cette espèce de croyance?*'* he demanded; and there is no type used by mortal printers large enough to qualify his accent.

I humbly indicated that I had no design of changing.

But he could not away with such a monstrous attitude.

'No, no,' he cried, 'you must change. You have come here, God has led you here, and you must embrace the opportunity.'

I made a slip in policy; I appealed to the family affections, though I was speaking to a priest and a soldier, two classes of men circumstantially divorced from the kind and homely ties of life.

'Your father and mother?' cried the priest. 'Very well; you will convert them in their turn when you go home.'

I think I see my father's face! I would rather tackle the Gætulian lion* in his den than embark on such an enterprise against the family theologian.

But now the hunt was up; priest and soldier were in full cry for my conversion; and the Work of the Propagation of the Faith, for which the people of Cheylard subscribed forty-eight francs ten centimes during 1877, was being gallantly pursued against myself. It was an odd but most effective proselytising. They never sought to convince me in argument, where I might have attempted some defence, but took it for granted that I was both ashamed and terrified at my position, and urged me solely on the point of time. Now, they said, when God had led me to Our Lady of the Snows, now was the appointed hour.

'Do not be withheld by false shame,' observed the priest, for my encouragement.

For one who feels very similarly to all sects of religion, and who has never been able, even for a moment, to weigh seriously the merit of this or that creed on the eternal side of things, however much he may see to praise or blame upon the secular and temporal side, the situation thus created was both unfair and painful. I committed my second fault in tact, and tried to plead that it was all the same thing in the end, and we were all drawing near by different sides to the same kind and undiscriminating Friend and Father. That, as it seems to lay spirits, would be the only gospel worthy of the name. But different men think differently; and this revolutionary aspiration brought down the priest with all the terrors of the law. He launched into harrowing details of hell. The damned, he said—on the authority of a little book which he had read not a week before, and which, to add conviction to conviction, he had fully intended to bring along with him in his pocket—were to occupy the same attitude through all eternity in the midst of dismal tortures. And as he thus expatiated, he grew in nobility of aspect with his enthusiasm.

As a result the pair concluded that I should seek out the Prior, since the Abbot was from home, and lay my case immediately before him.

'*C'est mon conseil comme ancien militaire,*' observed the commandant; '*et celui de monsieur comme prêtre.*'*

'*Oui,*' added the *curé,* sententiously nodding; '*comme ancien militaire—et comme prêtre.*'

At this moment, whilst I was somewhat embarrassed how to answer, in came one of the monks, a little brown fellow, as lively as a grig, and with an Italian accent, who threw himself at once into the contention, but in a milder and more persuasive vein, as befitted one of these pleasant brethren. Look at *him,* he said. The rule was very hard; he would have dearly liked to stay in his own country, Italy—it was well known how beautiful it was, the beautiful Italy; but then there were no Trappists in Italy; and he had a soul to save; and here he was.

I am afraid I must be at bottom, what a cheerful Indian critic has dubbed me, 'a faddling hedonist'; for this descrip-

tion of the brother's motives gave me somewhat of a shock.
I should have preferred to think he had chosen the life for
its own sake, and not for ulterior purposes; and this shows
how profoundly I was out of sympathy with these good
Trappists, even when I was doing my best to sympathise.
But to the *curé* the argument seemed decisive.

'Hear that!' he cried. 'And I have seen a marquis here,
a marquis, a marquis'—he repeated the holy word three
times over—'and other persons high in society; and generals. And here, at your side, is this gentleman, who has been
so many years in armies—decorated, an old warrior. And
here he is, ready to dedicate himself to God.'

I was by this time so thoroughly embarrassed that I
pleaded cold feet, and made my escape from the apartment.
It was a furious windy morning, with a sky much cleared,
and long and potent intervals of sunshine; and I wandered
until dinner in the wild country towards the east, sorely
staggered and beaten upon by the gale, but rewarded with
some striking views.

At dinner the Work of the Propagation of the Faith was
recommenced, and on this occasion still more distastefully
to me. The priest asked me many questions as to the
contemptible faith of my fathers, and received my replies
with a kind of ecclesiastical titter.

'Your sect,' he said once; 'for I think you will admit it
would be doing it too much honour to call it a religion.'

'As you please, monsieur,' said I. '*La parole est à vous.*'*

At length I grew annoyed beyond endurance; and
although he was on his own ground, and, what is more to
the purpose, an old man, and so holding a claim upon my
toleration, I could not avoid a protest against this uncivil
usage. He was sadly discountenanced.

'I assure you,' he said, 'I have no inclination to laugh in
my heart. I have no other feeling but interest in your soul.'

And there ended my conversion. Honest man! He was
no dangerous deceiver; but a country parson, full of zeal
and faith. Long may he tread Gévaudan with his kilted
skirts—a man strong to walk and strong to comfort his
parishioners in death! I dare say he would beat bravely

through a snowstorm where his duty called him; and it is not always the most faithful believer who makes the cunningest apostle.

UPPER GÉVAUDAN, CONTINUED

'The bed was made, the room was fit,
By punctual eve the stars were lit:
The air was sweet, the water ran;
No need was there, for maid or man,
When we put up, my ass and I,
At God's green caravanserai.'*

ACROSS THE GOULET

The wind fell during dinner, and the sky remained clear;
so it was under better auspices that I loaded Modestine
before the monastery gate. My Irish friend accompanied
me so far on the way. As we came through the wood, there
was Père Apollinaire hauling his barrow; and he too quitted
his labours to go with me for perhaps a hundred yards,
holding my hand between both of his in front of him. I
parted first from one and then from the other with unfeigned regret, but yet with the glee of the traveller who
shakes off the dust of one stage before hurrying forth upon
another. Then Modestine and I mounted the course of the
Allier, which here led us back into Gévaudan towards its
sources in the forest of Mercoire. It was but an inconsiderable burn before we left its guidance. Thence, over a hill,
our way lay through a naked plateau, until we reached
Chasseradès at sundown.

The company in the inn kitchen that night were all men
employed in survey for one of the projected railways.
They were intelligent and conversible, and we decided
the future of France over hot wine, until the state of
the clock frightened us to rest. There were four beds in
the little upstairs room; and we slept six. But I had a bed to
myself, and persuaded them to leave the window open.

'*Hé, bourgeois; il est cinq heures!*'* was the cry that wakened
me in the morning (Saturday, September 28th). The room
was full of a transparent darkness, which dimly showed me

the other three beds and the five different nightcaps on the pillows. But out of the window the dawn was growing ruddy in a long belt over the hill-tops, and day was about to flood the plateau. The hour was inspiriting; and there seemed a promise of calm weather, which was perfectly fulfilled. I was soon under way with Modestine. The road lay for a while over the plateau, and then descended through a precipitous village into the valley of the Chassezac. This stream ran among green meadows, well hidden from the world by its steep banks; the broom was in flower, and here and there was a hamlet sending up its smoke.

At last the path crossed the Chassezac upon a bridge, and, forsaking this deep hollow, set itself to cross the mountain of La Goulet. It wound up through Lestampes by upland fields and woods of beech and birch, and with every corner brought me into an acquaintance with some new interest. Even in the gully of the Chassezac my ear had been struck by a noise like that of a great bass bell ringing at the distance of many miles; but this, as I continued to mount and draw nearer to it, seemed to change in character, and I found at length that it came from some one leading flocks afield to the note of a rural horn. The narrow street of Lestampes stood full of sheep, from wall to wall—black sheep and white, bleating like the birds in spring, and each one accompanying himself upon the sheep-bell round his neck. It made a pathetic concert, all in treble. A little higher, and I passed a pair of men in a tree with pruning-hooks, and one of them was singing the music of a *bourrée*. Still further, and when I was already threading the birches, the crowing of cocks came cheerfully up to my ears, and along with that the voice of a flute discoursing a deliberate and plaintive air from one of the upland villages. I pictured to myself some grizzled, apple-cheeked, country schoolmaster fluting in his bit of a garden in the clear autumn sunshine. All these beautiful and interesting sounds filled my heart with an unwonted expectation; and it appeared to me that, once past this range which I was mounting, I should descend into the garden of the world. Nor was I deceived, for I was now done with rains and winds and a bleak country. The first part of my journey ended here; and this was like an induction of sweet sounds into the other and more beautiful.

There are other degrees of *feyness*, as of punishment, besides the capital; and I was now led by my good spirits into an adventure which I relate in the interest of future donkey-drivers. The road zigzagged so widely on the hillside that I chose a short cut by map and compass, and struck through the dwarf woods to catch the road again upon a higher level. It was my one serious conflict with Modestine. She would none of my short cut; she turned in my face, she backed, she reared; she, whom I had hitherto imagined to be dumb, actually brayed with a loud hoarse flourish, like a cock crowing for the dawn. I plied the goad with one hand; with the other, so steep was the ascent, I had to hold on the pack-saddle. Half a dozen times she was nearly over backwards on the top of me; half a dozen times, from sheer weariness of spirit, I was nearly giving it up, and leading her down again to follow the road. But I took the thing as a wager, and fought it through. I was surprised, as I went on my way again, by what appeared to be chill rain-drops falling on my hand, and more than once looked up in wonder at the cloudless sky. But it was only sweat which came dropping from my brow.

Over the summit of the Goulet there was no marked road—only upright stones posted from space to space to guide the drovers. The turf underfoot was springy and well scented. I had no company but a lark or two, and met but one bullock-cart between Lestampes and Bleymard. In front of me I saw a shallow valley, and beyond that the range of the Lozère, sparsely wooded and well enough modelled in the flanks, but straight and dull in outline. There was scarce a sign of culture; only about Bleymard, the white highroad from Villefort to Mende traversed a range of meadows, set with spiry poplars, and sounding from side to side with the bells of flocks and herds.

A NIGHT AMONG THE PINES

From Bleymard after dinner, although it was already late, I set out to scale a portion of the Lozère. An ill-marked stony drove-road guided me forward; and I met nearly half a dozen bullock-carts descending from the woods, each laden with a whole pine-tree for the winter's firing. At the top of the woods, which do not climb very high upon this cold ridge, I struck leftward by a path among the pines, until I hit on a dell of green turf, where a streamlet made a little spout over some stones to serve me for a water-tap. 'In a more sacred or sequestered bower—nor nymph nor faunus haunted.'* The trees were not old, but they grew thickly round the glade: there was no outlook, except north-eastward upon distant hill-tops, or straight upward to the sky; and the encampment felt secure and private like a room. By the time I had made my arrangements and fed Modestine, the day was already beginning to decline. I buckled myself to the knees into my sack and made a hearty meal; and as soon as the sun went down, I pulled my cap over my eyes and fell asleep.

Night is a dead monotonous period under a roof; but in the open world it passes lightly, with its stars and dews and perfumes, and the hours are marked by changes in the face of Nature. What seems a kind of temporal death to people choked between walls and curtains, is only a light and living slumber to the man who sleeps afield. All night long he can hear Nature breathing deeply and freely; even as she takes her rest she turns and smiles; and there is one stirring hour unknown to those who dwell in houses, when a wakeful influence goes abroad over the sleeping hemisphere, and all the outdoor world are on their feet. It is then that the cock first crows, not this time to announce the dawn, but like a cheerful watchman speeding the course of night. Cattle awake on the meadows; sheep break their fast on dewy hillsides, and change to a new lair among the ferns; and houseless men, who have lain down with the fowls, open their dim eyes and behold the beauty of the night.

At what inaudible summons, at what gentle touch of Nature, are all these sleepers thus recalled in the same hour to life? Do the stars rain down an influence, or do we share some thrill of mother earth below our resting bodies? Even shepherds and old country-folk, who are the deepest read in these arcana, have not a guess as to the means or purpose of this nightly resurrection. Towards two in the morning they declare the thing takes place; and neither know nor inquire further. And at least it is a pleasant incident. We are disturbed in our slumber, only, like the luxurious Montaigne, 'that we may the better and more sensibly relish it.'* We have a moment to look upon the stars, and there is a special pleasure for some minds in the reflection that we share the impulse with all outdoor creatures in our neighbourhood, that we have escaped out of the Bastille of civilisation, and are become, for the time being, a mere kindly animal and a sheep of Nature's flock.

When that hour came to me among the pines, I wakened thirsty. My tin was standing by me half full of water. I emptied it at a draught; and feeling broad awake after this internal cold aspersion, sat upright to make a cigarette. The stars were clear, coloured, and jewel-like, but not frosty. A faint silvery vapour stood for the Milky Way. All around me the black fir-points stood upright and stock-still. By the whiteness of the pack-saddle, I could see Modestine walking round and round at the length of her tether; I could hear her steadily munching at the sward; but there was not another sound, save the indescribable quiet talk of the runnel over the stones. I lay lazily smoking and studying the colour of the sky, as we call the void of space, from where it showed a reddish grey behind the pines to where it showed a glossy blue-black between the stars. As if to be more like a pedlar, I wear a silver ring. This I could see faintly shining as I raised or lowered the cigarette; and at each whiff the inside of my hand was illuminated, and became for a second the highest light in the landscape.

A faint wind, more like a moving coolness than a stream of air, passed down the glade from time to time; so that even in my great chamber the air was being renewed all night long. I though with horror of the inn at Chasseradès and the congregated nightcaps; with horror of the nocturnal prowesses of clerks and students, of hot theatres and pass-keys and close rooms. I have not often enjoyed a more serene possession of myself, nor felt more independent of material aids. The outer world, from which we cower into our houses, seemed after all a gentle habitable place; and night after night a man's bed, it seemed, was laid and waiting for him in the fields, where God keeps an open house. I thought I had rediscovered one of those truths which are revealed to savages and hid from political econ-omists: at the least, I had discovered a new pleasure for myself. And yet even while I was exulting in my solitude I became aware of a strange lack. I wished a companion to lie near me in the starlight, silent and not moving, but ever within touch. For there is a fellowship more quiet even than solitude, and which, rightly understood, is solitude made perfect. And to live out of doors with the woman a man loves is of all lives the most complete and free.

As I thus lay, between content and longing, a faint noise stole towards me through the pines. I thought, at first, it was the crowing of cocks or the barking of dogs at some very distant farm; but steadily and gradually it took articu-late shape in my ears, until I became aware that a passenger was going by upon the highroad in the valley, and singing loudly as he went. There was more of goodwill than grace in his performance; but he trolled with ample lungs; and the sound of his voice took hold upon the hillside and set the air shaking in the leafy glens. I have heard people passing by night in sleeping cities; some of them sang; one, I remember, played loudly on the bagpipes. I have heard the rattle of a cart or carriage spring up suddenly after hours of stillness, and pass, for some minutes, within the range of my hearing as I lay abed. There is a romance about all who are abroad in the black hours, and with something of a thrill we try to guess their business. But here the romance was double: first, this glad passenger, lit internally with wine, who sent up his voice in music through the night; and then I, on the other hand, buckled into my sack, and smoking alone in the pinewoods between four and five thousand feet towards the stars.

When I awoke again (Sunday, 29th September), many of the stars had disappeared; only the stronger companions of the night still burned visibly overhead; and away towards the east I saw a faint haze of light upon the horizon, such as had been the Milky Way when I was last awake. Day was at hand. I lit my lantern, and by its glowworm light put on my boots and gaiters; then I broke up some bread for Modestine, filled my can at the water-tap, and lit my spirit-lamp to boil myself some chocolate. The blue darkness lay long in the glade where I had so sweetly slumbered; but soon there was a broad streak of orange melting into gold along the mountain-tops of Vivarais. A solemn glee possessed my mind at this gradual and lovely coming in of day. I heard the runnel with delight; I looked round me for something beautiful and unexpected; but the still black pine-trees, the hollow glade, the munching ass, remained unchanged in figure. Nothing had altered but the light, and that, indeed, shed over all a spirit of life and of breathing peace, and moved me to a strange exhilaration.

I drank my water-chocolate, which was hot if it was not rich, and strolled here and there, and up and down about the glade. While I was thus delaying, a gush of steady wind, as long as a heavy sigh, poured direct out of the quarter of the morning. It was cold, and set me sneezing. The trees near at hand tossed their black plumes in its passage; and I could see the thin distant spires of pine along the edge of the hill rock slightly to and fro against the golden east. Ten minutes after, the sunlight spread at a gallop along the hillside, scattering shadows and sparkles, and the day had come completely.

I hastened to prepare my pack, and tackle the steep ascent that lay before me; but I had something on my mind. It was only a fancy; yet a fancy will sometimes be importunate. I had been most hospitably received and punctually

served in my green caravanserai. The room was airy, the
water excellent, and the dawn had called me to a moment.
I say nothing of the tapestries or the inimitable ceiling, nor
yet of the view which I commanded from the windows; but
I felt I was in some one's debt for all this liberal entertainment. And so it pleased me, in a half-laughing way, to leave
pieces of money on the turf as I went along, until I had
left enough for my night's lodging. I trust they did not fall
to some rich and churlish drover.

THE COUNTRY OF THE CAMISARDS

'We travelled in the print of olden wars;
    Yet all the land was green;
    And love we found, and peace,
    Where fire and war had been.
They pass and smile, the children of the sword—
    No more the sword they wield:
    And O, how deep the corn
    Along the battlefield!'

W. P. BANNATYNE.*

ACROSS THE LOZÈRE

The track that I had followed in the evening soon died out, and I continued to follow over a bald turf ascent a row of stone pillars, such as had conducted me across the Goulet. It was already warm. I tied my jacket on the pack, and walked in my knitted waistcoat. Modestine herself was in high spirits, and broke of her own accord, for the first time in my experience, into a jolting trot that sent the oats swashing in the pocket of my coat. The view, back upon the northern Gévaudan, extended with every step; scarce a tree, scarce a house, appeared upon the fields of wild hill that ran north, east, and west, all blue and gold in the haze and sunlight of the morning. A multitude of little birds kept sweeping and twittering about my path; they perched on the stone pillars, they pecked and strutted on the turf, and I saw them circle in volleys in the blue air, and show, from time to time, translucent flickering wings between the sun and me.

Almost from the first moment of my march a faint large noise, like a distant surf, had filled my ears. Sometimes I was tempted to think it the voice of a neighbouring water-fall, and sometimes a subjective result of the utter stillness of the hill. But as I continued to advance, the noise increased and became like the hissing of an enormous tea-urn, and at the same time breaths of cool air began to reach me from the direction of the summit. At length I understood. It was blowing stiffly from the south upon the other slope of the Lozère, and every step that I took I was drawing nearer to the wind.

Although it had been long desired, it was quite unexpectedly at last that my eyes rose above the summit. A step that seemed no way more decisive than many other steps that had preceded it—and, 'like stout Cortez when, with eagle eyes, he stared at the Pacific,'* I took possession, in my own name, of a new quarter of the world. For behold, instead of the gross turf rampart I had been mounting for so long, a view into the hazy air of heaven, and a land of intricate blue hills below my feet.

The Lozère lies nearly east and west, cutting Gévaudan into two unequal parts; its highest point, this Pic de Finiels, on which I was then standing, rises upwards of five thousand six hundred feet above the sea, and in clear weather commands a view over all lower Languedoc to the Mediterranean Sea. I have spoken with people who either pretended or believed that they had seen, from the Pic de Finiels, white ships sailing by Montpellier and Cette. Behind was the upland northern country through which my way had lain, peopled by a dull race, without wood, without much grandeur of hill-form, and famous in the past for little besides wolves. But in front of me, half-veiled in sunny haze, lay a new Gévaudan, rich, picturesque, illustrious for stirring events. Speaking largely, I was in the Cevennes at Monastier, and during all my journey; but there is a strict and local sense in which only this confused and shaggy country at my feet has any title to the name, and in this sense the peasantry employ the word. These are the Cevennes with an emphasis: the Cevennes of the Cevennes. In that undecipherable labyrinth of hills, a war of bandits, a war of wild beasts, raged for two years between the Grand Monarch* with all his troops and marshals on the one hand, and a few thousand Protestant mountaineers upon the other. A hundred and eighty years ago, the Camisards* held a station even on the Lozère, where I stood; they had an organisation, arsenals, a military and religious hierarchy; their affairs were 'the discourse of every coffee-house' in London; England sent fleets in their support; their leaders prophesied and murdered; with colours and drums, and the singing of old French psalms, their bands sometimes affronted daylight, marched before walled cities, and dispersed the generals of the king; and sometimes at night, or in masquerade, possessed themselves of strong castles, and avenged treachery upon their allies and cruelty upon their foes. There, a hundred and eighty years ago, was the chivalrous Roland, 'Count and Lord Roland* generalissimo of the Protestants in France,' grave, silent, imperious, pockmarked ex-dragoon, whom a lady followed in his wanderings out of love. There was Cavalier* a baker's apprentice with a genius for war, elected brigadier of Camisards at seventeen, to die at fifty-five the English governor of Jersey. There again was Castanet,* a partisan leader in a voluminous peruke and with a taste for controversial divinity. Strange generals, who moved apart to take counsel with the God of Hosts, and fled or offered battle, set sentinels or slept in an unguarded camp, as the Spirit whispered to their hearts! And there, to follow these and other leaders, was the rank and file of prophets and disciples, bold, patient, indefatigable, hardy to run upon the mountains, cheering their rough life with psalms, eager to fight, eager to pray, listening devoutly to the oracles of brain-sick children, and mystically putting a grain of wheat among the pewter balls with which they charged their muskets.

I had travelled hitherto through a dull district and in the track of nothing more notable than the child-eating Beast of Gévaudan, the Napoleon Bonaparte of wolves. But now I was to go down into the scene of a romantic chapter—or, better, a romantic foot-note—in the history of the world. What was left of all this bygone dust and heroism? I was told that Protestantism still survived in this head seat of Protestant resistance; so much the priest himself had told me in the monastery parlour. But I had yet to learn if it were a bare survival, or a lively and generous tradition. Again, if in the northern Cevennes the people are narrow in religious judgments, and more filled with zeal than charity, what was I to look for in this land of persecution and reprisal—in a land where the tyranny of the Church produced the Camisard rebellion, and the terror of the Camisards threw the Catholic peasantry into legalised revolt upon the other side, so that Camisard and Florentin* skulked for each other's lives among the mountains?

Just on the brow of the hill, where I paused to look before me, the series of stone pillars came abruptly to an end; and only a little below, a sort of track appeared and began to go down a break-neck slope, turning like a corkscrew as it went. It led into a valley between falling hills, stubbly with rocks like a reaped field of corn, and floored farther down with green meadows. I followed the track with precipitation; the steepness of the slope, the continual agile turning of the line of descent, and the old unwearied hope of finding something new in a new country, all conspired to lend me wings. Yet a little lower and a stream began, collecting itself together out of many fountains, and soon making a glad noise among the hills. Sometimes it would cross the track in a bit of waterfall, with a pool, in which Modestine refreshed her feet.

The whole descent is like a dream to me, so rapidly was it accomplished. I had scarcely left the summit ere the valley had closed round my path, and the sun beat upon me, walking in a stagnant lowland atmosphere. The track became a road, and went up and down in easy undulations. I passed cabin after cabin, but all seemed deserted; and I saw not a human creature nor heard any sound except that of the stream. I was, however, in a different country from the day before. The stony skeleton of the world was here vigorously displayed to sun and air. The slopes were steep and changeful. Oak-trees clung along the hills, well grown, wealthy in leaf, and touched by the autumn with strong and luminous colours. Here and there another stream would fall in from the right or the left, down a gorge of snow-white and tumultuary boulders. The river in the bottom (for it was rapidly growing a river, collecting on all hands as it trotted on its way) here foamed a while in desperate rapids, and there lay in pools of the most enchanting sea-green shot with watery browns. As far as I have gone, I have never seen a river of so changeful and delicate a hue; crystal was not more clear, the meadows were not by half so green; and at every pool I saw I felt a thrill of longing to be out of these hot, dusty, and material garments, and bathe my naked body in the mountain air and water. All the time as I went on I never forgot it was the Sabbath; the stillness was a perpetual reminder; and I heard in spirit the church-bells clamouring all over Europe, and the psalms of a thousand churches.

At length a human sound struck upon my ear—a cry strangely modulated between pathos and derision; and looking across the valley, I saw a little urchin sitting in a meadow, with his hands about his knees, and dwarfed to almost comical smallness by the distance. But the rogue had picked me out as I went down the road, from oak wood on to oak wood, driving Modestine; and he made me the compliments of the new country in this tremulous high-pitched salutation. And as all noises are lovely and natural at a sufficient distance, this also, coming through so much clean hill air and crossing all the green valley, sounded pleasant to my ear, and seemed a thing rustic, like the oaks or the river.

A little after, the stream that I was following fell into the Tarn at Pont de Montvert of bloody memory.

PONT DE MONTVERT

One of the first things I encountered in Pont de Montvert was, if I remember rightly, the Protestant temple; but this was but the type of other novelties. A subtle atmosphere distinguishes a town in England from a town in France, or even in Scotland. At Carlisle you can see you are in one country; at Dumfries, thirty miles away, you are as sure that you are in the other. I should find it difficult to tell in what particulars Pont de Montvert differed from Monastier or Langogne or even Bleymard; but the difference existed, and spoke eloquently to the eyes. The place, with its houses, its lanes, its glaring river-bed, wore an indescribable air of the South.

All was Sunday bustle in the streets and in the public-house, as all had been Sabbath peace among the mountains. There must have been near a score of us at dinner by eleven before noon; and after I had eaten and drunken, and sat writing up my journal, I suppose as many more came dropping in one after another, or by twos and threes. In crossing the Lozère I had not only come among new natural features, but moved into the territory of a different race. These people, as they hurriedly despatched their viands in an intricate sword-play of knives, questioned and answered me with a degree of intelligence which excelled all that I had met, except among the railway folk at Chasseradès. They had open telling faces, and were lively both in speech and manner. They not only entered throughly into the spirit of my little trip, but more than one declared, if he were rich enough, he would like to set forth on such another.

Even physically there was a pleasant change. I had not seen a pretty woman since I left Monastier, and there but one. Now of the three who sat down with me to dinner, one was certainly not beautiful—a poor timid thing of forty, quite troubled at this roaring table-d'hôte, whom I squired and helped to wine, and pledged and tried generally to encourage, with quite a contrary effect; but the other two, both married, were both more handsome than the average of women. And Clarisse? What shall I say of Clarisse? She waited the table with a heavy placable nonchalance, like a performing cow; her great grey eyes were steeped in amorous languor; her features, although fleshy, were of an original and accurate design; her mouth had a curl; her nostril spoke of dainty pride; her cheek fell into strange and interesting lines. It was a face capable of strong emotion, and, with training, it offered the promise of delicate sentiment. It seemed pitiful to see so good a model left to country admirers and a country way of thought. Beauty should at least have touched society; then, in a moment, it throws off a weight that lay upon it, it becomes conscious of itself, it puts on an elegance, learns a gait and a carriage of the head, and, in a moment, *patet dea.** Before I left I assured Clarisse of my hearty admiration. She took it like milk, without embarrassment or wonder, merely looking at me steadily with her great eyes; and I own the result upon myself was some confusion. If Clarisse could read English, I should not dare to add that her figure was unworthy of her face. Hers was a case for stays; but that may perhaps grow better as she gets up in years.

Pont de Montvert, or Greenhill Bridge, as we might say at home, is a place memorable in the story of the Camisards. It was here that the war broke out; here that those southern Covenanters slew their Archbishop Sharpe.* The persecution on the one hand, the febrile enthusiasm on the other, are almost equally difficult to understand in these quiet modern days, and with our easy modern beliefs and disbeliefs. The Protestants were one and all beside their right minds with zeal and sorrow. They were all prophets and prophetesses. Children at the breast would exhort their parents to good works. 'A child of fifteen months at Quissac spoke from its mother's arms, agitated and sobbing, distinctly and with a loud voice.' Marshall Villars* has seen a town where all the women 'seemed possessed by the devil,' and had trembling fits, and uttered prophecies publicly upon the streets. A prophetess of Vivarais was hanged at Montpellier because blood flowed from her eyes and nose, and she declared that she was weeping tears of blood for the misfortunes of the Protestants. And it was not only women and children. Stalwart dangerous fellows, used to swing the sickle or to wield the forest axe, were likewise shaken with strange paroxysms, and spoke oracles with sobs and streaming tears. A persecution unsurpassed in violence had lasted near a score of years, and this was the result upon the persecuted; hanging, burning, breaking on the wheel, had been vain; the dragoons had left their hoof-marks over all the country-side; there were men rowing in the galleys, and women pining in the prisons of the Church; and not a thought was changed in the heart of any upright Protestant.

Now the head and forefront of the persecution—after Lamoignon de Bavile*—François de Langlade du Châyla* (pronounced Chéïla), Archpriest of the Cevennes and Inspector of Missions in the same country, had a house in which he sometimes dwelt in the town of Pont de Montvert. He was a conscientious person, who seems to have been intended by nature for a pirate, and now fifty-five, an age by which a man has learned all the moderation of which he is capable. A missionary in his youth in China, he there suffered martyrdom, was left for dead, and only succoured and brought back to life by the charity of a pariah. We must suppose the pariah devoid of second-sight, and not purposely malicious in this act. Such an experience, it might be thought, would have cured a man of the desire to persecute; but the human spirit is a thing strangely put together; and, having been a Christian martyr, Du Chayla became a Christian persecutor. The Work of the Propagation of the Faith went roundly forward in his hands. His house in Pont de Montvert served him as a prison. There he plucked out the hairs of the beard, and closed the hands of his prisoners upon live coal to convince them that they were deceived in their opinions. And yet had not he himself tried and proved the inefficacy of these carnal arguments among the Buddhists in China?

Not only was life made intolerable in Languedoc, but flight was rigidly forbidden. One Massip, a muleteer, and well acquainted with the mountain-paths, had already guided several troops of fugitives in safety to Geneva; and on him, with another convoy, consisting mostly of women dressed as men, Du Chayla, in an evil hour for himself, laid his hands. The Sunday following, there was a conventicle of Protestants in the woods of Altefage upon Mont Bougès; where there stood up one Séguier—Spirit Séguier, as his companions called him—a wool-carder, tall, black-faced, and toothless, but a man full of prophecy. He declared, in the name of God, that the time for submission had gone by, and they must betake themselves to arms for the deliverance of their brethren and the destruction of the priests.

The next night, 24th July, 1702, a sound disturbed the Inspector of Missions as he sat in his prison-house at Pont de Montvert; the voices of many men upraised in psalmody drew nearer and nearer through the town. It was ten at night; he had his court about him, priests, soldiers, and servants, to the number of twelve or fifteen; and now dreading the insolence of a conventicle below his very windows, he ordered forth his soldiers to report. But the psalm-singers were already at his door, fifty strong, led by the inspired Séguier, and breathing death. To their summons, the archpriest made answer like a stout old persecutor, and bade his garrison fire upon the mob. One Camisard (for, according to some, it was in this night's work that they came by the name) fell at this discharge; his comrades burst in the door with hatchets and a beam of wood, overran the lower story of the house, set free the prisoners, and finding one of them in the *vine*, a sort of Scavenger's Daughter* of the place and period, redoubled in fury against Du Chayla, and sought by repeated assaults to carry the upper floors. But he, on his side, had given absolution to his men, and they bravely held the staircase.

'Children of God,' cried the prophet, 'hold your hands. Let us burn the house, with the priest and the satellites of Baal.'

The fire caught readily. Out of an upper window Du Chayla and his men lowered themselves into the garden by means of knotted sheets; some escaped across the river under the bullets of the insurgents; but the archpriest himself fell, broke his thigh, and could only crawl into the hedge. What were his reflections as this second martyrdom drew near? A poor, brave, besotted, hateful man, who had done his duty resolutely according to his light both in the Cevennes and China. He found at least one telling word to say in his defence; for when the roof fell in and the upbursting flames discovered his retreat, and they came and dragged him to the public place of the town, raging and calling him damned—'If I be damned,' said he, 'why should you also damn yourselves?'

Here was a good reason for the last; but in the course of his inspectorship he had given many stronger which all told in a contrary direction; and these he was now to hear. One by one, Séguier first, the Camisards drew near and stabbed him. 'This,' they said, 'is for my father broken on the wheel. This for my brother in the galleys. That for my mother or my sister imprisoned in your cursed convents.' Each gave his blow and his reason; and then all kneeled and sang psalms around the body till the dawn. With the dawn, still singing, they defiled away towards Frugères, farther up the Tarn, to pursue the work of vengeance, leaving Du Chayla's prison-house in ruins, and his body pierced with two-and-fifty wounds upon the public place.

'T is a wild night's work, with its accompaniment of psalms; and it seems as if a psalm must always have a sound of threatening in that town upon the Tarn. But the story does not end, even so far as concerns Pont de Montvert, with the departure of the Camisards. The career of Séguier was brief and bloody. Two more priests and a whole family at Ladèveze, from the father to the servants, fell by his hand or by his orders; and yet he was but a day or two at large, and restrained all the time by the presence of the soldiery. Taken at length by a famous soldier of fortune, Captain Poul, he appeared unmoved before his judges.

'Your name?' they asked.

'Pierre Séguier.'

'Why are you called Spirit?'

'Because the Spirit of the Lord is with me.'

'Your domicile?'

'Lately in the desert, and soon in heaven.'

'Have you no remorse for your crimes?'

'I have committed none. *My soul is like a garden full of shelter and of fountains.*'

At Pont de Montvert, on the 12th of August, he had his right hand stricken from his body, and was burned alive. And his soul was like a garden? So perhaps was the soul of Du Chayla, the Christian martyr. And perhaps if you could read in my soul, or I could read in yours, our own composure might seem little less surprising.

Du Chayla's house still stands, with a new roof, beside one of the bridges of the town; and if you are curious you may see the terrace-garden into which he dropped.

IN THE VALLEY OF THE TARN

A new road leads from Pont de Montvert to Florac by the valley of the Tarn; a smooth sandy ledge, it runs about half-way between the summit of the cliffs and the river in the bottom of the valley; and I went in and out, as I followed it, from bays of shadow into promontories of afternoon sun. This was a pass like that of Killiecrankie;* a deep turning gully in the hills, with the Tarn making a wonderful hoarse uproar far below, and craggy summits standing in the sunshine high above. A thin fringe of ash-trees ran about the hill-tops, like ivy on a ruin; but on the lower slopes and far up every glen the Spanish chest-nut-trees stood each four-square to heaven under its tented foliage. Some were planted each on its own terrace, no larger than a bed; some, trusting in their roots, found strength to grow and prosper and be straight and large upon the rapid slopes of the valley; others, where there was a margin to the river, stood marshalled in a line and mighty like cedars of Lebanon. Yet even where they grew most thickly they were not to be thought of as a wood, but as a herd of stalwart individuals; and the dome of each tree stood forth separate and large, and as it were a little hill, from among the domes of its companions. They gave forth a faint sweet perfume which pervaded the air of the afternoon; autumn had put tints of gold and tarnish in the green; and the sun so shone through and kindled the broad foliage, that each chestnut was relieved against another, not in shadow, but in light. A humble sketcher here laid down his pencil in despair.

I wish I could convey a notion of the growth of these noble trees; of how they strike out boughs like the oak, and trail sprays of drooping foliage like the willow; of how they stand on upright fluted columns like the pillars of a church; or like the olive, from the most shattered bole can put out smooth and youthful shoots, and begin a new life upon the ruins of the old. Thus they partake of the nature of many different trees; and even their prickly top-knots, seen near at hand against the sky, have a certain palm-like air that impresses the imagination. But their individuality, although compounded of so many elements, is but the richer and the more original. And to look down upon a level filled with these knolls of foliage, or to see a clan of old unconquerable chestnuts cluster 'like herded elephants' upon the spur of a mountain, is to rise to higher thoughts of the powers that are in Nature.

Between Modestine's laggard humour and the beauty of the scene, we made little progress all that afternoon; and at last finding the sun, although still far from setting, was already beginning to desert the narrow valley of the Tarn, I began to cast about for a place to camp in. This was not easy to find; the terraces were too narrow, and the ground, where it was unterraced, was usually too steep for a man to lie upon. I should have slipped all night, and awakened towards morning with my feet or my head in the river.

After perhaps a mile, I saw, some sixty feet above the road, a little plateau large enough to hold my sack, and securely parapeted by the trunk of an aged and enormous chestnut. Thither, with infinite trouble, I goaded and kicked the reluctant Modestine, and there I hastened to unload her. There was only room for myself upon the plateau, and I had to go nearly as high again before I found so much as standing room for the ass. It was on a heap of rolling stones, on an artificial terrace, certainly not five feet square in all. Here I tied her to a chestnut, and having given her corn and bread and made a pile of chestnut- leaves, of which I found her greedy, I descended once more to my own encampment.

The position was unpleasantly exposed. One or two carts went by upon the road; and as long as daylight lasted I concealed myself, for all the world like a hunted Camisard, behind my fortification of vast chestnut trunk; for I was passionately afraid of discovery and the visit of jocular persons in the night. Moreover, I saw that I must be early awake; for these chestnut gardens had been the scene of industry no further gone than on the day before. The slope was strewn with lopped branches, and here and there a great package of leaves was propped against a trunk; for even the leaves are serviceable, and the peasants use them in winter by way of fodder for their animals. I picked a meal in fear and trembling, half lying down to hide myself from the road; and I daresay I was as much concerned as if I had been a scout from Joani's band above upon the Lozère or from Salomon's* across the Tarn in the old times of psalm-singing and blood. Or, indeed, perhaps more; for the Camisards had a remarkable confidence in God; and a tale comes back into my memory of how the Count of Gévaudan, riding with a party of dragoons and a notary at his saddlebow to enforce the oath of fidelity in all the country hamlets, entered a valley in the woods, and found Cavalier and his men at dinner, gaily seated on the grass, and their hats crowned with box-tree garlands, while fifteen women washed their linen in the stream. Such was a field festival in 1703; at that date Antony Watteau* would be painting similar subjects.

This was a very different camp from that of the night before in the cool and silent pine woods. It was warm and even stifling in the valley. The shrill song of frogs, like the tremolo note of a whistle with a pea in it, rang up from the river-side before the sun was down. In the growing dusk, faint rustling began to run to and fro among the fallen leaves; from time to time a faint chirping or cheeping noise would fall upon my ear; and from time to time I thought I could see the movement of something swift and indistinct between the chestnuts. A profusion of large ants swarmed upon the ground; bats whisked by, and mosquitoes droned overhead. The long boughs with their bunches of leaves hung against the sky like garlands; and those immediately above and around me had somewhat the air of a trellis which should have been wrecked and half overthrown in a gale of wind.

Sleep for a long time fled my eyelids; and just as I was beginning to feel quiet stealing over my limbs, and settling densely on my mind, a noise at my head startled me broad awake again, and, I will frankly confess it, brought my heart into my mouth. It was such a noise as a person would make scratching loudly with a finger-nail; it came from under the knapsack which served me for a pillow, and it was thrice repeated before I had time to sit up and turn about. Nothing was to be seen, nothing more was to be heard, but a few of these mysterious rustlings far and near, and the ceaseless accompaniment of the river and the frogs. I learned next day that the chestnut gardens are infested by rats; rustling, chirping, and scraping were probably all due to these; but the puzzle, for the moment, was insoluble, and I had to compose myself for sleep, as best I could, in wondering uncertainty about my neighbours.

I was wakened in the grey of the morning (Monday, 30th September) by the sound of footsteps not far off upon the stones, and opening my eyes, I beheld a peasant going by among the chestnuts by a footpath that I had not hitherto observed. He turned his head neither to the right nor to the left, and disappeared in a few strides among the foliage. Here was an escape! But it was plainly more than time to be moving. The peasantry were abroad; scarce less terrible to me in my nondescript position than the soldiers of Captain Poul to an undaunted Camisard. I fed Modestine with what haste I could; but as I was returning to my sack, I saw a man and a boy come down the hillside in a direction crossing mine. They unintelligibly hailed me, and I replied with inarticulate but cheerful sounds, and hurried forward to get into my gaiters.

The pair, who seemed to be father and son, came slowly up to the plateau, and stood close beside me for some time in silence. The bed was open, and I saw with regret my revolver lying patently disclosed on the blue wool. At last, after they had looked me all over, and the silence had grown laughably embarrassing, the man demanded in what seemed unfriendly tones:

'You have slept here?'

'Yes,' said I. 'As you see.'

'Why?' he asked.

'My faith!' I answered lightly, 'I was tired.'

He next inquired where I was going and what I had had for dinner; and then, without the least transition, '*C'est bien,*' he added. 'Come along.' And he and his son, without another word, turned off to the next chestnut-tree but one, which they set to pruning. The thing had passed off more simply than I hoped. He was a grave, respectable man; and his unfriendly voice did not imply that he thought he was speaking to a criminal, but merely to an inferior.

I was soon on the road, nibbling a cake of chocolate and seriously occupied with a case of conscience. Was I to pay for my night's lodging? I had slept ill, the bed was full of fleas in the shape of ants, there was no water in the room, the very dawn had neglected to call me in the morning. I might have missed a train, had there been any in the neighbourhood to catch. Clearly I was dissatisfied with my entertainment; and I decided I should not pay unless I met a beggar.

The valley looked even lovelier by morning; and soon the road descended to the level of the river. Here, in a place where many straight and prosperous chestnuts stood together, making an aisle upon a swarded terrace, I made my morning toilette in the water of the Tarn. It was marvellously clear, thrillingly cool; the soapsuds disappeared as if by magic in the swift current, and the white boulders gave one a model for cleanliness. To wash in one of God's rivers in the open air seems to me a sort of cheerful solemnity or semi-pagan act of worship. To dabble among dishes in a bedroom may perhaps make clean the body; but the imagination takes no share in such a cleansing. I went on with a light and peaceful heart and sang psalms to the spiritual ear as I advanced.

Suddenly up came an old woman, who point-blank demanded alms.

'Good!' thought I; 'here comes the waiter with the bill.' And I paid for my night's lodgings on the spot. Take it how you please, but this was the first and the last beggar that I met with during all my tour.

A step or two farther I was overtaken by an old man in a brown nightcap, clear-eyed, weather-beaten, with a faint, excited smile. A little girl followed him, driving two sheep and a goat; but she kept in our wake, while the old man walked beside me and talked about the morning and the valley. It was not much past six; and for healthy people who have slept enough, that is an hour of expansion and of open and trustful talk.

'*Connaissez-vous le Seigneur?*' he said at length.

I asked him what Seigneur he meant; but he only repeated the question with more emphasis and a look in his eyes denoting hope and interest.

'Ah!' said I, pointing upwards, 'I understand you now. Yes, I know Him; He is the best of acquaintances.'

The old man said he was delighted. 'Hold,' he added, striking his bosom; 'it makes me happy here.' There were a few who knew the Lord in these valleys, he went on to tell me; not many, but a few. 'Many are called,' he quoted, 'and few chosen.'*

'My father,' said I, 'it is not easy to say who know the Lord; and it is none of our business. Protestants and Catholics, and even those who worship stones, may know Him and be known by Him, for He has made all.'

I did not know I was so good a preacher.

The old man assured me he thought as I did, and repeated his expressions of pleasure at meeting me. 'We are so few,' he said. 'They call us Moravians* here; but down in the department of Gard, where there are also a good number, they are called Derbists* after an English pastor.'

I began to understand that I was figuring, in questionable taste, as a member of some sect to me unknown; but I was more pleased with the pleasure of my companion than embarrassed by my own equivocal position. Indeed I can see no dishonesty in not avowing a difference; and especially in these high matters, where we have all a sufficient assurance that, whoever may be in the wrong, we ourselves are not completely in the right. The truth is much talked about; but this old man in a brown nightcap showed himself so simple, sweet, and friendly that I am not unwilling to profess myself his convert. He was, as a matter of fact, a Plymouth Brother. Of what that involves in the way of doctrine I have no idea nor the time to inform myself; but I know right well that we are all embarked upon a troublesome world, the children of one Father, striving in many essential points to do and to become the same. And although it was somewhat in a mistake that he shook hands with me so often and showed himself so ready to receive my words, that was a mistake of the truth-finding sort. For charity begins blindfold; and only through a series of similar misapprehensions rises at length into a settled principle of love and patience, and a firm belief in all our fellow-men. If I deceived this good old man, in the like manner I would willingly go on to deceive others. And if ever at length, out of our separate and sad ways, we should all come together into one common house, I have a hope, to which I cling dearly, that my mountain Plymouth Brother will hasten to shake hands with me again.

Thus, talking like Christian and Faithful* by the way, he and I came down upon a hamlet by the Tarn. It was but a humble place, called La Vernède, with less than a dozen houses, and a Protestant chapel on a knoll. Here he dwelt; and here, at the inn, I ordered my breakfast. The inn was kept by an agreeable young man, a stone-breaker on the road, and his sister, a pretty and engaging girl. The village schoolmaster dropped in to speak with the stranger. And these were all Protestants—a fact which pleased me more than I should have expected; and, what pleased me still more, they seemed all upright and simple people. The Plymouth Brother hung round me with a sort of yearning interest, and returned at least thrice to make sure I was enjoying my meal. His behaviour touched me deeply at the time, and even now moves me in recollection. He feared to intrude, but he would not willingly forego one moment of my society; and he seemed never weary of shaking me by the hand.

When all the rest had drifted off to their day's work, I sat for near half an hour with the young mistress of the house, who talked pleasantly over her seam of the chestnut harvest, and the beauties of the Tarn, and old family affections, broken up when young folk go from home, yet still subsisting. Hers, I am sure, was a sweet nature, with a country plainness and much delicacy underneath; and he who takes her to his heart will doubtless be a fortunate young man.

The valley below La Vernède pleased me more and more as I went forward. Now the hills approached from either hand, naked and crumbling, and walled in the river between cliffs; and now the valley widened and became green. The road led me past the old castle of Miral on a steep; past a battlemented monastery, long since broken up and turned into a church and parsonage; and past a cluster of black roofs, the village of Cocurès, sitting among vineyards and meadows and orchards thick with red apples, and where, along the highway, they were knocking down walnuts from the roadside trees, and gathering them in sacks and baskets. The hills, however much the vale might open, were still tall and bare, with cliffy battlements and here and there a pointed summit; and the Tarn still rattled through the stones with a mountain noise. I had been led by bagmen of a picturesque turn of mind, to expect a horrific country after the heart of Byron; but to my Scotch eyes it seemed smiling and plentiful, as the weather still gave an impression of high summer to my Scotch body; although the chestnuts were already picked out by the autumn, and the poplars, that here began to mingle with them, had turned into pale gold against the approach of winter.

There was something in this landscape, smiling although wild, that explained to me the spirit of the Southern Covenanters. Those who took to the hills for conscience' sake in Scotland had all gloomy and bedevilled thoughts; for once that they received God's comfort they would be twice engaged with Satan; but the Camisards had only bright and supporting visions. They dealt much more in blood, both given and taken; yet I find no obsession of the Evil One in their records. With a light conscience, they pursued their life in these rough times and circumstances. The soul of Séguier, let us not forget, was like a garden. They knew they were on God's side, with a knowledge that has no parallel among the Scots; for the Scots, although they might be certain of the cause, could never rest confident of the person.

'We flew,' says one old Camisard, 'when we heard the sound of psalm-singing, we flew as if with wings. We felt within us an animating ardour, a transporting desire. The feeling cannot be expressed in words. It is a thing that must have been experienced to be understood. However weary we might be, we thought no more of our weariness and grew light, so soon as the psalms fell upon our ears.'

The valley of the Tarn and the people whom I met at La Vernède not only explain to me this passage, but the twenty years of suffering which those, who were so stiff and so bloody when once they betook themselves to war, endured with the meekness of children and the constancy of saints and peasants.

FLORAC

On a branch of the Tarn stands Florac, the seat of a sub-prefecture, with an old castle, an alley of planes, many quaint street-corners, and a live fountain welling from the hill. It is notable, besides, for handsome women, and as one of the two capitals, Alais being the other, of the country of the Camisards.

The landlord of the inn took me, after I had eaten, to an adjoining *café*, where I, or rather my journey, became the topic of the afternoon. Every one had some suggestion for my guidance; and the sub-prefectorial map was fetched from the sub-prefecture itself, and much thumbed among coffee-cups and glasses of liqueur. Most of these kind advisers were Protestant, though I observed that Protestant and Catholic intermingled in a very easy manner; and it surprised me to see what a lively memory still subsisted of the religious war. Among the hills of the south-west, by Mauchline, Cumnock, or Carsphairn,* in isolated farms or in the manse, serious Presbyterian people still recall the days of the great persecution, and the graves of local martyrs are still piously regarded. But in towns and among the so-called better classes, I fear that these old doings have become an idle tale. If you met a mixed company in the King's Arms at Wigtown, it is not likely that the talk would run on Covenanters. Nay, at Muirkirk of Glenluce, I found the beadle's wife had not so much as heard of Prophet Peden.* But these Cévenols were proud of their ancestors in quite another sense; the war was their chosen topic; its exploits were their own patent of nobility; and where a man or a race has had but one adventure, and that heroic, we must expect and pardon some prolixity of reference. They told me the country was still full of legends hitherto uncollected; I heard from them about Cavalier's descendants—not direct descendants, be it understood, but only cousins or nephews—who were still prosperous people in the scene of the boy-general's exploits; and one farmer had seen the bones of old combatants dug up into the air of an afternoon in the nineteenth century, in a field where the ancestors had fought, and the great-grandchildren were peaceably ditching.

Later in the day one of the Protestant pastors was so good as to visit me: a young man, intelligent and polite, with whom I passed an hour or two in talk. Florac, he told me, is part Protestant, part Catholic; and the difference in religion is usually doubled by a difference in politics. You may judge of my surprise, coming as I did from such a babbling purgatorial Poland of a place as Monastier, when I learned that the population lived together on very quiet terms, and there was even an exchange of hospitalities between households thus doubly separated. Black Camisard and White Camisard, militiaman and Miquelet and dragoon, Protestant prophet and Catholic cadet of the White Cross,* they had all been sabreing and shooting, burning, pillaging and murdering, their hearts hot with indignant passion; and here, after a hundred and seventy years, Protestant is still Protestant, Catholic still Catholic, in mutual toleration and mild amity of life. But the race of man, like that indomitable nature whence it sprang, has medicating virtues of its own; the years and seasons bring various harvests; the sun returns after the rain; and mankind outlives secular animosities, as a single man awakens from the passions of a day. We judge our ancestors from a more divine position; and the dust being a little laid with several centuries, we can see both sides adorned with human virtues and fighting with a show of right.

I have never thought it easy to be just, and find it daily even harder than I thought. I own I met these Protestants with delight and a sense of coming home. I was accustomed to speak their language, in another and deeper sense of the word than that which distinguishes between French and English; for the true Babel is a divergence upon morals. And hence I could hold more free communication with the Protestants, and judge them more justly, than the Catholics. Father Apollinaris may pair off with my mountain Plymouth Brother as two guileless and devout old men; yet I ask myself if I had as ready a feeling for the virtues of the Trappist; or had I been a Catholic, if I should have felt so warmly to the dissenter of La Vernède. With the first I was on terms of mere forbearance; but with the other, although only on a misunderstanding and by keeping on selected points, it was still possible to hold converse and exchange some honest thoughts. In this world of imperfection we gladly welcome even partial intimacies. If we find but one to whom we can speak out of our heart freely, with whom we can walk in love and simplicity without dissimulation, we have no ground of quarrel with the world or God.

IN THE VALLEY OF THE MIMENTE

On Tuesday, 1st October, we left Florac late in the afternoon, a tired donkey and tired donkey-driver. A little way
up the Tarnon, a covered bridge of wood introduced us
into the valley of the Mimente. Steep rocky red mountains
overhung the stream; great oaks and chestnuts grew upon
the slopes or in stony terraces; here and there was a red
field of millet or a few apple-trees studded with red apples;
and the road passed hard by two black hamlets, one with
an old castle atop to please the heart of the tourist.

It was difficult here again to find a spot fit for my
encampment. Even under the oaks and chestnuts the
ground had not only a very rapid slope, but was heaped
with loose stones; and where there was no timber the hills
descended to the stream in a red precipice tufted with
heather. The sun had left the highest peak in front of me,
and the valley was full of the lowing sound of herdsmen's
horns as they recalled the flocks into the stable, when I
spied a bight of meadow some way below the roadway in
an angle of the river. Thither I descended, and tying
Modestine provisionally to a tree, proceeded to investigate
the neighbourhood. A grey pearly evening shadow filled the
glen; objects at a little distance grew indistinct and melted
baffingly into each other; and the darkness was rising
steadily like an exhalation. I approached a great oak which
grew in the meadow, hard by the river's brink; when to my
disgust the voices of children fell upon my ear, and I beheld
a house round the angle on the other bank. I had half a
mind to pack and be gone again, but the growing darkness
moved me to remain. I had only to make no noise until
the night was fairly come, and trust to the dawn to call me
early in the morning. But it was hard to be annoyed by
neighbours in such a great hotel.

A hollow underneath the oak was my bed. Before I had
fed Modestine and arranged my sack, three stars were
already brightly shining, and the others were beginning

dimly to appear. I slipped down to the river, which looked very black among its rocks, to fill my can; and dined with a good appetite in the dark, for I scrupled to light a lantern while so near a house. The moon, which I had seen, a pallid crescent, all afternoon, faintly illuminated the summit of the hills, but not a ray fell into the bottom of the glen where I was lying. The oak rose before me like a pillar of darkness; and overhead the heartsome stars were set in the face of the night. No one knows the stars who has not slept, as the French happily put it, *à la belle étoile.* He may know all their names and distances and magnitudes, and yet be ignorant of what alone concerns mankind, their serene and gladsome influence on the mind. The greater part of poetry is about the stars; and very justly, for they are themselves the most classical of poets. These same far-away worlds, sprinkled like tapers or shaken together like a diamond dust upon the sky, had looked not otherwise to Roland or Cavalier, when, in the words of the latter, they had 'no other tent but the sky, and no other bed than my mother earth.'

All night a strong wind blew up the valley, and the acorns fell pattering over me from the oak. Yet, on this first night of October, the air was as mild as May, and I slept with the fur thrown back.

I was much disturbed by the barking of a dog, an animal that I fear more than any wolf. A dog is vastly braver, and is besides supported by the sense of duty. If you kill a wolf, you meet with encouragement and praise; but if you kill a dog, the sacred rights of property and the domestic affections come clamouring round you for redress. At the end of a fagging day, the sharp, cruel note of a dog's bark is in itself a keen annoyance; and to a tramp like myself, he represents the sedentary and respectable world in its most hostile form. There is something of the clergyman or the lawyer about this engaging animal; and if he were not amenable to stones, the boldest man would shrink from travelling afoot. I respect dogs much in the domestic circle; but on the highway or sleeping afield, I both detest and fear them.

I was wakened next morning (Wednesday, October 2nd) by the same dog—for I knew his bark—making a charge down the bank, and then, seeing me sit up, retreating again with great alacrity. The stars were not yet quite extinguished. The heaven was of that enchanting mild grey-blue of the early morn. A still clear light began to fall, and the trees on the hillside were outlined sharply against the sky. The wind had veered more to the north, and no longer reached me in the glen; but as I was going on with my preparations, it drove a white cloud very swiftly over the hill-top; and looking up, I was surprised to see the cloud dyed with gold. In these high regions of the air, the sun was already shining as at noon. If only the clouds travelled high enough, we should see the same thing all night long. For it is always daylight in the fields of space.

As I began to go up the valley, a draught of wind came down it out of the seat of the sunrise, although the clouds continued to run overhead in an almost contrary direction. A few steps farther, and I saw a whole hillside gilded with the sun; and still a little beyond, between two peaks, a centre of dazzling brilliancy appeared floating in the sky, and I was once more face to face with the big bonfire that occupies the kernel of our system.

I met but one human being that forenoon, a dark military-looking wayfarer, who carried a game-bag on a baldric; but he made a remark that seems worthy of record. For when I asked him if he were Protestant or Catholic——

'Oh,' said he, 'I make no shame of my religion. I am a Catholic.'

He made no shame of it! The phrase is a piece of natural statistics; for it is the language of one in a minority. I thought with a smile of Bavile and his dragoons, and how you may ride rough-shod over a religion for a century, and leave it only the more lively for the friction. Ireland is still Catholic; the Cevennes still Protestant. It is not a basketful of law-papers, nor the hoofs and pistol-butts of a regiment of horse, that can change one tittle of a ploughman's thoughts. Outdoor rustic people have not many ideas but such as they have are hardy plants and thrive flourishingly in persecution. One who has grown a long while in the sweat of laborious noons, and under the stars at night, a frequenter of hills and forests, an old honest countryman, has, in the end, a sense of communion with the powers of the universe, and amicable relations towards his God. Like my mountain Plymouth Brother, he knows the Lord. His religion does not repose upon a choice of logic; it is the poetry of the man's experience, the philosophy of the history of his life. God, like a great power, like a great shining sun, has appeared to this simple fellow in the course of years, and become the ground and essence of his least reflections; and you may change creeds and dogmas by authority, or proclaim a new religion with the sound of trumpets, if you will; but here is a man who has his own thoughts, and will stubbornly adhere to them in good and evil. He is a Catholic, a Protestant, or a Plymouth Brother, in the same indefeasible sense that a man is not a woman, or a woman not a man. For he could not vary from his faith, unless he could eradicate all memory of the past, and, in a strict and not a conventional meaning, change his mind.

THE HEART OF THE COUNTRY

I was now drawing near to Cassagnas, a cluster of black roofs upon the hillside, in this wild valley, among chestnut gardens, and looked upon in the clear air by many rocky peaks. The road along the Mimente is yet new, nor have the mountaineers recovered their surprise when the first cart arrived at Cassagnas. But although it lay thus apart from the current of men's business, this hamlet had already made a figure in the history of France. Hard by, in caverns of the mountain, was one of the five arsenals of the Camisards; where they laid up clothes and corn and arms against necessity, forged bayonets and sabres, and made themselves gunpowder with willow charcoal and saltpetre boiled in kettles. To the same caves, amid this multifarious industry, the sick and wounded were brought up to heal; and there they were visited by the two surgeons, Chabrier and Tavan, and secretly nursed by women of the neighbourhood.

Of the five legions into which the Camisards were divided, it was the oldest and the most obscure that had its magazines by Cassagnas. This was the band of Spirit Séguier; men who had joined their voices with his in the 68th Psalm as they marched down by night on the archpriest of the Cevennes. Séguier, promoted to heaven, was succeeded by Salomon Couderc, whom Cavalier treats in his memoirs as chaplain-general to the whole army of the Camisards. He was a prophet; a great reader of the heart, who admitted people to the sacrament or refused them by 'intentively viewing every man' between the eyes; and had the most of the Scriptures off by rote. And this was surely happy; since in a surprise in August, 1703, he lost his mule, his portfolios, and his Bible. It is only strange that they were not surprised more often and more effectually; for this legion of Cassagnas was truly patriarchal in its theory of war, and camped without sentries, leaving that duty to the angels of the God for whom they fought. This is a token, not only of their faith, but of the trackless country where they harboured. M.de Caladon, taking a stroll one fine day, walked into 'a flock of sheep in a plain,' and found some asleep and some awake and psalm-singing. A traitor had need of no recommendation to insinuate himself among their ranks, beyond 'his faculty of singing psalms'; and even the prophet Salomon 'took him into a particular friendship.' Thus, among their intricate hills, the rustic troop subsisted; and history can attribute few exploits to them but sacraments and ecstasies.

People of this tough and simple stock will not, as I have just been saying, prove variable in religion; nor will they get nearer to apostasy than a mere external conformity like that of Naaman* in the house of Rimmon. When Louis XVI, in the words of the edict, 'convinced by the uselessness of a century of persecutions, and rather from necessity than sympathy,' granted at last a royal grace of toleration,* Cassagnas was still Protestant; and to a man, it is so to this day. There is, indeed, one family that is not Protestant, but neither is it Catholic. It is that of a Catholic *curé* in revolt, who has taken to his bosom a schoolmistress. And his conduct, it is worth noting, is disapproved by the Protestant villagers.

'It is a bad idea for a man,' said one, 'to go back from his engagements.'

The villagers whom I saw seemed intelligent after a countrified fashion, and were all plain and dignified in manner. As a Protestant myself, I was well looked upon, and my acquaintance with history gained me further respect. For we had something not unlike a religious controversy at table, a gendarme and a merchant with whom I dined being both strangers to the place, and Catholics. The young men of the house stood round and supported me; and the whole discussion was tolerantly conducted, and surprised a man brought up among the infinitesimal and contentious differences of Scotland. The merchant, indeed, grew a little warm, and was far less pleased than some others with my historical acquirements. But the gendarme was mighty easy over it all.

'It's a bad idea for a man to change,' said he; and the remark was generally applauded.

That was not the opinion of the priest and soldier at Our Lady of the Snows. But this is a different race; and perhaps the same great-heartedness that upheld them to resist, now enables them to differ in a kind spirit. For courage respects courage; but where a faith has been trodden out, we may look for a mean and narrow population. The true work of Bruce and Wallace was the union of the nations; not that they should stand apart a while longer, skirmishing upon their borders; but that, when the time came, they might unite with self-respect.

The merchant was much interested in my journey, and thought it dangerous to sleep afield.

'There are the wolves,' said he; 'and then it is known you are an Englishman. The English have always long purses, and it might very well enter into some one's head to deal you an ill blow some night.'

I told him I was not much afraid of such accidents; and at any rate judged it unwise to dwell upon alarms or consider small perils in the arrangement of life. Life itself, I submitted, was a far too risky business as a whole to make each additional particular of danger worth regard. 'Something,' said I, 'might burst in your inside any day of the week, and there would be an end of you, if you were locked into your room with three turns of the key.'

'*Cependant*,' said he, '*coucher dehors!* '*

'God,' said I, 'is everywhere.'

'*Cependant, coucher dehors!* ' he repeated, and his voice was eloquent of terror.

He was the only person, in all my voyage, who saw anything hardy in so simple a proceeding; although many considered it superfluous. Only one, on the other hand, professed much delight in the idea; and that was my Plymouth Brother, who cried out, when I told him I sometimes preferred sleeping under the stars to a close and noisy alehouse, 'Now I see that you know the Lord!'

The merchant asked me for one of my cards as I was leaving, for he said I should be something to talk of in the future, and desired me to make a note of his request and reason; a desire with which I have thus complied.

A little after two I struck across the Mimente and took a rugged path southward up a hillside covered with loose stones and tufts of heather. At the top, as is the habit of the country, the path disappeared; and I left my she-ass munching heather, and went forward alone to seek a road.

I was now on the separation of two vast water-sheds; behind me all the streams were bound for the Garonne and the Western Ocean; before me was the basin of the Rhone. Hence, as from the Lozère, you can see in clear weather the shining of the Gulf of Lyons; and perhaps from here the soldiers of Salomon may have watched for the topsails of Sir Cloudesley Shovel,* and the long-promised aid from England. You may take this ridge as lying in the heart of the country of the Camisards: four of the five legions camped all round it and almost within view—Salomon and Joani to the north, Castanet and Roland to the south; and when Julien* had finished his famous work, the devastation of the High Cevennes, which lasted all through October and November, 1703, and during which four hundred and sixty villages and hamlets were, with fire and pickaxe, utterly subverted, a man standing on this eminence would have looked forth upon a silent, smokeless, and dispeopled land. Time and man's activity have now repaired these ruins; Cassagnas is once more roofed and sending up domestic smoke; and in the chestnut gardens, in low and leafy corners, many a prosperous farmer returns, when the day's work is done, to his children and bright hearth. And still it was perhaps the wildest view of all my journey. Peak upon peak, chain upon chain of hills ran surging southward, channelled and sculptured by the winter streams, feathered from head to foot with chestnuts, and here and there breaking out into a coronal of cliffs. The sun, which was still far from setting, sent a drift of misty gold across the hill-tops, but the valleys were already plunged in a profound and quiet shadow.

A very old shepherd, hobbling on a pair of sticks, and wearing a black cap of liberty, as if in honour of his nearness to the grave, directed me to the road for St Germain de Calberte. There was something solemn in the isolation of this infirm and ancient creature. Where he dwelt, how he got upon this high ridge, or how he proposed to get down again, were more than I could fancy. Not far off upon my right was the famous Plan de Font Morte, where Poul with his Armenian sabre slashed down the Camisards of Séguier. This, methought, might be some Rip van Winkle of the war, who had lost his comrades, fleeing before Poul, and wandered ever since upon the mountains. It might be news to him that Cavalier had surrendered, or Roland had fallen fighting with his back against an olive. And while I was thus working on my fancy, I heard him hailing in broken tones, and saw him waving me to come back, with one of his two sticks. I had already got some way past him; but, leaving Modestine once more, retraced my steps.

Alas, it was a very commonplace affair. The old gentleman had forgot to ask the pedlar what he sold, and wished to remedy this neglect.

I told him sternly, 'Nothing.'

'Nothing?' cried he.

I repeated 'Nothing,' and made off.

It's odd to think of, but perhaps I thus became as inexplicable to the old man as he had been to me.

The road lay under chestnuts, and though I saw a hamlet or two below me in the vale, and many lone houses of the chestnut farmers, it was a very solitary march all afternoon; and the evening began early underneath the trees. But I heard the voice of a woman singing some sad, old, endless ballad not far off. It seemed to be about love and a *bel amoureux*, her handsome sweetheart; and I wished I could have taken up the strain and answered her, as I went on upon my invisible woodland way, weaving, like Pippa* in the poem, my own thoughts with hers. What could I have told her? Little enough; and yet all the heart requires. How the world gives and takes away, and brings sweethearts near, only to separate them again into distant and strange lands; but to love is the great amulet which makes the world a garden; and 'hope, which comes to all,' outwears the accidents of life, and reaches with tremulous hand beyond the grave and death. Easy to say: yea, but also, by God's mercy, both easy and grateful to believe!

We struck at last into a wide white high-road, carpeted with noiseless dust. The night had come; the moon had been shining for a long while upon the opposite mountain, when on turning a corner my donkey and I issued ourselves into her light. I had emptied out my brandy at Florac, for I could bear the stuff no longer, and replaced it with some generous and scented Volnay; and now I drank to the moon's sacred majesty upon the road. It was but a couple of mouthfuls; yet I became thenceforth unconscious of my limbs, and my blood flowed with luxury. Even Modestine was inspired by this purified nocturnal sunshine, and bestirred her little hoofs as to a livelier measure. The road wound and descended swiftly among masses of chestnuts. Hot dust rose from our feet and flowed away. Our two shadows—mine deformed with the knapsack, hers comically bestridden by the pack—now lay before us clearly outlined on the road, and now, as we turned a corner, went off into the ghostly distance, and sailed along the mountain like clouds. From time to time a warm wind rustled down the valley, and set all the chestnuts dangling their bunches of foliage and fruit; the ear was filled with whispering music, and the shadows danced in/tune. And next moment the breeze had gone by, and in all the valley nothing moved except our travelling feet. On the opposite slope, the monstrous ribs and gullies of the mountain were faintly designed in the moonshine; and high overhead, in some lone house, there burned one lighted window, one square spark of red in the huge field of sad nocturnal colouring.

At a certain point, as I went downward, turning many acute angles, the moon disappeared behind the hill; and I pursued my way in great darkness, until another turning shot me without preparation into St Germain de Calberte. The place was asleep and silent, and buried in opaque night. Only from a single open door, some lamplight escaped upon the road to show me I was come among men's habitations. The two last gossips of the evening, still talking by a garden wall, directed me to the inn. The landlady was getting her chicks to bed; the fire was already out, and had, not without grumbling, to be rekindled; half an hour later, and I must have gone supperless to roost.

THE LAST DAY

When I awoke (Thursday, 3rd October), and, hearing a great flourishing of cocks and chuckling of contented hens, betook me to the window of the clean and comfortable room where I had slept the night, I looked forth on a sunshiny morning in a deep vale of chestnut gardens. It was still early, and the cockcrows, and the slanting lights, and the long shadows encouraged me to be out and look round me.

St Germain de Calberte is a great parish nine leagues round about. At the period of the wars, and immediately before the devastation, it was inhabited by two hundred and seventy-five families, of which only nine were Catholic; and it took the *curé* seventeen September days to go from house to house on horseback for a census. But the place itself, although capital of a canton, is scarce larger than a hamlet. It lies terraced across a steep slope in the midst of mighty chestnuts. The Protestant chapel stands below upon a shoulder; in the midst of the town is the quaint old Catholic church.

It was here that poor Du Chayla, the Christian martyr, kept his library and held a court of missionaries; here he had built his tomb, thinking to lie among a grateful population whom he had redeemed from error; and hither on the morrow of his death they brought the body, pierced with two-and-fifty wounds, to be interred. Clad in his priestly robes, he was laid out in state in the church. The *curé*, taking his text from Second Samuel, twentieth chapter and twelfth verse, 'And Amasa wallowed in his blood in the highway,' preached a rousing sermon, and exhorted his brethren to die each at his post, like their unhappy and illustrious superior. In the midst of this eloquence there came a breeze that Spirit Séguier was near at hand; and behold! all the assembly took to their horses' heels, some east, some west, and the *curé* himself as far as Alais.

Strange was the position of this little Catholic metropolis, a thimbleful of Rome, in such a wild and contrary neighbourhood. On the one hand, the legion of Salomon overlooked it from Cassagnas; on the other, it was cut off from assistance by the legion of Roland at Mialet. The *curé*, Louvrelenil, although he took a panic at the archpriest's funeral, and so hurriedly decamped to Alais, stood well by his isolated pulpit, and thence uttered fulminations against the crimes of the Protestants. Salomon besieged the village for an hour and a half, but was beaten back. The militiamen, on guard before the *curé's* door, could be heard, in the black hours, singing Protestant psalms and holding friendly talk with the insurgents. And in the morning, although not a shot had been fired, there would not be a round of powder in their flasks. Where was it gone? All handed over to the Camisards for a consideration. Untrusty guardians for an isolated priest!

That these continual stirs were once busy in St Germain de Calberte, the imagination with difficulty receives; all is now so quiet, the pulse of human life now beats so low and still in this hamlet of the mountains. Boys followed me a great way off, like a timid sort of lion-hunters; and people turned round to have a second look, or came out of their houses, as I went by. My passage was the first event, you would have fancied, since the Camisards. There was nothing rude or forward in this observation; it was but a pleased and wondering scrutiny, like that of oxen or the human infant; yet it wearied my spirits, and soon drove me from the street.

I took refuge on the terraces, which are here greenly carpeted with sward, and tried to imitate with a pencil the inimitable attitudes of the chestnuts as they bear up their canopy of leaves. Ever and again a little wind went by, and the nuts dropped all around me, with a light and dull sound, upon the sward. The noise was as of a thin fall of great hailstones; but there went with it a cheerful human sentiment of an approaching harvest and farmers rejoicing in their gains. Looking up, I could see the brown nut peering through the husk, which was already gaping; and between the stems the eye embraced an amphitheatre of hill, sunlit and green with leaves.

I have not often enjoyed a place more deeply. I moved in an atmosphere of pleasure, and felt light and quiet and content. But perhaps it was not the place alone that so disposed my spirit. Perhaps some one was thinking of me in another country; or perhaps some thought of my own had come and gone unnoticed, and yet done me good. For some thoughts, which sure would be the most beautiful, vanish before we can rightly scan their features; as though a god, travelling by our green highways, should but open the door, give one smiling look into the house, and go again forever. Was it Apollo, or Mercury, or Love with folded wings? Who shall say? But we go the lighter about our business, and feel peace and pleasure in our hearts.

I dined with a pair of Catholics. They agreed in the condemnation of a young man, a Catholic, who had married a Protestant girl and gone over to the religion of his wife. A Protestant born they could understand and respect; indeed, they seemed to be of the mind of an old Catholic woman who told me that same day there was no difference between the two sects, save that 'wrong was more wrong for the Catholic,' who had more light and guidance; but this of a man's desertion filled them with contempt.

'It's a bad idea for a man to change,' said one.

It may have been accidental, but you see how this phrase pursued me; and for myself, I believe it is the current philosophy in these parts. I have some difficulty in imagining a better. It's not only a great flight of confidence for a man to change his creed and go out of his family for heaven's sake; but the odds are—nay, and the hope is— that, with all this great transition in the eyes of man, he has not changed himself a hairsbreadth to the eyes of God. Honour to those who do so, for the wrench is sore. But it argues something narrow, whether of strength or weakness, whether of the prophet or the fool, in those who can take a sufficient interest in such infinitesimal and human operations, or who can quit a friendship for a doubtful process of the mind. And I think I should not leave my old creed for another, changing only words for other words; but by some brave reading, embrace it in spirit and truth, and find wrong as wrong for me as for the best of other communions.

The phylloxera was in the neighbourhood; and instead of wine we drank at dinner a more economical juice of the grape—La Parisienne, they call it. It is made by putting the fruit whole into a cask with water; one by one the berries ferment and burst; what is drunk during the day is supplied at night in water; so, with ever another pitcher from the well, and ever another grape exploding and giving out its strength, one cask of Parisienne may last a family till spring. It is, as the reader will anticipate, a feeble beverage, but very pleasant to the taste.

What with dinner and coffee, it was long past three before I left St Germain de Calberte. I went down beside the Gardon of Mialet, a great glaring watercourse devoid of water, and through St Étienne de Vallée Française, or Val Francesque, as they used to call it; and towards evening began to ascend the hill of St Pierre. It was a long and steep ascent. Behind me an empty carriage returning to St Jean du Gard kept hard upon my tracks, and near the summit overtook me. The driver, like the rest of the world, was sure I was a pedlar; but, unlike others, he was sure of what I had to sell. He had noticed the blue wool which hung out of my pack at either end; and from this he had decided, beyond my power to alter his decision, that I dealt in blue-wool collars, such as decorate the neck of the French draught-horse.

I had hurried to the topmost powers of Modestine, for I dearly desired to see the view upon the other side before the day had faded. But it was night when I reached the summit; the moon was riding high and clear; and only a few grey streaks of twilight lingered in the west. A yawning valley, gulfed in blackness, lay like a hole in created nature at my feet; but the outline of the hills was sharp against the sky. There was Mount Aigoal, the stronghold of Castanet. And Castanet, not only as an active undertaking leader, deserves some mention among Camisards; for there is a spray of rose among his laurel; and he showed how, even in a public tragedy, love will have its way. In the high tide of war he married, in his mountain citadel, a young and pretty lass called Mariette. There were great rejoicings; and the bridegroom released five-and-twenty prisoners in honour of the glad event. Seven months afterwards Mariette, the Princess of the Cevennes, as they called her in derision, fell into the hands of the authorities, where it was like to have gone hard with her. But Castanet was a man of execution, and loved his wife. He fell on Valleraugue, and got a lady there for a hostage; and for the first and last time in that war there was an exchange of prisoners. Their daughter, pledge of some starry night upon Mount Aigoal, has left descendants to this day.

Modestine and I—it was our last meal together—had a snack upon the top of St Pierre, I on a heap of stones, she standing by me in the moonlight and decorously eating bread out of my hand. The poor brute would eat more heartily in this manner; for she had a sort of affection for me, which I was soon to betray.

It was a long descent upon St Jean du Gard and we met no one but a carter, visible afar off by the glint of the moon on his extinguished lantern.

Before ten o'clock we had got in and were at supper; fifteen miles and a stiff hill in little beyond six hours!

FAREWELL, MODESTINE!

On examination, on the morning of October 4th, Modestine was pronounced unfit for travel. She would need at least two days' repose according to the ostler; but I was now eager to reach Alais for my letters; and, being in a civilised country of stage-coaches, I determined to sell my lady friend and be off by the diligence that afternoon. Our yesterday's march, with the testimony of the driver who had pursued us up the long hill of St Pierre, spread a favourable notion of my donkey's capabilities. Intending purchasers were aware of an unrivalled opportunity. Before ten I had an offer of twenty-five francs; and before noon, after a desperate engagement, I sold her, saddle and all, for five-and-thirty. The pecuniary gain is not obvious, but I had bought freedom into the bargain.

St Jean du Gard is a large place and largely Protestant. The maire, a Protestant, asked me to help him in a small matter which is itself characteristic of the country. The young women of the Cevennes profit by the common religion and the difference of the language to go largely as governesses into England; and here was one, a native of Mialet, struggling with English circulars from two different agencies in London. I gave what help I could; and volunteered some advice, which struck me as being excellent.

One thing more I note. The phylloxera has ravaged the vineyards in this neighbourhood; and in the early morning, under some chestnuts by the river, I found a party of men working with a cider-press. I could not at first make out what they were after, and asked one fellow to explain.

'Making cider,' he said. '*Oui, c'est comme ça. Comme dans le nord!*'

There was a ring of sarcasm in his voice; the country was going to the devil.

It was not until I was fairly seated by the driver, and rattling through a rocky valley with dwarf olives, that I became aware of my bereavement. I had lost Modestine.

Up to that moment I had thought I hated her; but now she was gone,

> 'And, Oh,
> The difference to me!'*

For twelve days we had been fast companions; we had travelled upwards of a hundred and twenty miles, crossed several respectable ridges, and jogged along with our six legs by many a rocky and many a boggy by-road. After the first day, although sometimes I was hurt and distant in manner, I still kept my patience; and as for her, poor soul! she had come to regard me as a god. She loved to eat out of my hand. She was patient, elegant in form, the colour of an ideal mouse, and inimitably small. Her faults were those of her race and sex; her virtues were her own. Farewell, and if forever——

Father Adam wept when he sold her to me; after I had sold her in my turn, I was tempted to follow his example; and being alone with a stage-driver and four or five agreeable young men, I did not hesitate to yield to my emotion.

MISCELLANEOUS ESSAYS

MISCELLANEOUS ESSAYS

ROADS*

(1873)

No amateur will deny that he can find more pleasure in a
single drawing, over which he can sit a whole quiet forenoon, and so gradually study himself into humour with the
artist, than he can ever extract from the dazzle and accumulation of incongruous impressions that send him, weary
and stupefied, out of some famous picture-gallery. But what
is thus admitted with regard to art is not extended to the
(so-called) natural beauties: no amount of excess in sublime
mountain outline or the graces of cultivated lowland can
do anything, it is supposed, to weaken or degrade the
palate. We are not at all sure, however, that moderation,
and a regimen tolerably austere, even in scenery, are not
healthful and strengthening to the taste; and that the best
school for a lover of nature is not to be found in one of
those countries where there is no stage effect—nothing
salient or sudden—but a quiet spirit of orderly and harmonious beauty pervades all the details, so that we can
patiently attend to each of the little touches that strike in
us, all of them together, the subdued note of the landscape.
It is in scenery such as this that we find ourselves in the
right temper to seek out small sequestered loveliness. The
constant recurrence of similar combinations of colour and
outline gradually forces upon us a sense of how the harmony has been built up, and we become familiar with
something of nature's mannerism. This is the true pleasure
of your 'rural voluptuary'—not to remain awe-stricken before a Mount Chimborazo;* not to sit deafened over the
big drum in the orchestra, but day by day to teach himself
some new beauty—to experience some new vague and
tranquil sensation that has before evaded him. It is not the
people who 'have pined and hungered after nature many
a year, in the great city pent,'* as Coleridge said in the
poem that made Charles Lamb so much ashamed of him-

self; it is not those who make the greatest progress in this intimacy with her, or who are most quick to see and have the greatest gusto to enjoy. In this, as in everything else, it is minute knowledge and long-continued loving industry that make the true dilettante. A man must have thought much over scenery before he begins fully to enjoy it. It is no youngling enthusiasm on hill-tops that can possess itself of the last essence of beauty. Probably most people's heads are growing bare before they can see all in a landscape that they have the capability of seeing; and, even then, it will be only for one little moment of consummation before the faculties are again on the decline, and they that look out of the windows begin to be darkened and restrained in sight. Thus the study of nature should be carried forward thoroughly and with system. Every gratification should be rolled long under the tongue, and we should be always eager to analyse and compare, in order that we may be able to give some plausible reason for our admirations. True, it is difficult to put even approximately into words the kind of feelings thus called into play. There is a dangerous vice inherent in any such intellectual refining upon vague sensation. The analysis of such satisfactions lends itself very readily to literary affectations; and we can all think of instances where it has shown itself apt to exercise a morbid influence, even upon an author's choice of language and the turn of his sentences. And yet there is much that makes the attempt attractive; for any expression, however imperfect, once given to a cherished feeling, seems a sort of legitimation of the pleasure we take in it. A common sentiment is one of those great goods that make life palatable and ever new. The knowledge that another has felt as we have felt, and seen things, even if they are little things, not much otherwise than we have seen them, will continue to the end to be one of life's choicest pleasures.

Let the reader, then, betake himself in the spirit we have recommended to some of the quieter kinds of English landscape. In those homely and placid agricultural districts, familiarity will bring into relief many things worthy of notice, and urge them pleasantly home to him by a sort of loving repetition; such as the wonderful life-giving speed of windmill sails above the stationary country; the occurrence and recurrence of the same church tower at the end of one long vista after another: and, conspicuous among these sources of quiet pleasure, the character and variety of the road itself, along which he takes his way. Not only near at hand, in the lithe contortions with which it adapts itself to the interchanges of level and slope, but far away also, when he sees a few hundred feet of it upheaved against a hill and shining in the afternoon sun, he will find it an object so changeful and enlivening that he can always pleasurably busy his mind about it. He may leave the riverside, or fall out of the way of villages, but the road he has always with him; and, in the true humour of observation, will find in that sufficient company. From its subtle windings and changes of level there arises a keen and continuous interest, that keeps the attention ever alert and cheerful. Every sensitive adjustment to the contour of the ground, every little dip and swerve, seems instinct with life and an exquisite sense of balance and beauty. The road rolls upon the easy slopes of the country, like a long ship in the hollows of the sea. The very margins of waste ground, as they trench a little farther on the beaten way, or recede again to the shelter of the hedge, have something of the same free delicacy of line—of the same swing and wilfulness. You might think for a whole summer's day (and not have thought it any nearer an end by evening) what concourse and succession of circumstances has produced the least of these deflections; and it is, perhaps, just in this that we should look for the secret of their interest. A footpath across a meadow—in all its human waywardness and unaccountability, in all the *grata protervitas** of its varying direction— will always be more to us than a railroad well engineered through a difficult country.* No reasoned sequence is thrust upon our attention: we seem to have slipped for one lawless little moment out of the iron rule of cause and effect; and so we revert at once to some of the pleasant old heresies of personification, always poetically orthodox, and attribute a sort of free will, an active and spontaneous life, to the white riband of road that lengthens out, and bends, and cunningly adapts itself to the inequalities of the land before our eyes. We remember, as we write, some miles of fine wide highway laid out with conscious æsthetic artifice through a broken and richly cultivated tract of country. It is said that the engineer had Hogarth's line of beauty in his mind as he laid them down. And the result is striking. One splendid satisfying sweep passes with easy transition into another, and there is nothing to trouble or dislocate the strong continuousness of the main line of the road. And yet there is something wanting. There is here no saving imperfection, none of those secondary curves and little trepidations of direction that carry, in natural roads, our curiosity actively along with them. One feels at once that this road has not grown like a natural road, but has been laboriously made to pattern; and that, while a model may be academically correct in outline, it will always be inanimate and cold. The traveller is also aware of a sympathy of mood between himself and the road he travels. We have all seen ways that have wandered into heavy sand near the sea-coast, and trail wearily over the dunes like a trodden serpent: here we too must plod forward at a dull, laborious pace; and so a sympathy is preserved between our frame of mind and the expression of the relaxed, heavy curves of the roadway. Such a phenomenon, indeed, our reason might perhaps resolve with a little trouble. We might reflect that the present road had been developed out of a track spontaneously followed by generations of primitive way-farers; and might see in its expression a testimony that those generations had been affected at the same ground, one after another, in the same manner as we are affected to-day. Or we might carry the reflection further, and remind ourselves that where the air is invigorating and the ground firm under the traveller's foot, his eye is quick to take advantage of small undulations, and he will turn carelessly aside from the direct way wherever there is anything beautiful to examine or some promise of a wider view; so that even a bush of wild roses may permanently bias and deform the

straight path over the meadow; whereas, where the soil is
heavy, one is preoccupied with the labour of mere progression, and goes with a bowed head heavily and unobservant-
ly forward. Reason, however, will not carry us the whole
way; for the sentiment often recurs in situations where it is
very hard to imagine any possible explanation; and indeed,
if we drive briskly along a good, well-made road in an open
vehicle, we shall experience this sympathy almost at its
fullest. We feel the sharp settle of the springs at some
curiously twisted corner; after a steep ascent, the fresh air
dances in our faces as we rattle precipitately down the other
side, and we find it difficult to avoid attributing something
headlong, a sort of *abandon*, to the road itself.

The mere winding of that path is enough to enliven a
long day's walk in even a commonplace or dreary country-
side. Something that we have seen from miles back, upon
an eminence, is so long hid from us, as we wander through
folded valleys or among woods, that our expectation of
seeing it again is sharpened into a violent appetite, and as
we draw nearer we impatiently quicken our steps and turn
every corner with a beating heart. It is through these
prolongations of expectancy, this succession of one hope to
another, that we live out long seasons of pleasure in a few
hours' walk. It is in following these capricious sinuosities
that we learn, only bit by bit and through one coquettish
reticence after another, much as we learn the heart of a
friend, the whole loveliness of the country. This disposition
always preserves something new to be seen, and takes us,
like a careful cicerone, to many different points of distant
view before it allows us finally to approach the hoped-for
destination.

In its connection with the traffic, and whole friendly
intercourse with the country, there is something very pleasant in that succession of saunterers and brisk and business-
like passers-by, that peoples our ways and helps to build up
what Walt Whitman calls 'the cheerful voice of the public
road, the gay, fresh sentiment of the road.'* But out of the
great network of ways that binds all life together from the
hill-farm to the city, there is something individual to most,

and, on the whole, nearly as much choice on the score of company as on the score of beauty or easy travel. On some we are never long without the sound of wheels, and folk pass us by so thickly that we lose the sense of their number. But on others, about little-frequented districts, a meeting is an affair of moment; we have the sight far off of some one coming towards us, the growing definiteness of the person, and then the brief passage and salutation, and the road left empty in front of us for perhaps a great while to come. Such encounters have a wistful interest that can hardly be understood by the dweller in places more populous. We remember standing beside a countryman once, in the mouth of a quiet by-street in a city that was more than ordinarily crowded and bustling; he seemed stunned and bewildered by the continual passage of different faces; and after a long pause, during which he appeared to search for some suitable expression, he said timidly that there seemed to be a *great deal of meeting thereabouts*. The phrase is significant. It is the expression of town-life in the language of the long, solitary country highways. A meeting of one with one was what this man had been used to in the pastoral uplands from which he came; and the concourse of the streets was in his eyes only an extraordinary multiplication of such 'meetings.'

And now we come to that last and most subtle quality of all, to that sense of prospect, of outlook, that is brought so powerfully to our minds by a road. In real nature as well as in old landscapes, beneath that impartial daylight in which a whole variegated plain is plunged and saturated, the line of the road leads the eye forth with the vague sense of desire up to the green limit of the horizon. Travel is brought home to us, and we visit in spirit every grove and hamlet that tempts us in the distance. *Sehnsucht*—the passion for what is ever beyond—is livingly expressed in that white riband of possible travel that severs the uneven country; not a ploughman following his plough up the shining furrow, not the blue smoke of any cottage in a hollow, but is brought to us with a sense of nearness and attainability by this wavering line of junction. There is a passionate paragraph in *Werther** that strikes the very key. 'When I came hither,' he writes, 'how the beautiful valley invited me on every side, as I gazed down into it from the hill-top! There the wood—ah, that I might mingle in its shadows! there the mountain summits—ah, that I might look down from them over the broad country! the interlinked hills! the secret valleys! O, to lose myself among their mysteries! I hurried into the midst, and came back without finding aught I hoped for. Alas! the distance is like the future. A vast whole lies in the twilight before our spirit; sight and feeling alike plunge and lose themselves in the prospect, and we yearn to surrender our whole being, and let it be filled full with all the rapture of one single glorious sensation; and alas! when we hasten to the fruition, when *there* is changed to *here*, all is afterwards as it was before, and we stand in our indigent and cramped estate, and our soul thirsts after a still ebbing elixir.' It is to this wandering and uneasy spirit of anticipation that roads minister. Every little vista, every little glimpse that we have of what lies before us, gives the impatient imagination rein, so that it can outstrip the body and already plunge into the shadow of the woods, and overlook from the hilltop the plain beyond it, and wander in the windings of the valleys that are still far in front. The road is already there—we shall not be long behind. It is as if we were marching with the rear of a great army, and, from far before, heard the acclamation of the people as the vanguard entered some friendly and jubilant city. Would not every man, through all the long miles of march, feel as if he also were within the gates?

ORDERED SOUTH*

By a curious irony of fate, the places to which we are sent
when health deserts us are often singularly beautiful. Often,
too, they are places we have visited in former years, or seen
briefly in passing by, and kept ever afterwards in pious
memory; and we please ourselves with the fancy that we
shall repeat many vivid and pleasurable sensations, and take
up again the thread of our enjoyment in the same spirit as
we let it fall. We shall now have an opportunity of finishing
many pleasant excursions, interrupted of yore before our
curiosity was fully satisfied. It may be that we have kept in
mind, during all these years, the recollection of some valley
into which we have just looked down for a moment before
we lost sight of it in the disorder of the hills; it may be
that we have lain awake at night, and agreeably tantalised
ourselves with the thought of corners we had never turned,
or summits we had all but climbed; we shall now be able,
as we tell ourselves, to complete all these unfinished pleasures, and pass beyond the barriers that confined our
recollections.

The promise is so great, and we are all so easily led away
when hope and memory are both in one story, that I dare
say the sick man is not very inconsolable when he receives
sentence of banishment, and is inclined to regard his ill-
health as not the least fortunate accident of his life. Nor is
he immediately undeceived. The stir and speed of the
journey, and the restlessness that goes to bed with him as
he tries to sleep between two days of noisy progress, fever
him, and stimulate his dull nerves into something of their
old quickness and sensibility. And so he can enjoy the faint
autumnal splendour of the landscape, as he sees hill and
plain, vineyard and forest, clad in one wonderful glory of
fairy gold, which the first great winds of winter will trans-
mute, as in the fable, into withered leaves. And so too he
can enjoy the admirable brevity and simplicity of such little
glimpses of country and country ways as flash upon him

through the windows of the train; little glimpses that have a character all their own; sights seen as a travelling swallow might see them from the wing, or Iris as she went abroad over the land on some Olympian errand. Here and there, indeed, a few children huzzah and wave their hands to the express; but for the most part, it is an interruption too brief and isolated to attract much notice; the sheep do not cease from browsing; a girl sits balanced on the projecting tiller of a canal boat, so precariously that it seems as if a fly or the splash of a leaping fish would be enough to overthrow the dainty equilibrium, and yet all these hundreds of tons of coal and wood and iron have been precipitated roaring past her very ear, and there is not a start, not a tremor, not a turn of the averted head, to indicate that she has been even conscious of its passage. Herein, I think, lies the chief attraction of railway travel. The speed is so easy, and the train disturbs so little the scenes through which it takes us, that our heart becomes full of the placidity and stillness of the country; and while the body is borne forward in the flying chain of carriages, the thoughts alight, as the humour moves them, at unfrequented stations; they make haste up the poplar alley that leads toward the town; they are left behind with the signalman as, shading his eyes with his hands, he watches the long train sweep away into the golden distance.

Moreover, there is still before the invalid the shock of wonder and delight with which he will learn that he has passed the indefinable line that separates South from North. And this is an uncertain moment; for sometimes the consciousness is forced upon him early, on the occasion of some slight association, a colour, a flower, or a scent; and sometimes not until, one fine morning, he wakes up with the southern sunshine peeping through the *persiennes*,* and the southern patois confusedly audible below the windows. Whether it come early or late, however, this pleasure will not end with the anticipation, as do so many others of the same family. It will leave him wider awake than it found him, and give a new significance to all he may see for many days to come. There is something in the mere name of the

South that carries enthusiasm along with it. At the sound of the word, he pricks up his ears; he becomes as anxious to seek out beauties and to get by heart the permanent lines and character of the landscape, as if he had been told that it was all his own—an estate out of which he had been kept unjustly, and which he was now to receive in free and full possession. Even those who have never been there before feel as if they had been; and everybody goes comparing, and seeking for the familiar, and finding it with such ecstasies of recognition, that one would think they were coming home after a weary absence, instead of travelling hourly farther abroad.

It is only after he is fairly arrived and settled down in his chosen corner, that the invalid begins to understand the change that has befallen him. Everything about him is as he had remembered, or as he had anticipated. Here, at his feet, under his eyes, are the olive gardens and the blue sea. Nothing can change the eternal magnificence of form of the naked Alps behind Mentone; nothing, not even the crude curves of the railway, can utterly deform the suavity of contour of one bay after another along the whole reach of the Riviera. And of all this, he has only a cold head-knowledge that is divorced from enjoyment. He recognises with his intelligence that this thing and that thing is beautiful, while in his heart of hearts he has to confess that it is not beautiful for him. It is in vain that he spurs his discouraged spirit; in vain that he chooses out points of view, and stands there, looking with all his eyes, and waiting for some return of the pleasure that he remembers in other days, as the sick folk may have awaited the coming of the angel at the pool of Bethesda.* He is like an enthusiast leading about with him a stolid, indifferent tourist. There is some one by who is out of sympathy with the scene, and is not moved up to the measure of the occasion; and that some one is himself. The world is disenchanted for him. He seems to himself to touch things with muffled hands, and to see them through a veil. His life becomes a palsied fumbling after notes that are silent when he has found and struck them. He cannot recognise that this phlegmatic and unimpressionable body with which he now goes burthened, is the same that he knew heretofore so quick and delicate and alive.

He is tempted to lay the blame on the very softness and amenity of the climate, and to fancy that in the rigours of the winter at home, these dead emotions would revive and flourish. A longing for the brightness and silence of fallen snow seizes him at such times. He is homesick for the hale rough weather; for the tracery of the frost upon his window-panes at morning, the reluctant descent of the first flakes, and the white roofs relieved against the sombre sky. And yet the stuff of which these yearnings are made, is of the flimsiest: if but the thermometer fall a little below its ordinary Mediterranean level, or a wind come down from the snow-clad Alps behind, the spirit of his fancies changes upon the instant, and many a doleful vignette of the grim wintry streets at home returns to him, and begins to haunt his memory. The hopeless, huddled attitude of tramps in doorways; the flinching gait of barefoot children on the icy pavement; the sheen of the rainy streets towards afternoon; the meagre anatomy of the poor defined by the clinging of wet garments; the high canorous note of the North-easter on days when the very houses seem to stiffen with cold: these, and such as these, crowd back upon him, and mockingly substitute themselves for the fanciful winter scenes with which he had pleased himself a while before. He cannot be glad enough that he is where he is. If only the others could be there also; if only those tramps could lie down for a little in the sunshine, and those children warm their feet, this once, upon a kindlier earth; if only there were no cold anywhere, and no nakedness, and no hunger; if only it were as well with all men as it is with him!

For it is not altogether ill with the invalid, after all. If it is only rarely that anything penetrates vividly into his numbed spirit, yet, when anything does, it brings with it a joy that is all the more poignant for its very rarity. There is something pathetic in these occasional returns of a glad activity of heart. In his lowest hours he will be stirred and awakened by many such; and they will spring perhaps from very trivial sources; as a friend once said to me, the 'spirit of delight' comes often on small wings. For the pleasure that we take in beautiful nature is essentially capricious. It comes sometimes when we least look for it; and sometimes, when we expect it most certainly, it leaves us to gape joylessly for days together, in the very home-land of the beautiful. We may have passed a place a thousand times and one; and on the thousand and second it will be transfigured, and stand forth in a certain splendour of reality from the dull circle of surroundings; so that we see it 'with a child's first pleasure,' as Wordsworth saw the daffodils by the lake side. And if this falls out capriciously with the healthy, how much more so with the invalid. Some day he will find his first violet, and be lost in pleasant wonder, by what alchemy the cold earth of the clods, and the vapid air and rain, can be transmuted into colour so rich and odour so touchingly sweet. Or perhaps he may see a group of washerwomen relieved, on a spit of shingle, against the blue sea, or a meeting of flower-gatherers in the tempered daylight of an olive-garden; and something significant or monumental in the grouping, something in the harmony of faint colour that is always characteristic of the dress of these southern women, will come home to him unexpectedly, and awake in him that satisfaction with which we tell ourselves that we are the richer by one more beautiful experience. Or it may be something even slighter: as when the opulence of the sunshine, which somehow gets lost and fails to produce its effect on the large scale, is suddenly revealed to him by the chance isolation—as he changes the position of his sunshade—of a yard or two of roadway with its stones and weeds. And then, there is no end to the infinite variety of the olive-yards themselves. Even the colour is indeterminate and continually shifting: now you would say it was green, now gray, now blue; now tree stands above tree, like 'cloud on cloud,' massed into filmy indistinctness; and now, at the wind's will, the whole sea of foliage is shaken and broken up with little momentary silverings and shadows. But every one sees the world in his own way. To some the glad moment may have arrived on other provocations; and their recollection may be most vivid of the stately gait of women carrying burthens on their heads; of tropical effects, with canes and naked rock and sunlight; of the relief of cypresses; of the troubled, busy-looking groups of sea-pines, that seem always as if they were being wielded and swept together by a whirlwind; of the air coming, laden with virginal perfumes, over the myrtles and the scented underwood; of the empurpled hills standing up, solemn and sharp, out of the green-gold air of the east at evening.

There go many elements, without doubt, to the making of one such moment of intense perception; and it is on the happy agreement of these many elements, on the harmonious vibration of many nerves, that the whole delight of the moment must depend. Who can forget how, when he has chanced upon some attitude of complete restfulness, after long uneasy rolling to and fro on grass or heather, the whole fashion of the landscape has been changed for him, as though the sun had just broken forth, or a great artist had only then completed, by some cunning touch, the composition of the picture? And not only a change of posture—a snatch of perfume, the sudden singing of a bird, the freshness of some pulse of air from an invisible sea, the light shadow of a travelling cloud, the merest nothing that sends a little shiver along the most infinitesimal nerve of a man's body—not one of the least of these but has a hand somehow in the general effect, and brings some refinement of its own into the character of the pleasure we feel.

And if the external conditions are thus varied and subtle, even more so are those within our own bodies. No man can find out the world, says Solomon, from beginning to end, because the world is in his heart; and so it is impossible for any of us to understand, from beginning to end, that agreement of harmonious circumstances that creates in us the highest pleasure of admiration, precisely because some of these circumstances are hidden from us for ever in the constitution of our own bodies. After we have reckoned up all that we can see or hear or feel, there still remains to be taken into account some sensibility more delicate than usual in the nerves affected, or some exquisite refinement in the architecture of the brain, which is indeed to the sense of the beautiful as the eye or the ear to the sense of hearing or sight. We admire splendid views and great pictures; and yet what is truly admirable is rather the mind within us, that gathers together these scattered details for its delight, and makes out of certain colours, certain distributions of graduated light and darkness, that intelligible whole which alone we call a picture or a view. Hazlitt, relating in one of his essays* how he went on foot from one great man's house to another's in search of works of art, begins suddenly to triumph over these noble and wealthy owners, because he was more capable of enjoying their costly possessions than they were; because they had paid the money and he had received the pleasure. And the occasion is a fair one for self-complacency. While the one man was working to be able to buy the picture, the other was working to be able to enjoy the picture. An inherited aptitude will have been diligently improved in either case; only the one man has made for himself a fortune, and the other has made for himself a living spirit. It is a fair occasion for self-complacency, I repeat, when the event shows a man to have chosen the better part, and laid out his life more wisely, in the long run, than those who have credit for most wisdom. And yet even this is not a good unmixed; and like all other possessions, although in a less degree, the possession of a brain that has been thus improved and cultivated, and made into the prime organ of a man's enjoyment, brings with it certain inevitable cares and disappointments. The happiness of such an one comes to depend greatly upon those fine shades of sensation that heighten and harmonise the coarser elements of beauty. And thus a degree of nervous prostration, that to other men would be hardly disagreeable, is enough to overthrow for him the whole fabric of his life, to take, except at rare moments, the edge off his pleasures, and to meet him wherever he goes with failure, and the sense of want, and disenchantment of the world and life.

It is not in such numbness of spirit only that the life of the invalid resembles a premature old age. Those excursions that he had promised himself to finish, prove too long or too arduous for his feeble body; and the barrier-hills are as impassable as ever. Many a white town that sits far out on the promontory, many a comely fold of wood on the mountain-side, beckons and allures his imagination day after day, and is yet as inaccessible to his feet as the clefts and gorges of the clouds. The sense of distance grows upon him wonderfully; and after some feverish efforts and the fretful uneasiness of the first few days, he falls contentedly in with the restrictions of his weakness. His narrow round becomes pleasant and familiar to him as the cell to a contented prisoner. Just as he has fallen already out of the mid- race of active life, he now falls out of the little eddy that circulates in the shallow waters of the sanatorium. He sees the country people come and go about their every-day affairs, the foreigners stream out in goodly pleasure parties; the stir of man's activity is all about him, as he suns himself inertly in some sheltered corner; and he looks on with a patriarchal impersonality of interest, such as a man may feel when he pictures to himself the fortunes of his remote descendants, or the robust old age of the oak he has planted overnight.

In this falling aside, in this quietude and desertion of other men, there is no inharmonious prelude to the last quietude and desertion of the grave; in this dulness of the senses there is a gentle preparation for the final insensibility of death. And to him the idea of mortality comes in a shape less violent and harsh than is its wont, less as an abrupt catastrophe than as a thing of infinitesimal gradation, and the last step on a long decline of way. As we turn to and fro in bed, and every moment the movements grow feebler and smaller and the attitude more restful and easy, until sleep overtakes us at a stride and we move no more, so desire after desire leaves him; day by day his strength decreases, and the circle of his activity grows even nar- rower; and he feels, if he is to be thus tenderly weaned from the passion of life, thus gradually inducted into the slumber of death, that when at last the end comes, it will come quietly and fitly. If anything is to reconcile poor spirits to the coming of the last enemy, surely it should be such a mild approach as this; not to hale us forth with violence, but to persuade us from a place we have no further pleasure in. It is not so much, indeed, death that approaches as life that withdraws and withers up from round about him. He has outlived his own usefulness, and almost his own enjoyment; and if there is to be no recovery; if never again will he be young and strong and passionate, if the actual present shall be to him always like a thing read in a book or remembered out of the far-away past; if, in fact, this be veritably nightfall, he will not wish greatly for the continuance of a twilight that only strains and disappoints the eyes, but steadfastly await the perfect darkness. He will pray for Medea when she comes, let her either rejuvenate or slay.

And yet the ties that still attach him to the world are many and kindly. The sight of children has a significance for him such as it may have for the aged also, but not for others. If he has been used to feel humanely, and to look upon life somewhat more widely than from the narrow loophole of personal pleasure and advancement, it is strange how small a portion of his thoughts will be changed or embittered by this proximity of death. He knows that already, in English counties, the sower follows the ploughman up the face of the field, and the rooks follow the sower; and he knows also that he may not live to go home again and see the corn spring and ripen, and be cut down at last, and brought home with gladness. And yet the future of this harvest, the continuance of drought or the coming of rain unseasonably, touch him as sensibly as ever. For he has long been used to wait with interest the issue of events in which his own concern was nothing; and to be joyful in a plenty, and sorrowful for a famine, that did not increase or diminish, by one half-loaf, the equable sufficiency of his own supply. Thus there remain unaltered all the disinterested hopes for mankind and a better future which have been the solace and inspiration of his life. These he has set beyond the reach of any fate that only menaces himself; and it makes small difference whether he die five thousand years, or five thousand and fifty years, before the good epoch for which he faithfully labours. He has not deceived himself; he has known from the beginning that he followed the pillar of fire and cloud, only to perish himself in the wilderness, and that it was reserved for others to enter joyfully into possession of the land. And so, as everything grows grayer and quieter about him, and slopes towards extinction, these unfaded visions accompany his sad decline, and follow him, with friendly voices and hopeful words, into the very vestibule of death. The desire of love or of fame scarcely moved him, in his days of health, more strongly than these generous aspirations move him now; and so life is carried forward beyond life, and a vista kept open for the eyes of hope, even when his hands grope already on the face of the impassable.

Lastly, he is bound tenderly to life by the thought of his friends; or shall we not say rather, that by their thought for him, by their unchangeable solicitude and love, he remains woven into the very stuff of life, beyond the power of bodily dissolution to undo? In a thousand ways will he survive and be perpetuated. Much of Etienne de la Boetie* survived during all the years in which Montaigne continued to converse with him on the pages of the ever-delightful essays. Much of what was truly Goethe was dead already when he revisited places that knew him no more, and found no better consolation than the promise of his own verses, that soon he too would be at rest. Indeed, when we think of what it is that we most seek and cherish, and find most pride and pleasure in calling ours, it will sometimes seem to us as if our friends, at our decease, would suffer loss more truly than ourselves. As a monarch who should care more for the outlying colonies he knows on the map or through the report of his vicegerents, than for the trunk of his empire under his eyes at home, are we not more concerned about the shadowy life that we have in the hearts of others, and that portion in their thoughts and fancies which, in a certain far-away sense, belongs to us, than about the real knot of our identity—that central metropolis of self, of which alone we are immediately aware—or the diligent service of arteries and veins and infinitesimal activity of ganglia, which we know (as we know a proposition in Euclid) to be the source and substance of the whole? At the death of every one whom we love, some fair and honourable portion of our existence falls away, and we are dislodged from one of these dear provinces; and they are not, perhaps, the most fortunate who survive a long series of such impoverishments, till their life and influence narrow gradually into the meagre limit of their own spirits, and death, when he comes at last, can destroy them at one blow.

NOTE.* To this essay I must in honesty append a word or two of qualification; for this is one of the points on which a slightly greater age teaches us a slightly different wisdom:

A youth delights in generalities, and keeps loose from particular obligations; he jogs on the footpath way, himself pursuing butterflies, but courteously lending his applause to the advance of the human species and the coming of the kingdom of justice and love. As he grows older, he begins to think more narrowly of man's action in the general, and perhaps more arrogantly of his own in the particular. He has not that same unspeakable trust in what he would have done had he been spared, seeing finally that that would have been little; but he has a far higher notion of the blank that he will make by dying. A young man feels himself one too many in the world; his is a painful situation; he has no calling; no obvious utility; no ties, but to his parents, and these he is sure to disregard. I do not think that a proper allowance has been made for this true cause of suffering in youth; but by the mere fact of a prolonged existence, we outgrow either the fact or else the feeling. Either we become so callously accustomed to our own useless figure in the world, or else—and this, thank God, in the majority of cases—we so collect about us the interest or the love of our fellows, so multiply our effective part in the affairs of life, that we need to entertain no longer the question of our right to be.

And so in the majority of cases, a man who fancies himself dying, will get cold comfort from the very youthful view expressed in this essay. He, as a living man, has some to help, some to love, some to correct; it may be, some to punish. These duties cling, not upon humanity, but upon the man himself. It is he, not another, who is one woman's son and a second woman's husband and a third woman's father. That life which began so small, has now grown, with a myriad filaments, into the lives of others. It is not indispensable; another will take the place and shoulder the discharged responsibility; but the better the man and the nobler his purposes, the more will he be tempted to regret the extinction of his powers and the deletion of his personality. To have lived a generation, is not only to have grown at home in that perplexing medium, but to have assumed innumerable duties. To die at such an age, has, for all but the entirely base, something of the air of a betrayal. A man does not only reflect upon what he might have done in a future that is never to be his; but beholding himself so early a deserter from the fight, he eats his heart for the good he might have done already. To have been so useless and now to lose all hope of being useful any more—there it is that death and memory assail him. And even if mankind shall go on, founding heroic cities, practising heroic virtues, rising steadily from strength to strength; even if his work shall be fulfilled, his friends consoled, his wife remarried by a better than he; how shall this alter, in one jot, his estimation of a career which was his only business in this world, which was so fitfully pursued, and which is now so ineffectively to end?

WALKING TOURS*

It must not be imagined that a walking tour, as some would have us fancy, is merely a better or worse way of seeing the country. There are many ways of seeing landscape quite as good; and none more vivid, in spite of canting dilettantes, than from a railway train. But landscape on a walking tour is quite accessory. He who is indeed of the brotherhood does not voyage in quest of the picturesque, but of certain jolly humours—of the hope and spirit with which the march begins at morning, and the peace and spiritual repletion of the evening's rest. He cannot tell whether he puts his knapsack on, or takes it off, with more delight. The excitement of the departure puts him in key for that of the arrival. Whatever he does is not only a reward in itself, but will be further rewarded in the sequel; and so pleasure leads on to pleasure in an endless chain. It is this that so few can understand; they will either be always lounging or always at five miles an hour; they do not play off the one against the other, prepare all day for the evening, and all evening for the next day. And, above all, it is here that your overwalker fails of comprehension. His heart rises against those who drink their curaçoa in liqueur glasses, when he himself can swill it in a brown John. He will not believe that the flavour is more delicate in the smaller dose. He will not believe that to walk this unconscionable distance is merely to stupefy and brutalise himself, and come to his inn, at night, with a sort of frost on his five wits, and a starless night of darkness in his spirit. Not for him the mild luminous evening of the temperate walker! He has nothing left of man but a physical need for bedtime and a double nightcap; and even his pipe, if he be a smoker, will be savourless and disenchanted. It is the fate of such an one to take twice as much trouble as is needed to obtain happiness, and miss the happiness in the end; he is the man of the proverb, in short, who goes further and fares worse.

Now, to be properly enjoyed, a walking tour should be gone upon alone. If you go in a company, or even in pairs, it is no longer a walking tour in anything but name; it is something else and more in the nature of a picnic. A walking tour should be gone upon alone, because freedom is of the essence; because you should be able to stop and go on, and follow this way or that, as the freak takes you; and because you must have your own pace, and neither trot alongside a champion walker, nor mince in time with a girl. And then you must be open to all impressions and let your thoughts take colour from what you see. You should be as a pipe for any wind to play upon. 'I cannot see the wit,' says Hazlitt, 'of walking and talking at the same time. When I am in the country I wish to vegetate like the country,'*—which is the gist of all that can be said upon the matter. There should be no cackle of voices at your elbow, to jar on the meditative silence of the morning. And so long as a man is reasoning he cannot surrender himself to that fine intoxication that comes of much motion in the open air, that begins in a sort of dazzle and sluggishness of the brain, and ends in a peace that passes comprehension.

During the first day or so of any tour there are moments of bitterness, when the traveller feels more than coldly towards his knapsack, when he is half in a mind to throw it bodily over the hedge and, like Christian on a similar occasion, 'give three leaps and go on singing.'* And yet it soon acquires a property of easiness. It becomes magnetic; the spirit of the journey enters into it. And no sooner have you passed the straps over your shoulder than the lees of sleep are cleared from you, you pull yourself together with a shake, and fall at once into your stride. And surely, of all possible moods, this, in which a man takes the road, is the best. Of course, if he *will* keep thinking of his anxieties, if he *will* open the merchant Abudah's chest and walk arm-in-arm with the hag—why, wherever he is, and whether he walk fast or slow, the chances are that he will not be happy. And so much the more shame to himself! There are perhaps thirty men setting forth at that same hour, and I would lay a large wager there is not another dull face among the thirty. It would be a fine thing to follow, in a coat of darkness, one after another of these wayfarers, some summer morning, for the first few miles upon the road. This one, who walks fast, with a keen look in his eyes, is all concentrated in his own mind; he is up at his loom, weaving and weaving, to set the landscape to words. This one peers about, as he goes, among the grasses; he waits by the canal to watch the dragon-flies; he leans on the gate of the pasture, and cannot look enough upon the complacent kine. And here comes another, talking, laughing, and gesticulating to himself. His face changes from time to time, as indignation flashes from his eyes or anger clouds his forehead. He is composing articles, delivering orations, and conducting the most impassioned interviews by the way. A little farther on, and it is as like as not he will begin to sing. And well for him, supposing him to be no great master in that art, if he stumble across no stolid peasant at a corner; for on such an occasion, I scarcely know which is the more troubled, or whether it is worse to suffer the confusion of your troubadour, or the unfeigned alarm of your clown. A sedentary population, accustomed, besides, to the strange mechanical bearing of the common tramp, can in no wise explain to itself the gaiety of these passers-by. I knew one man who was arrested as a runaway lunatic, because, although a full-grown person with a red beard, he skipped as he went like a child. And you would be astonished if I were to tell you all the grave and learned heads who have confessed to me that, when on walking tours, they sang—and sang very ill—and had a pair of red ears when, as described above, the inauspicious peasant plumped into their arms from round a corner. And here, lest you should think I am exaggerating, is Hazlitt's own confession, from his essay *On Going a Journey*, which is so good that there should be a tax levied on all who have not read it:

'Give me the clear blue sky over my head,' says he, 'and the green turf beneath my feet, a winding road before me, and a three hours' march to dinner—and then to thinking!

It is hard if I cannot start some game on these lone heaths. I laugh, I run, I leap, I sing for joy.'

Bravo! After that adventure of my friend with the policeman, you would not have cared, would you, to publish that in the first person? But we have no bravery nowadays, and, even in books, must all pretend to be as dull and foolish as our neighbours. It was not so with Hazlitt. And notice how learned he is (as, indeed, throughout the essay) in the theory of walking tours. He is none of your athletic men in purple stockings, who walk their fifty miles a day: three hours' march is his ideal. And then he must have a winding road, the epicure!

Yet there is one thing I object to in these words of his, one thing in the great master's practice that seems to me not wholly wise. I do not approve of that leaping and running. Both of these hurry the respiration; they both shake up the brain out of its glorious open-air confusion; and they both break the pace. Uneven walking is not so agreeable to the body, and it distracts and irritates the mind. Whereas, when once you have fallen into an equable stride, it requires no conscious thought from you to keep it up, and yet it prevents you from thinking earnestly of anything else. Like knitting, like the work of a copying clerk, it gradually neutralises and sets to sleep the serious activity of the mind. We can think of this or that, lightly and laughingly, as a child thinks, or as we think in a morning doze; we can make puns or puzzle out acrostics, and trifle in a thousand ways with words and rhymes; but when it comes to honest work, when we come to gather ourselves together for an effort, we may sound the trumpet as loud and long as we please; the great barons of the mind will not rally to the standard, but sit, each one, at home, warming his hands over his own fire and brooding on his own private thought!

In the course of a day's walk, you see, there is much variance in the mood. From the exhilaration of the start, to the happy phlegm of the arrival, the change is certainly great. As the day goes on, the traveller moves from the one extreme towards the other. He becomes more and more incorporated with the material landscape, and the open-air drunkenness grows upon him with great strides, until he posts along the road, and sees everything about him, as in a cheerful dream. The first is certainly brighter, but the second stage is the more peaceful. A man does not make so many articles towards the end, nor does he laugh aloud; but the purely animal pleasures, the sense of physical well-being, the delight of every inhalation, of every time the muscles tighten down the thigh, console him for the absence of the others, and bring him to his destination still content.

Nor must I forget to say a word on bivouacs. You come to a milestone on a hill, or some place where deep ways meet under trees; and off goes the knapsack, and down you sit to smoke a pipe in the shade. You sink into yourself, and the birds come round and look at you; and your smoke dissipates upon the afternoon under the blue dome of heaven; and the sun lies warm upon your feet, and the cool air visits your neck and turns aside your open shirt. If you are not happy, you must have an evil conscience. You may dally as long as you like by the roadside. It is almost as if the millennium were arrived, when we shall throw our clocks and watches over the housetop, and remember time and seasons no more. Not to keep hours for a lifetime is, I was going to say, to live for ever. You have no idea, unless you have tried it, how endlessly long is a summer's day, that you measure out only by hunger, and bring to an end only when you are drowsy. I know a village where there are hardly any clocks, where no one knows more of the days of the week than by a sort of instinct for the fête on Sundays, and where only one person can tell you the day of the month, and she is generally wrong; and if people were aware how slow Time journeyed in that village, and what armfuls of spare hours he gives, over and above the bargain, to its wise inhabitants, I believe there would be a stampede out of London, Liverpool, Paris, and a variety of large towns, where the clocks lose their heads, and shake the hours out each one faster than the other, as though they were all in a wager. And all these foolish pilgrims would each bring his own misery along with him, in a watch-pocket! It is to be noticed, there were no clocks and watches in the much-vaunted days before the flood. It follows, of course, there were no appointments, and punctuality was not yet thought upon. 'Though ye take from a covetous man all his treasure,' says Milton, 'he has yet one jewel left; ye cannot deprive him of his covetousness.'* And so I would say of a modern man of business, you may do what you will for him, put him in Eden, give him the elixir of life—he has still a flaw at heart, he still has his business habits. Now, there is no time when business habits are more mitigated than on a walking tour. And so during these halts, as I say, you will feel almost free.

But it is at night, and after dinner, that the best hour comes. There are no such pipes to be smoked as those that follow a good day's march; the flavour of the tobacco is a thing to be remembered, it is so dry and aromatic, so full and so fine. If you wind up the evening with grog, you will own there was never such grog; at every sip a jocund tranquillity spreads about your limbs, and sits easily in your heart. If you read a book—and you will never do so save by fits and starts—you find the language strangely racy and harmonious; words take a new meaning; single sentences possess the ear for half an hour together; and the writer endears himself to you, at every page, by the nicest coincidence of sentiment. It seems as if it were a book you had written yourself in a dream. To all we have read on such occasions we look back with special favour. 'It was on the 10th of April, 1798,' says Hazlitt, with amorous precision, 'that I sat down to a volume of the new *Héloïse*,* at the Inn at Llangollen, over a bottle of sherry and a cold chicken.' I should wish to quote more, for though we are mighty fine fellows nowadays, we cannot write like Hazlitt. And, talking of that, a volume of Hazlitt's essays would be a capital pocket-book on such a journey; so would a volume of Heine's songs; and for *Tristram Shandy* I can pledge a fair experience.

If the evening be fine and warm, there is nothing better in life than to lounge before the inn door in the sunset, or lean over the parapet of the bridge, to watch the weeds and the quick fishes. It is then, if ever, that you taste Joviality to the full significance of that audacious word. Your muscles are so agreeably slack, you feel so clean and so strong and so idle, that whether you move or sit still, whatever you do is done with pride and a kingly sort of pleasure. You fall in talk with any one, wise or foolish, drunk or sober. And it seems as if a hot walk purged you, more than of anything else, of all narrowness and pride, and left curiosity to play its part freely, as in a child or a man of science. You lay aside all your own hobbies, to watch provincial humours develop themselves before you, now as a laughable farce, and now grave and beautiful like an old tale.

Or perhaps you are left to your own company for the night, and surly weather imprisons you by the fire. You may remember how Burns, numbering past pleasures, dwells upon the hours when he has been 'happy thinking.'* It is a phrase that may well perplex a poor modern, girt about on every side by clocks and chimes, and haunted, even at night, by flaming dial-plates. For we were all so busy, and have so many far-off projects to realise, and castles in the fire to turn into solid habitable mansions on a gravel soil, that we can find no time for pleasure trips into the Land of Thought and among the Hills of Vanity. Changed times, indeed, when we must sit all night, beside the fire, with folded hands; and a changed world for most of us, when we find we can pass the hours without discontent, and be happy thinking. We are in such haste to be doing, to be writing, to be gathering gear, to make our voice audible a moment in the derisive silence of eternity, that we forget that one thing, of which these are but the parts—namely, to live. We fall in love, we drink hard, we run to and fro upon the earth like frightened sheep. And now you are to ask yourself if, when all is done, you would not have been better to sit by the fire at home and be happy thinking. To sit still and contemplate—to remember the faces of women without desire, to be pleased by the great deeds of men without envy, to be everything and everywhere in sympathy, and yet content to remain where and what you are—is not this to know both wisdom and virtue, and to dwell with happiness? After all, it is not they who carry flags, but they who look upon it from a private chamber, who have the fun of the procession. And once you are at that, you are in the very humour of all social heresy. It is no time for shuffling, or for big, empty words. If you ask yourself what you mean by fame, riches, or learning, the answer is far to seek; and you go back into that kingdom of light imaginations, which seem so vain in the eyes of Philistines perspiring after wealth, and so momentous to those who are stricken with the disproportions of the world, and, in the face of the gigantic stars, cannot stop to split differences between two degrees of the infinitesimally small, such as a tobacco-pipe or the Roman Empire, a million of money or a fiddlestick's end.

You lean from the window, your last pipe reeking whitely into the darkness, your body full of delicious pains, your mind enthroned in the seventh circle of content; when suddenly the moon changes, the weathercock goes about, and you ask yourself one question more: whether, for the interval, you have been the wisest philosopher or the most egregious of donkeys? Human experience is not yet able to reply; but at least you have had a fine moment, and looked down upon all the kingdoms of the earth. And whether it was wise or foolish, to-morrow's travel will carry you, body and mind, into some different parish of the infinite.

MEMORIES OF FONTAINEBLEAU

FOREST NOTES*

(1875–6)

ON THE PLAIN

Perhaps the reader knows already the aspect of the great levels of the Gâtinais, where they border with the wooded hills of Fontainebleau. Here and there a few grey rocks creep out of the forest as if to sun themselves. Here and there a few apple-trees stand together on a knoll. The quaint, undignified tartan of a myriad small fields dies out into the distance; the strips blend and disappear; and the dead flat lies forth open and empty, with no accident save perhaps a thin line of trees or faint church spire against the sky. Solemn and vast at all times, in spite of pettiness in the near details, the impression becomes more solemn and vast towards evening. The sun goes down, a swollen orange, as it were into the sea. A blue-clad peasant rides home, with a harrow smoking behind him among the dry clods. Another still works with his wife in their little strip. An immense shadow fills the plain; these people stand in it up to their shoulders; and their heads, as they stoop over their work and rise again, are relieved from time to time against the golden sky.

These peasant farmers are well off nowadays, and not by any means overworked; but somehow you always see in them the historical representative of the serf of yore, and think not so much of present times, which may be prosperous enough, as of the old days when the peasant was taxed beyond possibility of payment, and lived, in Michelet's image, like a hare between two furrows. These very people now weeding their patch under the broad sunset, that very man and his wife, it seems to us, have suffered all the wrongs of France. It is they who have been their country's scapegoat for long ages; they who, generation after generation, have sowed and not reaped, reaped and another has garnered; and who have now entered into their reward, and enjoy their good things in their turn. For the days are gone by when the Seigneur ruled and profited. 'Le Seigneur,' says the old formula, 'enferme ses manants comme sous porte et gonds, du ciel à la terre. Tout est à lui, forêt chenue, oiseau dans l'air, poisson dans l'eau, bête au buisson, l'onde qui coule, la cloche dont le son au loin roule.'* Such was his old state of sovereignty, a local god rather than a mere king. And now you may ask yourself where he is, and look round for vestiges of my late lord, and in all the country-side there is no trace of him but his forlorn and fallen mansion. At the end of a long avenue, now sown with grain, in the midst of a close full of cypresses and lilacs, ducks and crowing chanticleers and droning bees, the old château lifts its red chimneys and peaked roofs and turning vanes into the wind and sun. There is a glad spring bustle in the air, perhaps, and the lilacs are all in flowers, and the creepers green about the broken balustrade; but no spring shall revive the honour of the place. Old women of the people, little children of the people, saunter and gambol in the walled court or feed the ducks in the neglected moat. Plough-horses, mighty of limb, browse in the long stables. The dial-hand on the clock waits for some better hour. Out on the plain, where hot sweat trickles into men's eyes, and the spade goes in deep and comes up slowly, perhaps the peasant may feel a movement of joy at his heart when he thinks that these spacious chimneys are now cold, which have so often blazed and flickered upon gay folk at supper, while he and his hollow-eyed children watched through the night with empty bellies and cold feet. And perhaps as he raises his head and sees the forest lying like a coast-line of low hills along the sea-like level of the plain, perhaps forest and château hold no unsimilar place in his affections.

If the château was my lord's the forest was my lord the king's; neither of them for this poor Jacques. If he thought to eke out his meagre way of life by some petty theft of wood for the fire, or for a new roof-tree, he found himself face to face with a whole department, from the Grand

Master of the Woods and Waters, who was a high-born lord, down to the common sergeant, who was a peasant like himself, and wore stripes or a bandoleer by way of uniform. For the first offence, by the Salic law, there was a fine of fifteen sols; and should a man be taken more than once in fault, or circumstances aggravate the colour of his guilt, he might be whipped, branded, or hanged. There was a hangman over at Melun, and, I doubt not, a fine tall gibbet hard by the town gate, where Jacques might see his fellows dangle against the sky as he went to market.

And then, if he lived near to a cover, there would be the more hares and rabbits to eat out his harvest, and the more hunters to trample it down. My lord has a new horn from England. He has laid out seven francs in decorating it with silver and gold, and fitting it with a silken leash to hang about his shoulder. The hounds have been on a pilgrimage to the shrine of Saint Mesmer, or Saint Hubert in the Ardennes, or some other holy intercessor who has made a speciality of the health of hunting-dogs. In the grey dawn the game was turned and the branch broken by our best piqueur. A rare day's hunting lies before us. Wind a jolly flourish, sound the *bien-aller* with all your lungs. Jacques must stand by, hat in hand, while the quarry and hound and huntsman sweep across his field, and a year's sparing and labouring is as though it had not been. If he can see the ruin with a good enough grace, who knows but he may fall in favour with my lord; who knows but his son may become the last and least among the servants at his lord-ship's kennel—one of the two poor varlets who get no wages and sleep at night among the hounds?*

For all that, the forest has been of use to Jacques, not only warming him with fallen wood, but giving him shelter in days of sore trouble, when my lord of the château, with all his troopers and trumpets, had been beaten from field after field into some ultimate fastness, or lay overseas in an English prison. In these dark days, when the watch on the church steeple saw the smoke of burning villages on the sky-line, or a clump of spears and fluttering pennons draw-ing nigh across the plain, these good folk gat them up, with all their household gods, into the wood, whence, from some high spur, their timid scouts might overlook the coming and going of the marauders, and see the harvest ridden down, and church and cottage go up to heaven all night in flame. It was but an unhomely refuge that the woods afforded, where they might abide all change of weather and keep house with wolves and vipers. Often there was none left alive, when they returned, to show the old divisions of field from field. And yet, as times went, when the wolves entered at night into depopulated Paris, and perhaps De Retz* was passing by with a company of demons like himself, even in these caves and thickets there were glad hearts and grateful prayers.

Once or twice, as I say, in the course of the ages, the forest may have served the peasant well, but at heart it is a royal forest, and noble by old association. These woods have rung to the horns of all the kings of France, from Philip Augustus downwards. They have seen Saint Louis exercise the dogs he brought with him from Egypt; Francis I. go a-hunting with ten thousand horses in his train; and Peter of Russia following his first stag. And so they are still haunted for the imagination by royal hunts and progresses, and peopled with the faces of memorable men of yore. And this distinction is not only in virtue of the pastime of dead monarchs. Great events, great revolutions, great cycles in the affairs of men, have here left their note, here taken shape in some significant and dramatic situation. It was hence that Guise and his leaguers led Charles the Ninth a prisoner to Paris. Here, booted and spurred, and with all his dogs about him, Napoleon met the Pope beside a woodland cross. Here, on his way to Elba not so long after, he kissed the eagle of the Old Guard, and spoke words of passionate farewell to his soldiers. And here, after Waterloo, rather than yield its ensign to the new power, one of his faithful regiments burned that memorial of so much toil and glory on the Grand Master's table, and drank its dust in brandy, as a devout priest consumes the remnants of the Host.

IN THE SEASON

Close into the edge of the forest, so close that the trees of the *bornage* stand pleasantly about the last houses, sits a certain small and very quiet village. There is but one street, and that, not long ago, was a green lane, where the cattle browsed between the door-steps. As you go up this street, drawing ever nearer the beginning of the wood, you will arrive at last before an inn where artists lodge. To the door (for I imagine it to be six o'clock on some fine summer's even), half a dozen, or maybe half a score, of people have brought out chairs, and now sit sunning themselves, and waiting the omnibus from Melun. If you go on into the court you will find as many more, some in the billiard-room over absinthe and a match of corks, some without over a last cigar and a vermouth. The doves coo and flutter from the dovecote; Hortense is drawing water from the well; and as all the rooms open into the court, you can see the white-capped cook over the furnace in the kitchen, and some idle painter, who has stored his canvases and washed his brushes, jangling a waltz on the crazy, tongue-tied piano in the salle-à-manger. '*Edmond, encore un vermouth,*' cries a man in velveteen, adding in a tone of apologetic afterthought, '*un double, s'il vous plaît.*' 'Where are you working?' asks one in pure white linen from top to toe. 'At the Carrefour de l'Épine,' returns the other in corduroy (they are all gaitered, by the way). 'I couldn't do a thing to it. I ran out of white. Where were you?' 'I wasn't working, I was looking for motives.' Here is an outbreak of jubilation, and a lot of men clustering together about some new-comer with outstretched hands; perhaps the 'correspondence' has come in and brought So-and-so from Paris, or perhaps it is only So-and-so who has walked over from Chailly to dinner.

'*A table, Messieurs!*' cries M. Siron, bearing through the court the first tureen of soup. And immediately the company begins to settle down about the long tables in the dining-room, framed all round with sketches of all degrees of merit and demerit. There's the big picture of the huntsman winding a horn, with a dead boar between his legs, and his legs—well, his legs in stockings. And here is the little picture of a raw mutton-chop, in which Such-a-one knocked a hole last summer with no worse a missile than a plum from the dessert. And under all these works of art so much eating goes forward, so much drinking, so much jabbering in French and English, that it would do your heart good merely to peep and listen at the door. One man is telling how they all went last year to the fête at Fleury, and another how well So-and-so would sing of an evening; and here are a third and fourth making plans for the whole future of their lives; and there is a fifth imitating a conjurer and making faces on his clenched fist, surely of all arts the most difficult and admirable! A sixth has eaten his fill, lights a cigarette, and resigns himself to digestion. A seventh has just dropped in, and calls for soup. Number eight, meanwhile, has left the table, and is once more trampling the poor piano under powerful and uncertain fingers.

Dinner over, people drop outside to smoke and chat. Perhaps we go along to visit our friends at the other end of the village, where there is always a good welcome and a good talk, and perhaps some pickled oysters and white wine to close the evening. Or a dance is organised in the dining-room, and the piano exhibits all its paces under manful jockeying, to the light of the three or four candles and a lamp or two, while the waltzers move to and fro upon the wooden floor, and sober men, who are not given to such light pleasures, get up on the table or the sideboard, and sit there looking on approvingly over a pipe and a tumbler of wine. Or sometimes—suppose my lady moon looks forth, and the court from out the half-lit dining-room seems nearly as bright as by day, and the light picks out the window-panes, and makes a clear shadow under every vine-leaf on the wall—sometimes a picnic is proposed, and a basket made ready, and a good procession formed in front of the hotel. The two trumpeters in honour go before; and as we file down the long alley, and up through devious footpaths among rocks and pine-trees, with every here and there a dark passage of shadow, and every here and there a spacious outlook over moonlit woods, these two precede us and sound many a jolly flourish as they walk. We gather ferns and dry boughs into the cavern, and soon a good blaze flutters the shadows of the old bandits' haunt, and shows shapely beards and comely faces and toilettes ranged about the wall. The bowl is lit, and the punch is burnt and sent round in scalding thimblefuls. So a good hour or two may pass with song and jest. And then we go home in the moonlight morning, straggling a good deal among the birch tufts and the boulders, but ever called together again, as one of our leaders winds his horn. Perhaps some one of the party will not heed the summons, but chooses out some by-way of his own. As he follows the winding sandy road, he hears the flourishes grow fainter and fainter in the distance, and die finally out, and still walks on in the strange coolness and silence and between the crisp lights and shadows of the moonlit woods, until suddenly the bell rings out the hour from far-away Chailly, and he starts to find himself alone. No surf-bell on forlorn and perilous shores, no passing knoll over the busy market-place, can speak with a more heavy and disconsolate tongue to human ears. Each stroke calls up a host of ghostly reverberations in his mind. And as he stands rooted, it has grown once more so utterly silent that it seems to him he might hear the church bells ring the hour out all the world over, not at Chailly only, but in Paris, and away in outlandish cities, and in the village on the river, where his childhood passed between the sun and flowers.

IDLE HOURS

The woods by night, in all their uncanny effect, are not rightly to be understood until you can compare them with the woods by day. The stillness of the medium, the floor of glittering sand, these trees that go streaming up like monstrous sea-weeds and waver in the moving winds like

the weeds in submarine currents, all these set the mind
working on the thought of what you may have seen off a
foreland or over the side of a boat, and make you feel like
a diver, down in the quiet water, fathoms below the tum-
bling, transitory surface of the sea. And yet in itself, as I
say, the strangeness of these nocturnal solitudes is not to
be felt fully without the sense of contrast. You must have
risen in the morning and seen the woods as they are by
day, kindled and coloured in the sun's light; you must have
felt the odour of innumerable trees at even, the unsparing
heat along the forest roads, and the coolness of the groves.

And on the first morning you will doubtless rise betimes.
If you have not been wakened before by the visit of some
adventurous pigeon, you will be wakened as soon as the
sun can reach your window—for there are no blinds or
shutters to keep him out—and the room, with its bare wood
floor and bare whitewashed walls, shines all round you in
a sort of glory of reflected lights. You may doze a little
while longer by snatches, or lie awake to study the charcoal
men and dogs and horses with which former occupants
have defiled the partitions: Thiers, with wily profile; local
celebrities, pipe in hand; or maybe, a romantic landscape
splashed in oil. Meanwhile artist after artist drops into the
salle-à-manger for coffee, and then shoulders easel, sunshade, stool, and paint-box, bound into a faggot, and sets
off for what he calls his 'motive.' And artist after artist, as
he goes out of the village, carries with him a little following
of dogs. For the dogs, who belong only nominally to any
special master, hang about the gate of the forest all day
long, and whenever anyone goes by who hits their fancy,
profit by his escort, and go forth with him to play an hour
or two at hunting. They would like to be under the trees
all day. But they cannot go alone. They require a pretext.
And so they take the passing artist as an excuse to go into
the woods, as they might take a walking-stick as an excuse
to bathe. With quick ears, long spines, and bandy legs, or
perhaps as tall as a greyhound and with a bulldog's head,
this company of mongrels will trot by your side all day and
come home with you at night, still showing white teeth and

wagging stunted tail. Their good-humour is not to be exhausted. You may pelt them with stones if you please, and all they will do is to give you a wider berth. If once they come out with you, to you they will remain faithful, and with you return; although if you meet them next morning in the street, it is as like as not they will cut you with a countenance of brass.

The forest—a strange thing for an Englishman—is very destitute of birds. This is no country where every patch of wood among the meadows gives up an incense of song, and every valley wandered through by streamlet rings and reverberates from side to side with a profusion of clear notes. And this rarity of birds is not to be regretted on its own account only. For the insects prosper in their absence, and become as one of the plagues of Egypt. Ants swarm in the hot sand; mosquitoes drone their nasal drone; wherever the sun finds a hole in the roof of the forest, you see a myriad transparent creatures coming and going in the shaft of light; and even between-whiles, even where there is no incursion of sun-rays into the dark arcade of the wood, you are conscious of a continual drift of insects, an ebb and flow of infinitesimal living things between the trees. Nor are insects the only evil creatures that haunt the forest. For you may plump into a cave among the rocks, and find yourself face to face with a wild boar, or see a crooked viper slither across the road.

Perhaps you may set yourself down in the bay between two spreading beech-roots with a book on your lap, and be awakened all of a sudden by a friend: 'I say, just keep where you are, will you? You make the jolliest motive.' And you reply: 'Well, I don't mind, if I may smoke.' And thereafter the hours go idly by. Your friend at the easel labours doggedly a little way off, in the wide shadow of the tree; and yet farther, across a strait of glaring sunshine, you see another painter, encamped in the shadow of another tree, and up to his waist in the fern. You cannot watch your own effigy growing out of the white trunk, and the trunk beginning to stand forth from the rest of the wood, and the whole picture getting dappled over with the flecks of sun that slip through the leaves overhead, and, as a wind goes by and sets the trees a-talking, flicker hither and thither like butterflies of light. But you know it is going forward; and, out of emulation with the painter, get ready your own palette, and lay out the colour for a woodland scene in words.

Your tree stands in a hollow paved with fern and heather, set in a basin of low hills, and scattered over with rocks and junipers. All the open is steeped in pitiless sunlight. Everything stands out as though it were cut in cardboard, every colour is strained into its highest key. The boulders are some of them upright and dead like monolithic castles, some of them prone like sleeping cattle. The junipers— looking, in their soiled and ragged mourning, like some funeral procession that has gone seeking the place of se- pulchre three hundred years, and more, in wind and rain— are daubed in forcibly against the glowing ferns and heather. Every tassel of their rusty foliage is defined with pre-Raphaelite minuteness. And a sorry figure they make out there in the sun, like misbegotten yew-trees! The scene is all pitched in a key of colour so peculiar, and lit up with such a discharge of violent sunlight, as a man might live fifty years in England and not see.

Meanwhile at your elbow some one tunes up a song, words of Ronsard to a pathetic tremulous air, of how the poet loved his mistress long ago, and pressed on her the flight of time, and told her how white and quiet the dead lay under the stones, and how the boat dipped and pitched as the shades embarked for the passionless land. Yet a little while, sang the poet, and there shall be no more love; only to sit and remember loves that might have been. There is a falling flourish in the air that remains in the memory and comes back in incongruous places, on the seat of hansoms or in the warm bed at night, with something of a forest savour.

'You can get up now,' says the painter; 'I'm at the background.'

And so up you get, stretching yourself, and go your way into the wood, the daylight becoming richer and more golden, and the shadows stretching farther into the open. A cool air comes along the highways, and the scents awaken. The fir-trees breathe abroad their ozone. Out of unknown thickets comes forth the soft, secret, aromatic odour of the woods, not like a smell of the free heaven, but as though court ladies, who had known these paths in ages long gone by, still walked in the summer evenings, and shed from their brocades a breath of musk or bergamot upon the woodland winds. One side of the long avenues is still kindled with the sun, the other is plunged in transparent shadow. Over the trees the west begins to burn like a furnace; and the painters gather up their chattels, and go down, by avenue or footpath, to the plain.

A PLEASURE PARTY

As this excursion is a matter of some length, and, moreover, we go in force, we have set aside our usual vehicle, the pony-cart, and ordered a large wagonette from Lejosne's. It has been waiting for near an hour, while one went to pack a knapsack, and t'other hurried over his toilette and coffee; but now it is filled from end to end with merry folk in summer attire, the coachman cracks his whip, and amid much applause from round the inn door off we rattle at a spanking trot. The way lies through the forest, up hill and down dale, and by beech and pine wood, in the cheerful morning sunshine. The English get down at all the ascents and walk on ahead for exercise; the French are mightily entertained at this, and keep coyly underneath the tilt. As we go we carry with us a pleasant noise of laughter and light speech, and some one will be always breaking out into a bar or two of opera bouffe. Before we get to the Route Ronde here comes Desprez, the colour-man from Fontaine-bleau, trudging across on his weekly peddle with a case of merchandise; and it is 'Desprez, leave me some malachite green'; 'Desprez, leave me so much canvas'; 'Desprez, leave me this, or leave me that'; M. Desprez standing the while in the sunlight with grave face and many salutations. The next interruption is more important. For some time back we have had the sound of cannon in our ears; and now, a little past Franchard, we find a mounted trooper holding a led horse, who brings the wagonette to a stand. The artillery is practising in the Quadrilateral, it appears; passage along the Route Ronde formally interdicted for the moment. There is nothing for it but to draw up at the glaring crossroads, and get down to make fun of the notorious Cocardon, the most ungainly and ill-bred dog of all the ungainly and ill-bred dogs of Barbizon, or clamber about the sandy banks. And meanwhile the Doctor, with sun umbrella, wide Panama, and patriarchal beard, is busy wheedling and (for aught the rest of us know) bribing the too facile sentry. His speech is smooth and dulcet, his manner dignified and insinuating. It is not for nothing that the Doctor has voyaged all the world over, and speaks all languages from French to Patagonian. He has not come home from perilous journeys to be thwarted by a corporal of horse. And so we soon see the soldier's mouth relax, and his shoulders imitate a relenting heart. '*En voiture, Messieurs, Mesdames,*'* sings the Doctor; and on we go again at a good round pace, for black care follows hard after us, and discretion prevails not a little over valour in some timorous spirits of the party. At any moment we may meet the sergeant, who will send us back. At any moment we may encounter a flying shell, which will send us somewhere farther off than Grez.

Grez—for that is our destination—has been highly recommended for its beauty. '*Il y a de l'eau,*'* people have said, with an emphasis, as if that settled the question, which, for a French mind, I am rather led to think it does. And Grez, when we get there, is indeed a place worthy of some praise. It lies out of the forest, a cluster of houses, with an old bridge, an old castle in ruin, and a quaint old church. The inn garden descends in terraces to the river; stable-yard, kailyard, orchard, and a space of lawn, fringed with rushes and embellished with a green arbour. On the opposite bank there is a reach of English-looking plain, set thickly with willows and poplars. And between the two lies the river, clear and deep, and full of reeds and floating lilies. Water-plants cluster about the sterlings of the long low bridge, and stand half-way up upon the piers in green luxuriance. They catch the dipped oar with long antennæ, and chequer the slimy bottom with the shadow of their leaves. And the river wanders hither and thither among the islets, and is smothered and broken up by the reeds, like an old building in the lithe, hardy arms of the climbing ivy. You may watch the box where the good man of the inn keeps fish alive for his kitchen, one oily ripple following another over the top of the yellow deal. And you can hear a splashing and a prattle of voices from the shed under the old kirk, where the village women wash and wash all day among the fish and water-lilies. It seems as if linen washed there should be specially cool and sweet.

We have come here for the river. And no sooner have we all bathed than we board the two shallops and push off gaily, and go gliding under the trees and gathering a great treasure of water-lilies. Some one sings; some trail their hands in the cool water; some lean over the gunwale to see the image of the tall poplars far below, and the shadow of the boat, with the balanced oars and their own head protruded, glide smoothly over the yellow floor of the stream. At last, the day declining—all silent and happy, and up to the knees in the wet lilies—we punt slowly back again to the landing-place beside the bridge. There is a wish for solitude on all. One hides himself in the ar-bour with a cigarette; another goes a walk in the country with Cocardon; a third inspects the church. And it is not till dinner is on the table, and the inn's best wine goes round from glass to glass, that we begin to throw off the restraint and fuse once more into a jolly fellowship.

Half the party are to return to-night with the wagonette, and some of the others, loath to break up good company, will go with them a bit of the way and drink a stirrup-cup at Marlotte. It is dark in the wagonette, and not so merry as it might have been. The coachman loses the road. So-and-so tries to light fireworks with the most indifferent

success. Some sing, but the rest are too weary to applaud;
and it seems as if the festival were fairly at an end—

> 'Nous avons fait la noce,
> Rentrons à nos foyers!'

And such is the burthen, even after we have come to
Marlotte and taken our places in the court at Mother
Antonie's. There is punch on the long table out in the open
air, where the guests dine in summer weather. The candles
flare in the night wind, and the faces round the punch are
lit up, with shifting emphasis, against a background of
complete and solid darkness. It is all picturesque enough;
but the fact is, we are a-weary. We yawn; we are out of
the vein; we have made the wedding, as the song says, and
now, for pleasure's sake, let's make an end on't. When here
comes striding into the court, booted to mid-thigh, spurred
and splashed, in a jacket of green cord, the great, famous,
and redoubtable Blank; and in a moment the fire kindles
again, and the night is witness of our laughter as he imitates
Spaniards, Germans, Englishmen, picture-dealers, all eccentric ways of speaking and thinking, with a possession, a fury,
a strain of mind and voice, that would rather suggest a
nervous crisis than a desire to please. We are as merry as
ever when the trap sets forth again, and say farewell noisily
to all the good folk going farther. Then, as we are far
enough from thoughts of sleep, we visit Blank in his quaint
house, and sit an hour or so in a great tapestried chamber,
laid with furs, littered with sleeping hounds, and lit up, in
fantastic shadow and shine, by a wood fire in a mediæval
chimney. And then we plod back through the darkness to
the inn beside the river.

How quick bright things come to confusion! When we
arise next morning, the grey showers fall steadily, the trees
hang limp, and the face of the stream is spoiled with
dimpling raindrops. Yesterday's lilies encumber the garden
walk, or begin, dismally enough, their voyage towards the
Seine and the salt sea. A sickly shimmer lies upon the
dripping house-roofs, and all the colour is washed out of
the green and golden landscape of last night, as though an

envious man had taken a water-colour sketch and blotted it together with a sponge. We go out a-walking in the wet roads. But the roads about Grez have a trick of their own. They go on for a while among clumps of willows and patches of vine, and then, suddenly and without any warning, cease and determine in some miry hollow or upon some bald knowe; and you have a short period of hope, then right-about face, and back the way you came! So we draw about the kitchen fire and play a round game of cards for ha'pence, or go to the billiard-room for a match at corks; and by one consent a messenger is sent over for the wagonette—Grez shall be left to-morrow.

To-morrow dawns so fair that two of the party agree to walk back for exercise, and let their knapsacks follow by the trap. I need hardly say they are neither of them French; for, of all English phrases, the phrase 'for exercise' is the least comprehensible across the Strait of Dover. All goes well for a while with the pedestrians. The wet woods are full of scents in the noontide. At a certain cross, where there is a guardhouse, they make a halt, for the forester's wife is the daughter of their good host at Barbizon. And so there they are hospitably received by the comely woman, with one child in her arms and another prattling and tottering at her gown, and drink some syrup of quince in the back parlour, with a map of the forest on the wall, and some prints of love affairs and the great Napoleon hunting. As they draw near the Quadrilateral, and hear once more the report of the big guns, they take a by-road to avoid the sentries, and go on a while somewhat vaguely, with the sound of the cannon in their ears and the rain beginning to fall. The ways grow wider and sandier; here and there there are real sand-hills, as though by the sea-shore; the fir-wood is open and grows in clumps upon the hillocks, and the race of signposts is no more. One begins to look at the other doubtfully. 'I am sure we should keep more to the right,' says one; and the other is just as certain they should hold to the left. And now, suddenly the heavens open, and the rain falls 'sheer and strong and loud,' as out of a shower-bath. In a moment they are as wet as shipwrecked sailors. They cannot see out of their eyes for the drift, and the water churns and gurgles in their boots. They leave the track and try across country with a gambler's desperation, for it seems as if it were impossible to make the situation worse; and, for the next hour, go scrambling from boulder to boulder, or plod along paths that are now no more than rivulets, and across waste clearings where the scattered shells and broken fir-trees tell all too plainly of the cannon in the distance. And meantime the cannon grumble out responses to the grumbling thunder. There is such a mixture of melodrama and sheer discomfort about all this, it is at once so grey and so lurid, that it is far more agreeable to read and write about by the chimney-corner than to suffer in the person. At last they chance on the right path, and make Franchard in the early evening, the sorriest pair of wanderers that ever welcomed English ale. Thence, by the Bois d'Hyver, the Ventes-Alexandre, and the Pins Brulés, to the clean hostelry, dry clothes, and dinner.

THE WOODS IN SPRING

I think you will like the forest best in the sharp early springtime, when it is just beginning to re-awaken, and innumerable violets peep from among the fallen leaves; when two or three people at most sit down to dinner, and, at table, you will do well to keep a rug about your knees, for the nights are chill, and the salle-à-manger opens on the court. There is less to distract the attention, for one thing, and the forest is more itself. It is not bedotted with artists' sunshades as with unknown mushrooms, nor be-strewn with the remains of English picnics. The hunting still goes on, and at any moment your heart may be brought into your mouth as you hear far-away horns; or you may be told by an agitated peasant that the Vicomte has gone up the avenue, not ten minutes since, '*à fond de train, monsieur, et avec douze piqueurs.*'*

If you go up to some coign of vantage in the system of low hills that permeates the forest, you will see many different tracts of country, each of its own cold and melancholy neutral tint, and all mixed together and mingled the one into the other at the seams. You will see tracts of leafless beeches of a faint yellowish grey, and leafless oaks a little ruddier in the hue. Then zones of pine of a solemn green; and, dotted among the pines, or standing by themselves in rocky clearings, the delicate, snow-white trunks of birches, spreading out into snow-white branches yet more delicate, and crowned and canopied with a purple haze of twigs. And then a long, bare ridge of tumbled boulders, with bright sand-breaks between them, and wavering sandy roads among the bracken and brown heather. It is all rather cold and unhomely. It has not the perfect beauty, nor the gem-like colouring, of the wood in the later year, when it is no more than one vast colonnade of verdant shadow, tremulous with insects, intersected here and there by lanes of sunlight set in purple heather. The loveliness of the woods in March is not, assuredly, of this blowzy rustic type. It is made sharp with a grain of salt, with a touch of ugliness. It has a sting like the sting of bitter ale; you acquire the love of it as men acquire a taste for olives. And the wonderful clear, pure air wells into your lungs the while by voluptuous inhalations, and makes the eyes bright, and sets the heart tinkling to a new tune—or, rather, to an old tune; for you remember in your boyhood something akin to this spirit of adventure, this thirst for exploration, that now takes you masterfully by the hand, plunges you into many a deep grove, and drags you over many a stony crest. It is as if the whole wood were full of friendly voices calling you farther in, and you turn from one side to another, like Buridan's donkey, in a maze of pleasure.

Comely beeches send up their white, straight, clustered branches, barred with green moss, like so many fingers from a half-clenched hand. Mighty oaks stand to the ankles in a fine tracery of underwood; thence the tall shaft climbs upwards, and the great forest of stalwart boughs spreads out into the golden evening sky, where the rooks are flying and calling. On the sward of the Bois d'Hyver the firs stand well asunder with outspread arms, like fencers saluting; and the air smells of resin all around, and the sound of the axe is rarely still. But strangest of all, and in appearance oldest of all, are the dim and wizard upland districts of young wood. The ground is carpeted with fir-tassel, and strewn with fir-apples and flakes of fallen bark. Rocks lie crouching in the thicket, guttered with rain, tufted with lichen, white with years and the rigours of the changeful seasons. Brown and yellow butterflies are sown and carried away again by the light air—like thistledown. The loneliness of these coverts is so excessive, that there are moments when pleasure draws to the verge of fear. You listen and listen for some noise to break the silence, till you grow half mesmerised by the intensity of the strain; your sense of your own identity is troubled; your brain reels, like that of some gymnosophist poring on his own nose in Asiatic jungles; and should you see your own outspread feet, you see them, not as anything of yours, but as a feature of the scene around you.

Still the forest is always, but the stillness is not always unbroken. You can hear the wind pass in the distance over the tree-tops; sometimes briefly, like the noise of a train; sometimes with a long steady rush, like the breaking of waves. And sometimes, close at hand, the branches move, a moan goes through the thicket, and the wood thrills to its heart. Perhaps you may hear a carriage on the road to Fontainebleau, a bird gives a dry continual chirp, the dead leaves rustle underfoot, or you may time your steps to the steady recurrent strokes of the woodman's axe. From time to time over the low grounds, a flight of rooks goes by; and from time to time the cooing of wild doves falls upon the ear, not sweet and rich and near at hand as in England, but a sort of voice of the woods, thin and far away, as fits these solemn places. Or you hear suddenly the hollow, eager, violent barking of dogs; scared deer flit past you through the fringes of the wood; then a man or two running, in green blouse, with gun and game-bag on a bandoleer; and then, out of the thick of the trees, comes the jar of rifle-shots. Or perhaps the hounds are out, and horns are blown, and scarlet-coated huntsmen flash through the clearings, and the solid noise of horses galloping passes below you, where you sit perched among the rocks and heather. The boar is afoot, and all over the forest, and in all neighbouring villages, there is a vague excitement and a vague hope; for who knows whither the chase may lead? and even to have seen a single piqueur, or spoken to a single sportsman, is to be a man of consequence for the night.

Besides men who shoot and men who ride with the hounds, there are few people in the forest, in the early spring, save wood-cutters plying their axes steadily, and old women and children gathering wood for the fire. You may meet such a party coming home in the twilight: the old woman laden with a faggot of chips, and the little ones hauling a long branch behind them in her wake. That is the worst of what there is to encounter; and if I tell you of what once happened to a friend of mine, it is by no means to tantalise you with false hopes; for the adventure was unique. It was on a very cold, still, sunless morning with a flat grey sky and a frosty tingle in the air, that this friend (who shall here be nameless) heard the notes of a key-bugle played with much hesitation, and saw the smoke of a fire spread out along the green pine-tops, in a remote uncanny glen, hard by a hill of naked boulders. He drew near warily, and beheld a picnic party seated under a tree in the open. The old father knitted a sock, the mother sat staring at the fire. The eldest son, in the uniform of a private of dragoons, was choosing out notes on a key-bugle. Two or three daughters lay in the neighbourhood, picking violets. And the whole party as grave and silent as the woods around them! My friend watched for a long time, he says; but all held their peace; not one spoke or smiled; only the dragoon kept choosing out single notes upon the bugle, and the father knitted away at his work and made strange movements the while with his flexible eyebrows. They took no notice whatever of my friend's presence, which was disquieting in itself, and increased the resemblance of the whole party to mechanical waxworks. Certainly, he affirms, a wax figure might have played the bugle with more spirit than that strange dragoon. And as this hypothesis of his became more certain, the awful insolubility of why they should be left out there in the woods with nobody to wind them up again when they ran down, and a growing disquietude of what might happen next, became too much for his courage, and he turned tail, and fairly took to his heels. It might have been a singing in his ears, but he fancies he was followed as he ran by a peal of Titanic laughter. Nothing has ever transpired to clear up the mystery; it may be they were automata; or it may be (and this is the theory to which I lean myself) that this is all another chapter of Heine's *Gods in Exile;* that the upright old man with the eyebrows was no other than Father Jove, and the young dragoon with the taste for music either Apollo or Mars.

MORALITY

Strange indeed is the attraction of the forest for the minds of men. Not one or two only, but a great chorus of grateful voices have arisen to spread abroad its fame. Half the famous writers of modern France have had their word to say about Fontainebleau. Chateaubriand, Michelet, Béranger, George Sand, de Senancour, Flaubert, Murger, the brothers Goncourt, Théodore de Banville, each of these has done something to the eternal praise and memory of these woods. Even at the very worst of times, even when the picturesque was anathema in the eyes of all Persons of Taste, the forest still preserved a certain reputation for beauty. It was in 1730 that the Abbé Guilbert published his Historical Description of the Palace, Town, and Forest of Fontainebleau. And very droll it is to see him, as he tries to set forth his admiration in terms of what was then permissible. The monstrous rocks, etc., says the Abbé, '*sont admirées avec surprise des voyageurs qui s'écrient aussitôt avec Horace: Ut mihi devio rupes et vacuum nemus mirari libet.*'* The good man is not exactly lyrical in his praise; and you see how he sets his back against Horace as against a trusty oak.

Horace, at any rate, was classical. For the rest, however, the Abbé likes places where many alleys meet; or which, like the Belle-Étoile, are kept up 'by a special gardener,' and admires at the Table du Roi the labours of the Grand Master of Woods and Waters, the Sieur de la Falure, '*qui a fait faire ce magnifique endroit.*'

But indeed, it is not so much for its beauty that the forest makes a claim upon men's hearts, as for that subtle something, that quality of the air, that emanation from the old trees, that so wonderfully changes and renews a weary spirit. Disappointed men, sick Francis Firsts and vanquished Grand Monarchs, time out of mind have come here for consolation. Hither perplexed folk have retired out of the press of life, as into a deep bay-window on some night of masquerade, and here found quiet and silence, and rest, the mother of wisdom. It is the great moral spa; this forest without a fountain is itself the great fountain of Juventus. It is the best place in the world to bring an old sorrow that has been a long while your friend and enemy; and if, like Béranger's, your gaiety has run away from home and left open the door for sorrow to come in, of all covers in Europe, it is here you may expect to find the truant hid. With every hour you change. The air penetrates through your clothes, and nestles to your living body. You love exercise and slumber, long fasting and full meals. You forget all your scruples and live a while in peace and freedom, and for the moment only. For here, all is absent that can stimulate to moral feeling. Such people as you see may be old, or toil-worn, or sorry; but you see them framed in the forest, like figures on a painted canvas; and for you, they are not people in any living and kindly sense. You forget the grim contrariety of interests. You forget the narrow lane where all men jostle together in unchivalrous contention, and the kennel, deep and unclean, that gapes on either hand for the defeated. Life is simple enough, it seems, and the very idea of sacrifice becomes like a mad fancy out of a last night's dream.

Your ideal is not perhaps high, but it is plain and possible. You become enamoured of a life of change and movement and the open air, where the muscles shall be more exercised than the affections. When you have had your will of the forest, you may visit the whole round world. You may buckle on your knapsack and take the road on foot. You may bestride a good nag, and ride forth, with a pair of saddle-bags, into the enchanted East. You may cross the Black Forest, and see Germany wide-spread before you, like a map, dotted with old cities, walled and spired, that dream all day on their own reflections in the Rhine or Danube. You may pass the spinal cord of Europe and go down from Alpine glaciers to where Italy extends her marble moles and glasses her marble palaces in the midland sea. You may sleep in flying trains or wayside taverns. You may be awakened at dawn by the scream of the express or the small pipe of the robin in the hedge. For you the rain should allay the dust of the beaten road; the wind dry your clothes upon you as you walk. Autumn should hang out russet pears and purple grapes along the lane; inn after inn proffer you their cups of raw wine; river after river receive your body in the sultry noon. Wherever you went warm valleys and high trees and pleasant villages should compass you about; and light fellowships should take you by the arm, and walk with you an hour upon your way. You may see from afar off what it will come to in the end—the weather-beaten red-nosed vagabond, consumed by a fever of the feet, cut off from all near touch of human sympathy, a waif, an Ishmael, and an outcast. And yet it will seem well—and yet, in the air of the forest, this will seem the best—to break all the network bound about your feet by birth and old companionship and loyal love, and bear your shovelful of phosphates to and fro, in town and country, until the hour of the great dissolvent.

Or, perhaps, you will keep to the cover. For the forest is by itself, and forest life owns small kinship with life in the dismal land of labour. Men are so far sophisticated that they cannot take the world as it is given to them by the sight of their eyes. Not only what they see and hear, but what they know to be behind, enter into their notion, of a place. If the sea, for instance, lie just across the hills, sea-thoughts will come to them at intervals, and the tenor of their dreams from time to time will suffer a sea-change. And so here, in this forest, a knowledge of its greatness is for much in the effect produced. You reckon up the miles that lie between you and intrusion. You may walk before you all day long, and not fear to touch the barrier of your Eden, or stumble out of fairyland into the land of gin and steam-hammers. And there is an old tale enhances for the imagination the grandeur of the woods of France, and secures you in the thought of your seclusion. When Charles VI. hunted in the time of his wild boyhood near Senlis, there was captured an old stag, having a collar of bronze about his neck, and these words engraved on the collar: 'Cæsar mihi hoc donavit.' It is no wonder if the minds of men were moved at this occurrence and they stood aghast to find themselves thus touching hands with forgotten ages, and following an antiquity with hound and horn. And even for you, it is scarcely in an idle curiosity that you ponder how many centuries this stag had carried its free antlers through the wood, and how many summers and winters have shone and snowed on the imperial badge. If the extent of solemn wood could thus safeguard a tall stag from the hunters' hounds and horses, might not you also play hide-and-seek, in these groves, with all the pangs and trepidations of man's life, and elude Death, the mighty hunter, for more than the span of human years? Here, also, crash his arrows; here, in the farthest glade, sounds the gallop of the pale horse. But he does not hunt this cover with all his hounds, for the game is thin and small: and if you are but alert and wary, if you lodged ever in the deepest thickets, you too might live on into later generations and astonish men by your stalwart age and the trophies of an immemorial success.

For the forest takes away from you all excuse to die. There is nothing here to cabin or thwart your free desires. Here all the impudences of the brawling world reach you no more. You may count your hours, like Endymion, by the strokes of the lone wood-cutter, or by the progression of the lights and shadows and the sun wheeling his wide circuit through the naked heavens. Here shall you see no enemies but winter and rough weather. And if a pang comes to you at all, it will be a pang of healthful hunger. All the puling sorrows, all the carking repentance, all this talk of duty that is no duty, in the great peace, in the pure daylight of these woods, fall away from you like a garment. And if perchance you come forth upon an eminence, where the wind blows upon you large and fresh, and the pines knock their long stems together, like an ungainly sort of puppets, and see far away over the plain a factory chimney defined against the pale horizon—it is for you, as for the staid and simple peasant when, with his plough, he upturns old arms and harness from the furrow of the glebe. Ay, sure enough, there was a battle there in the old times; and, sure enough, there is a world out yonder where men strive together with a noise of oaths and weeping and clamorous dispute. So much you apprehend by an athletic act of the imagination. A faint far-off rumour as of Merovingian wars, a legend as of some dead religion.

FONTAINEBLEAU

VILLAGE COMMUNITIES OF PAINTERS

I

The charm of Fontainebleau is a thing apart. It is a place that people love even more than they admire. The vigorous forest air, the silence, the majestic avenues of highway, the wilderness of tumbled boulders, the great age and dignity of certain groves—these are but ingredients, they are not the secret of the philtre. The place is sanative; the air, the light, the perfumes, and the shapes of things concord in happy harmony. The artist may be idle and not fear the 'blues.' He may dally with his life. Mirth, lyric mirth, and a vivacious classical contentment are of the very essence of the better kind of art; and these, in that most smiling forest, he has the chance to learn or to remember. Even on the plain of Bière, where the Angelus of Millet* still tolls upon the ear of fancy, a larger air, a higher heaven, something ancient and healthy in the face of nature, purify the mind alike from dulness and hysteria. There is no place where the young are more gladly conscious of their youth, or the old better contented with their age.

The fact of its great and special beauty further recommends this country to the artist. The field was chosen by men in whose blood there still raced some of the gleeful or solemn exultation of great art—Millet who loved dignity like Michelangelo, Rousseau* whose modern brush was dipped in the glamour of the ancients. It was chosen before the day of that strange turn in the history of art, of which we now perceive the culmination in impressionistic tales and pictures—that voluntary aversion of the eye from all speciously strong and beautiful effects—that disinterested love of dulness which has set so many Peter Bells to paint the river-side primrose. It was then chosen for its proximity to Paris. And for the same cause, and by the force of tradition, the painter of to-day continues to inhabit and to paint it. There is in France scenery incomparable for romance and harmony. Provence, and the valley of the Rhone from Vienne to Tarascon, are one succession of masterpieces waiting for the brush. The beauty is not merely beauty; it tells, besides, a tale to the imagination, and surprises while it charms. Here you shall see castellated towns that would befit the scenery of dreamland; streets that glow with colour like cathedral windows; hills of the most exquisite proportions; flowers of every precious colour, growing thick like grass. All these, by the grace of railway travel, are brought to the very door of the modern painter; yet he does not seek them; he remains faithful to Fontainebleau, to the eternal bridge of Grez, to the watering-pot cascade in Cernay valley. Even Fontainebleau was chosen for him; even in Fontainebleau he shrinks from what is sharply charactered. But one thing, at least, is certain, whatever he may choose to paint and in whatever manner, it is good for the artist to dwell among graceful shapes. Fontainebleau, if it be but quiet scenery, is classically graceful; and though the student may look for different qualities, this quality, silently present, will educate his hand and eye.

But, before all its other advantages—charm, loveliness, or proximity to Paris—comes the great fact that it is already colonised. The institution of a painters' colony is a work of time and tact. The population must be conquered. The innkeeper has to be taught, and he soon learns, the lesson of unlimited credit; he must be taught to welcome as a favoured guest a young gentleman in a very greasy coat, and with little baggage beyond a box of colours and a canvas; and he must learn to preserve his faith in customers who will eat heartily and drink of the best, borrow money to buy tobacco, and perhaps not pay a stiver for a year. A colour merchant has next to be attracted. A certain vogue must be given to the place, lest the painter, most gregarious of animals, should find himself alone. And no sooner are these first difficulties overcome, than fresh perils spring up upon the other side; and the bourgeois and the tourist are knocking at the gate. This is the crucial moment for the colony. If these intruders gain a footing, they not only banish freedom and amenity; pretty soon, by means of their long purses, they will have undone the education of the innkeeper; prices will rise and credit shorten; and the poor painter must fare farther on and find another hamlet. 'Not here, O Apollo!' will become his song. Thus Trouville and, the other day, St Raphael were lost to the arts. Curious and not always edifying are the shifts that the French student uses to defend his lair; like the cuttlefish, he must sometimes blacken the waters of his chosen pool; but at such a time and for so practical a purpose Mrs Grundy must allow him license. Where his own purse and credit are not threatened, he will do the honours of his village generously. Any artist is made welcome, through whatever medium he may seek expression; science is respected; even the idler, if he prove, as he so rarely does, a gentleman, will soon begin to find himself at home. And when that essentially modern creature, the English or American girl-student, began to walk calmly into his favourite inns as if into a drawing-room at home, the French painter owned himself defenceless; he submitted or he fled. His French respectability, quite as precise as ours, though covering different provinces of life, recoiled aghast before the innovation. But the girls were painters; there was nothing to be done; and Barbizon, when I last saw it and for the time at least, was practically ceded to the fair invader. Paterfamilias, on the other hand, the common tourist, the holiday shopman, and the cheap young gentleman upon the spree, he hounded from his villages with every circumstance of contumely.

This purely artistic society is excellent for the young artist. The lads are mostly fools; they hold the latest orthodoxy in its crudeness; they are at that stage of education, for the most part, when a man is too much occupied with style to be aware of the necessity for any matter; and this, above all for the Englishman, is excellent. To work grossly at the trade, to forget sentiment, to think of his material and nothing else, is, for a while at least, the king's highway of progress. Here, in England, too many painters and writers dwell dispersed, unshielded, among the intelligent bourgeois. These, when they are not merely indifferent, prate to him about the lofty aims and moral influence of art. And this is the lad's ruin. For art is, first of all and last of all, a trade. The love of words and not a desire to publish new discoveries, the love of form and not a novel reading of historical events, mark the vocation of the writer and the painter. The arabesque, properly speaking, and even in literature, is the first fancy of the artist; he first plays with his material as a child plays with a kaleidoscope; and he is already in a second stage when he begins to use his pretty counters for the end of representation. In that, he must pause long and toil faithfully; that is his apprenticeship; and it is only the few who will really grow beyond it, and go forward, fully equipped, to do the business of real art—to give life to abstractions and significance and charm to facts. In the meanwhile, let him dwell much among his fellow-craftsmen. They alone can take a serious interest in the childish tasks and pitiful successes of these years. They alone can behold with equanimity this fingering of the dumb keyboard, this polishing of empty sentences, this dull and literal painting of dull and insignificant subjects. Outsiders will spur him on. They will say, 'Why do you not write a great book? paint a great picture?' If his guardian angel fail him, they may even persuade him to the attempt, and, ten to one, his hand is coarsened and his style falsified for life.

And this brings me to a warning. The life of the apprentice to any art is both unstrained and pleasing; it is strewn with small successes in the midst of a career of failure, patiently supported; the heaviest scholar is conscious of a certain progress; and if he come not appreciably nearer to the art of Shakespeare, grows letter-perfect in the domain of A-B, ab. But the time comes when a man should cease prelusory gymnastic, stand up, put a violence upon his will, and for better or worse, begin the business of creation. This evil day there is a tendency continually to postpone: above all with painters. They have made so many studies that it has become a habit; they make more, the walls of exhibitions blush with them; and death finds these aged students still busy with their horn-book. This class of man finds a congenial home in artist villages; in the slang of the English colony at Barbizon we used to call them 'Snoozers.' Continual returns to the city, the society of men farther advanced, the study of great works, a sense of humour or, if such a thing is to be had, a little religion or philosophy, are the means of treatment. It will be time enough to think of curing the malady after it has been caught; for to catch it is the very thing for which you seek that dreamland of the painters' village. 'Snoozing' is a part of the artistic education; and the rudiments must be learned stupidly, all else being forgotten, as if they were an object in themselves.

Lastly, there is something, or there seems to be something, in the very air of France that communicates the love of style. Precision, clarity, the cleanly and crafty employment of material, a grace in the handling, apart from any value in the thought, seem to be acquired by the mere residence; or if not acquired, become at least the more appreciated. The air of Paris is alive with this technical inspiration. And to leave that airy city and awake next day upon the borders of the forest is but to change externals. The same spirit of dexterity and finish breathes from the long alleys and the lofty groves, from the wildernesses that are still pretty in their confusion, and the great plain that contrives to be decorative in its emptiness.

II

In spite of its really considerable extent, the forest of Fontainebleau is hardly anywhere tedious. I know the whole western side of it with what, I suppose, I may call thoroughness; well enough at least to testify that there is no square mile without some special character and charm. Such quarters, for instance, as the Long Rocher, the Bas-Bréau, and the Reine Blanche, might be a hundred miles apart; they have scarce a point in common beyond the silence of the birds. The two last are really conterminous; and in both are tall and ancient trees that have outlived a thousand political vicissitudes. But in the one the great oaks prosper placidly upon an even floor; they be-shadow a great field; and the air and the light are very free below their stretching boughs. In the other the trees find difficult footing; castles of white rock lie tumbled one upon another, the foot slips, the crooked viper slumbers, the moss clings in the crevice; and above it all the great beech goes spiring and casting forth her arms, and, with a grace beyond church architecture, canopies this rugged chaos. Meanwhile, dividing the two cantons, the broad white causeway of the Paris road runs in an avenue: a road conceived for pageantry and for triumphal marches, an avenue for an army; but, its days of glory over, it now lies grilling in the sun between cool groves, and only at intervals the vehicle of the cruising tourist is seen far away and faintly audible along its ample sweep. A little upon one side, and you find a district of sand and birch and boulder; a little upon the other lies the valley of Apremont, all juniper and heather; and close beyond that you may walk into a zone of pine-trees. So artfully are the ingredients mingled. Nor must it be forgotten that, in all this part, you come continually forth upon a hill-top, and behold the plain, northward and westward, like an unrefulgent sea; nor that all day long the shadows keep changing; and at last, to the red fires of sunset, night succeeds, and with the night a new forest, full of whisper, gloom, and fragrance. There are few things more renovating than to leave Páris, the lamplit arches of the Carrousel, and the long alignment of the glittering streets, and to bathe the senses in this fragrant darkness of the wood.

In this continual variety the mind is kept vividly alive. It is a changeful place to paint, a stirring place to live in. As fast as your foot carries you, you pass from scene to scene, each vigorously painted in the colours of the sun, each endeared by that hereditary spell of forests on the mind of man who still remembers and salutes the ancient refuge of his race.

And yet the forest has been civilised throughout. The most savage corners bear a name, and have been cherished like antiquities; in the most remote, Nature has prepared and balanced her effects as if with conscious art; and man, with his guiding arrows of blue paint, has countersigned the picture. After your farthest wandering, you are never surprised to come forth upon the vast avenue of highway, to strike the centre point of branching alleys, or to find the aqueduct trailing, thousand-footed, through the brush. It is not a wilderness; it is rather a preserve. And, fitly enough, the centre of the maze is not a hermit's cavern. In the midst a little mirthful town lies sunlit, humming with the business of pleasure; and the palace, breathing distinction and peopled by historic names, stands smokeless among gardens.

Perhaps the last attempt at savage life was that of the harmless humbug who called himself the hermit. In a great tree, close by the high road, he had built himself a little cabin after the manner of the Swiss Family Robinson; thither he mounted at night, by the romantic aid of a rope ladder; and if dirt be any proof of sincerity, the man was savage as a Sioux. I had the pleasure of his acquaintance; he appeared grossly stupid, not in his perfect wits, and interested in nothing but small change; for that he had a great avidity. In the course of time he proved to be a chicken-stealer, and vanished from his perch; and perhaps from the first he was no true votary of forest freedom, but an ingenious, theatrically minded beggar, and his cabin in the tree was only stock-in-trade to beg withal. The choice of his position would seem to indicate so much; for if in the forest there are no places still to be discovered, there are many that have been forgotten and that lie unvisited. There, to be sure, are the blue arrows waiting to reconduct you, now blazed upon a tree, now posted in the corner of a rock. But your security from interruption is complete; you might camp for weeks, if there were only water, and not a soul suspect your presence; and if I may suppose the reader to have committed some great crime and come to me for aid, I think I could still find my way to a small cavern, fitted with a hearth and chimney, where he might lie perfectly concealed. A confederate landscape-painter might daily supply him with food; for water, he would have to make a nightly tramp as far as to the nearest pond; and at last, when the hue and cry began to blow over, he might get gently on the train at some side station, work round by a series of junctions, and be quietly captured at the frontier.

Thus Fontainebleau, although it is truly but a pleasure-ground, and although, in favourable weather, and in the more celebrated quarters, it literally buzzes with the tourist, yet has some of the immunities and offers some of the repose of natural forests. And the solitary, although he must return at night to his frequented inn, may yet pass the day with his own thoughts in the companionable silence of the trees. The demands of the imagination vary; some can be alone in a back garden looked upon by windows; others, like the ostrich, are content with a solitude that meets the eye; and others, again, expand in fancy to the very borders of their desert, and are irritably conscious of a hunter's camp in an adjacent county. To these last, of course, Fontainebleau will seem but an extended tea-garden: a Rosherville on a by-day. But to the plain man it offers solitude: an excellent thing in itself, and a good whet for company.

III

I was for some time a consistent Barbizonian; *et ego in Arcadia vixi*, it was a pleasant season; and that noiseless hamlet lying close among the borders of the wood is for me, as for so many others, a green spot in memory. The great Millet was just dead, the green shutters of his modest house were closed; his daughters were in mourning. The date of my first visit was thus an epoch in the history of the Latin Quarter. The *Petit Cénacle** was dead and buried; Murger* and his crew of sponging vagabonds were all at rest from their expedients; the tradition of their real life was nearly lost, and the petrified legend of the *Vie de Bohème* had become a sort of gospel, and still gave the cue to zealous imitators. But if the book be written in rose-water, the imitation was still further expurgated; honesty was the rule; the innkeepers gave, as I have said, almost unlimited credit; they suffered the seediest painter to depart, to take all his belongings, and to leave his bill unpaid; and if they sometimes lost, it was by English and Americans alone. At the same time, the great influx of Anglo-Saxons had begun to affect the life of the studious. There had been disputes; and, in one instance at least, the English and the Americans had made common cause to prevent a cruel pleasantry. It would be well if nations and races could communicate their qualities; but in practice when they look upon each other, they have an eye to nothing but defects. The Anglo-Saxon is essentially dishonest; the French is devoid by nature of the principle that we call 'Fair Play.' The Frenchman marvelled at the scruples of his guest, and, when the defender of innocence retired overseas and left his bills unpaid, he marvelled once again; the good and evil were, in his eyes, part and parcel of the same eccentricity; a shrug expressed his judgment upon both.

At Barbizon there was no master, no pontiff in the arts. Palizzi bore rule at Grez—urbane, superior rule—his memory rich in anecdotes of the great men of yore, his mind fertile in theories; sceptical, composed, and venerable to the eye; and yet beneath these outworks, all twittering with Italian superstition, his eye scouting for omens, and the whole fabric of his manners giving way on the appearance of a hunchback. Cernay had Pelouse, the admirable, placid Pelouse, smilingly critical of youth, who, when a full-blown commercial traveller, suddenly threw down his samples, bought a colour-box, and became the master whom we have all admired. Marlotte, for a central figure, boasted Olivier de Penne. Only Barbizon, since the death of Millet, was a headless commonwealth. Even its secondary lights, and those who in my day made the stranger welcome, have since deserted it. The good Lachèvre has departed, carrying his household gods; and long before that Gaston Lafenestre was taken from our midst by an untimely death. He died before he had deserved success; it may be, he would never have deserved it; but his kind, comely, modest countenance still haunts the memory of all who knew him. Another—whom I will not name—has moved farther on, pursuing the strange Odyssey of his decadence. His days of royal favour had departed even then; but he still retained, in his narrower life at Barbizon, a certain stamp of conscious importance, hearty, friendly, filling the room, the occupant of several chairs; nor had he yet ceased his losing battle, still labouring upon great canvases that none would buy, still waiting the return of fortune. But these days also were too good to last; and the former favourite of two sovereigns fled, if I heard the truth, by night. There was a time when he was counted a great man, and Millet but a dauber; behold, how the whirligig of time brings in his revenges! To pity Millet is a piece of arrogance; if life be hard for such resolute and pious spirits, it is harder still for us, had we the wit to understand it; but we may pity his unhappier rival, who, for no apparent merit, was raised to opulence and momentary fame, and, through no apparent fault, was suffered step by step to sink again to nothing. No misfortune can exceed the bitterness of such back foremost progress, even bravely supported as it was; but to those also who were taken early from the easel, a regret is due. From all the young men of this period, one stood out by the vigour of his promise; he was in the age of fermentation, enamoured of eccentricities. 'Il faut faire de la peinture nouvelle,' was his watchword; but if time and experience had continued his education, if he had been granted health to return from these excursions to the steady and the central, I must believe that the name of Hills had become famous.

Siron's inn, that excellent artists' barrack, was managed upon easy principles. At any hour of the night, when you returned from wandering in the forest, you went to the billiard-room and helped yourself to liquors, or descended to the cellar and returned laden with beer or wine. The Sirons were all locked in slumber; there was none to check your inroads; only at the week's end a computation was made, the gross sum was divided, and a varying share set down to every lodger's name under the rubric: *estrats*. Upon the more long-suffering the larger tax was levied; and your bill lengthened in a direct proportion to the easiness of your disposition. At any hour of the morning, again, you could get your coffee or cold milk, and set forth into the forest. The doves had perhaps wakened you, fluttering into your chamber; and on the threshold of the inn you were met by the aroma of the forest. Close by were the great aisles, the mossy boulders, the interminable field of forest shadow. There you were free to dream and wander. And at noon, and again at six o'clock, a good meal awaited you on Siron's table. The whole of your accommodation, set aside that varying item of the *estrats*, cost you five francs a day; your bill was never offered you until you asked it; and if you were out of luck's way, you might depart for where you pleased and leave it pending.

IV

Theoretically, the house was open to all comers; practically, it was a kind of club. The guests protected themselves, and, in so doing, they protected Siron. Formal manners being laid aside, essential courtesy was the more rigidly exacted; the new arrival had to feel the pulse of the society; and a breach of its undefined observances was promptly punished. A man might be as plain, as dull, as slovenly, as free of speech as he desired; but to a touch of presumption or a word of hectoring these free Barbizonians were as sensitive as a tea-party of maiden ladies. I have seen people driven forth from Barbizon; it would be difficult to say in words what they had done, but they deserved their fate. They had shown themselves unworthy to enjoy these corporate freedoms; they had pushed themselves; they had 'made their head'; they wanted tact to appreciate the 'fine shades' of Barbizonian etiquette. And once they were condemned, the process of extrusion was ruthless in its cruelty; after one evening with the formidable Bodmer, the Baily of our commonwealth, the erring stranger was beheld no more; he rose exceedingly early the next day, and the first coach conveyed him from the scene of his discomfiture. These sentences of banishment were never, in my knowledge, delivered against an artist; such would, I believe, have been illegal; but the odd and pleasant fact is this, that they were never needed. Painters, sculptors, writers, singers, I have seen all of these in Barbizon; and some were sulky and some blatant and inane; but one and all entered at once into the spirit of the association. This singular society is purely French, a creature of French virtues, and possibly of French defects. It cannot be imitated by the English. The roughness, the impatience, the more obvious selfishness, and even the more ardent friendship of the Anglo-Saxon, speedily dismember such a commonwealth. But this random gathering of young French painters, with neither apparatus nor parade of government, yet kept the life of the place upon a certain footing, insensibly imposed their etiquette upon the docile, and by caustic speech enforced their edicts against the unwelcome. To think of it is to wonder the more at the strange failure of their race upon the larger theatre. This inbred civility—to use the word in its completest meaning—this natural and facile adjustment of contending liberties, seems all that is required to make a governable nation and a just and prosperous country.

Our society, thus purged and guarded, was full of high spirits, of laughter, and of the initiative of youth. The few elder men who joined us were still young at heart, and took the key from their companions. We returned from long stations in the fortifying air, our blood renewed by the sunshine, our spirits refreshed by the silence of the forest; the Babel of loud voices sounded good; we fell to eat and play like the natural man; and in the high inn chamber, panelled with indifferent pictures and lit by candles guttering in the night air, the talk and laughter sounded far into the night. It was a good place and a good life for any naturally-minded youth; better yet for the student of painting, and perhaps best of all for the student of letters. He, too, was saturated in this atmosphere of style; he was shut out from the disturbing currents of the world, he might forget that there existed other and more pressing interests than that of art. But, in such a place, it was hardly possible to write; he could not drug his conscience, like the painter, by the production of listless studies; he saw himself idle among many who were apparently, and some who were really, employed; and what with the impulse of increasing health and the continual provocation of romantic scenes, he became tormented with the desire to work. He enjoyed a strenuous idleness full of visions, hearty meals, long, sweltering walks, mirth among companions; and still floating like music through his brain, foresights of great works that Shakespeare might be proud to have conceived, headless epics, glorious torsos of dramas, and words that were alive with import. So in youth, like Moses from the mountain, we have sights of that House Beautiful of art which we shall never enter. They are dreams and unsubstantial; visions of style that repose upon no base of human meaning; the last heart-throbs of that excited amateur who has to die in all of us before the artist can be born. But they come to us in such a rainbow of glory that all subsequent achievement appears dull and earthly in comparison. We were all artists; almost all in the age of illusion, cultivating an imaginary genius, and walking to the strains of some deceiving Ariel; small wonder, indeed, if we were happy! But art, of whatever nature, is a kind mistress; and though these dreams of youth fall by their own baselessness, others succeed, graver and more substantial; the symptoms change, the amiable malady endures; and still, at an equal distance, the House Beautiful shines upon its hill-top.

V

Grez lies out of the forest, down by the bright river. It boasts a mill, an ancient church, a castle, and a bridge of many sterlings. And the bridge is a piece of public property; anonymously famous; beaming on the incurious dilettante from the walls of a hundred exhibitions. I have seen it in the Salon; I have seen it in the Academy; I have seen it in the last French Exposition, excellently done by Bloomer; in a black-and-white, by Mr A. Henley, it once adorned this essay in the pages of the *Magazine of Art*. Long-suffering bridge! And if you visit Grez to-morrow, you shall find another generation camped at the bottom of Chevillon's garden under their white umbrellas, and doggedly painting it again.

The bridge taken for granted, Grez is a less inspiring place than Barbizon. I give it the palm over Cernay. There is something ghastly in the great empty village square of Cernay, with the inn tables standing in one corner, as though the stage were set for rustic opera, and in the early morning all the painters breaking their fast upon white wine under the windows of the villagers. It is vastly different to awake in Grez, to go down the green inn-garden, to find the river streaming through the bridge, and to see the dawn begin across the poplared level. The meals are laid in the cool arbour, under fluttering leaves. The splash of oars and bathers, the bathing costumes out to dry, the trim canoes beside the jetty, tell of a society that has an eye to pleasure. There is 'something to do' at Grez. Perhaps, for that very reason, I can recall no such enduring ardours, no such glories of exhilaration, as among the solemn groves and uneventful hours of Barbizon. This 'something to do' is a great enemy to joy; it is a way out of it; you wreak your high spirits on some cut-and-dry employment, and behold them gone! But Grez is a merry place after its kind: pretty to see, merry to inhabit. The course of its pellucid river, whether up or down, is full of gentle attractions for the navigator: islanded reed-mazes where, in autumn, the red berries cluster; the mirrored and inverted images of trees; lilies, and mills, and the foam and thunder of weirs. And of all noble sweeps of roadway, none is nobler, on a windy dusk, than the high road to Nemours between its lines of talking poplar.

But even Grez is changed. The old inn, long shored and trussed and buttressed, fell at length under the mere weight of years, and the place as it was is but a fading image in the memory of former guests. They, indeed, recall the ancient wooden stair; they recall the rainy evening, the wide hearth, the blaze of the twig fire, and the company that gathered round the pillar in the kitchen. But the material fabric is now dust; soon, with the last of its inhabitants, its very memory shall follow; and they, in their turn, shall suffer the same law, and, both in name and lineament, vanish from the world of men. 'For remembrance of the old house' sake,' as Pepys once quaintly put it, let me tell one story. When the tide of invasion swept over France, two foreign painters were left stranded and penniless in Grez; and there, until the war was over, the Chevillons ungrudgingly harboured them. It was difficult to obtain supplies; but the two waifs were still welcome to the best, sat down daily with the family to table, and at the due intervals were supplied with clean napkins, which they scrupled to employ. Madame Chevillon observed the fact and reprimanded them. But they stood firm; eat they must, but having no money they would soil no napkins.

VI

Nemours and Moret, for all they are so picturesque, have been little visited by painters. They are, indeed, too populous; they have manners of their own, and might resist the drastic process of colonisation. Montigny has been somewhat strangely neglected; I never knew it inhabited but once, when Will H. Low installed himself there with a barrel of *piquette*, and entertained his friends in a leafy trellis above the weir, in sight of the green country and to the music of the falling water. It was a most airy, quaint, and pleasant place of residence, just too rustic to be stagey; and from my memories of the place in general, and that garden trellis in particular—at morning, visited by birds, or at night, when the dew fell and the stars were of the party—I am inclined to think perhaps too favourably of the future of Montigny. Chailly-en-Biere has outlived all things, and lies dustily slumbering in the plain—the cemetery of itself. The great road remains to testify of its former bustle of postillions and carriage bells; and, like memorial tablets, there still hang in the inn room the paintings of a former generation, dead or decorated long ago. In my time, one man only, greatly daring, dwelt there. From time to time he would walk over to Barbizon, like a shade revisiting the glimpses of the moon, and after some communication with flesh and blood return to his austere hermitage. But even he, when I last revisited the forest, had come to Barbizon for good, and closed the roll of Chaillyites. It may revive—but I much doubt it. Achères and Recloses still wait a pioneer; Bourron is out of the question, being merely Grez over again, without the river, the bridge, or the beauty; and of all the possible places on the western side, Marlotte alone remains to be discussed. I scarcely know Marlotte, and, very likely for that reason, am not much in love with it. It seems a glaring and unsightly hamlet. The inn of Mother Antonie is unattractive; and its more reputable rival, though comfortable enough, is commonplace. Marlotte has a name; it is famous; if I were the young painter I would leave it alone in its glory.

VII

These are the words of an old stager; and though time is a good conservative in forest places, much may be untrue to-day. Many of us have passed Arcadian days there and moved on, but yet left a portion of our souls behind us buried in the woods. I would not dig for these reliquiæ; they are incommunicable treasures that will not enrich the finder; and yet there may lie, interred below great oaks or scattered along forest paths, stores of youth's dynamite and dear remembrances. And as one generation passes on and renovates the field of tillage for the next, I entertain a fancy that when the young men of to-day go forth into the forest, they shall find the air still vitalised by the spirits of their predecessors, and, like those 'unheard melodies' that are the sweetest of all, the memory of our laughter shall still haunt the field of trees. Those merry voices that in woods call the wanderer farther, those thrilling silences and whispers of the groves, surely in Fontainebleau they must be vocal of me and my companions? We are not content to pass away entirely from the scenes of our delight; we would leave, if but in gratitude, a pillar and a legend.

One generation after another fall like honey-bees upon this memorable forest, rifle its sweets, pack themselves with vital memories, and when the theft is consummated depart again into life richer, but poorer also. The forest, indeed, they have possessed, from that day forward it is theirs indissolubly, and they will return to walk in it at night in the fondest of their dreams, and use it for ever in their books and pictures. Yet when they make their packets, and put up their notes and sketches, something, it should seem, had been forgotten. A projection of themselves shall appear to haunt unfriended these scenes of happiness, a natural child of fancy, begotten and forgotten unawares. Over the whole field of our wanderings such fetches are still travelling like indefatigable bagmen; but the imps of Fontainebleau, as of all beloved spots, are very long of life, and memory is piously unwilling to forget their orphanage. If anywhere about that wood you meet my airy bantling, greet him with tenderness. He was a pleasant lad, though now abandoned. And when it comes to your own turn to quit the forest may you leave behind you such another; no Antony or Werther, let us hope, no tearful whipster, but, as becomes this not uncheerful and most active age in which we figure, the child of happy hours.

No art, it may be said, was ever perfect, and not many noble, that has not been mirthfully conceived. And no man, it may be added, was ever anything but a wet blanket and a cross to his companions who boasted not a copious spirit of enjoyment. Whether as man or artist, let the youth make haste to Fontainebleau, and once there let him address himself to the spirit of the place; he will learn more from exercise than from studies, although both are necessary; and if he can get into his heart the gaiety and inspiration of the woods he will have gone far to undo the evil of his sketches. A spirit once well strung up to the concert-pitch of the primeval out-of-doors will hardly dare to finish a study and magniloquently ticket it a picture. The incommunicable thrill of things, that is the tuning-fork by which we test the flatness of our art. Here it is that Nature teaches and condemns, and still spurs up to further effort and new failure. Thus it is that she sets us blushing at our ignorant and tepid works; and the more we find of these inspiring shocks the less shall we be apt to love the literal in our productions. In all sciences and senses the letter kills; and to-day, when cackling human geese express their ignorant condemnation of all studio pictures, it is a lesson most useful to be learnt. Let the young painter go to Fontainebleau, and while he stupefies himself with studies that teach him the mechanical side of his trade, let him walk in the great air, and be a servant of mirth, and not pick and botanise, but wait upon the moods of nature. So he will learn—or learn not to forget—the poetry of life and earth, which, when he has acquired his frock, will save him from joyless reproduction.

SWISS NOTES*

HEALTH AND MOUNTAINS

There has come a change in medical opinion, and a change has followed in the lives of sick folk. A year or two ago and the wounded soldiery of mankind were all shut up together in some basking angle of the Riviera, walking a dusty promenade or sitting in dusty olive-yards within earshot of the interminable and unchanging surf—idle among spiritless idlers; not perhaps dying; yet hardly living either; and aspiring, sometimes fiercely, after livelier weather and some vivifying change. These were certainly beautiful places to live in, and the climate was wooing in its softness. Yet there was a latent shiver in the sunshine; you were not certain whether you were being wooed; and these mild shores would sometimes seem to you to be the shores of death. There was a lack of manly element; the air was not reactive; you might write bits of poetry and practise resignation, but you did not feel that here was a good spot to repair your tissue or regain your nerve. And it appears, after all, that there was something just in these appreciations. The invalid is now asked to lodge on wintry Alps; a ruder air shall medicine him; the demon of cold is no longer to be fled from, but bearded in his den. For even Winter has his 'dear domestic cave,' and in those places where he may be said to dwell for ever, tempers his austerities.

Anyone who has travelled westward by the great transcontinental railroad of America, must remember the joy with which he perceived, after the tedious prairies of Nebraska and across the vast and dismal moorlands of Wyoming, a few snowy mountain summits along the southern sky. It is among these mountains, in the new state of Colorado, that the sick man may find, not merely an alleviation of his ailments, but the possibility of an active life and an honest livelihood. There, no longer as a lounger in a plaid, but as a working farmer, sweating at his work, he may prolong and begin anew his life. Instead of the bath-chair, the spade; instead of the regulated walk, rough journeys in the forest; and the pure, rare air of the open mountains from the miasma of the sick-room—these are the changes offered him, with what promise of pleasure and self- respect, with what a revolution in all his hopes and terrors, none but an invalid can know. Resignation, the cowardice that apes a kind of courage and that lives in the very air of health resorts, is cast aside at a breath of such a prospect. The man can open the door; he can be up and doing; he can be a kind of a man after all and not merely an invalid.

But it is a far cry to the Rocky Mountains. We cannot all of us go farming in Colorado; and there is yet a middle term, which combines the medical benefits of the new system with the moral drawbacks of the old. Again the invalid has to lie aside from life and its wholesome duties; again he has to be an idler among idlers; but this time at a great altitude, far among mountains, with the snow piled before his door and the frost-flowers every morning on his window. The mere fact is tonic to the nerves. His choice of a place of wintering has somehow to his own eyes the air of an act of bold conduct; and, since he has wilfully sought low temperatures, he is not so apt to shudder at a touch of chill. He came for that, he looked for it, and he throws it from him with the thought.

A long straight reach of valley, wall-like mountains upon either hand that rise higher and shoot up new summits the higher you climb; a few noble peaks seen even from the valley; a village of hotels; a world of black and white—black pine-woods clinging to the sides of the valley, and white snow flouring it, and papering it between the pine-woods, and covering all the mountains with a dazzling curd; add a few score invalids marching to and fro upon the snowy road, or skating on the ice-rinks, possibly to music, or sitting under sunshades by the door of the hotel—and you have the larger features of a mountain sanatorium. A certain furious river runs curving down the valley; its pace never varies, it has not a pool for as far as you can follow it; and its unchanging, senseless hurry is strangely tedious to wit-ness. It is a river that a man could grow to hate. Day after day breaks with the rarest gold upon the mountain spires, and creeps, growing and glowing, down into the valley. From end to end the snow reverberates the sunshine; from end to end the air tingles with the light, clear and dry like crystal. Only along the course of the river, but high above it, there hangs far into the noon one waving scarf of vapour. It were hard to fancy a more engaging feature in a landscape; perhaps it is harder to believe that delicate, long-lasting phantom of the atmosphere a creature of the incontinent stream whose course it follows. By noon the sky is arrayed in an unrivalled pomp of colour—mild and pale melting in the north, but towards the zenith dark with an intensity of purple blue. What with this darkness of heaven and the intolerable lustre of the snow, space is reduced again to chaos. An English painter, coming to France late in life, declared with natural anger that 'the values were all wrong.' Had he got among the Alps on a bright day he might have lost his reason. And even to anyone who has looked at landscape with any care, and in any way through the spectacles of representative art, the scene has a character of insanity. The distant shining mountain peak is here beside your eye; the neighbouring dull-coloured house in comparison is miles away; the summit, which is all of splendid snow, is close at hand; the nigh slopes, which are black with pine trees, bear it no relation, and might be in another sphere. Here there are none of those delicate gradations, those intimate, misty joinings-on and spreadings-out into the distance, nothing of that art of air and light by which the face of nature explains and veils itself in climes which we may be allowed to think more lovely. A glaring piece of crudity, where everything that is not white is a solecism and defies the judgment of the eyesight; a scene of blinding definition; a parade of daylight, almost scenically vulgar, more than scenically trying, and yet hearty and healthy, making the nerves to tighten and the mouth to smile: such is the winter daytime in the Alps. With the approach of evening all is changed. A mountain will suddenly intercept the sun; a shadow fall upon the valley; in ten minutes the thermometer will drop as many degrees; the peaks that are no longer shone upon dwindle into ghosts; and meanwhile, overhead, if the weather be rightly characteristic of the place, the sky fades towards night through a surprising key of colours. The latest gold leaps from the last mountain. Soon, perhaps, the moon shall rise, and in her gentler light the valley shall be mellowed and misted, with here and there a wisp of silver cloud upon a hill-top, and here and there a warmly glowing window in a house, between fire and starlight, kind and homely in the fields of snow.

But the valley is not seated so high among the clouds to be eternally exempt from changes. The clouds gather black as ink; the wind bursts rudely in; day after day the mists drive overhead, the snow-flakes flutter down in blinding disarray; daily the mail comes in later from the top of the pass; people peer through their windows and forsee no end but an entire seclusion from Europe and death by gradual dry-rot, each in his indifferent inn; and when at last the storm goes, and the sun comes again, behold a world of unpolluted snow, glossy like fur, bright like daylight, a joy to wallowing dogs and cheerful to the souls of men. Or perhaps, from across storied and malarious Italy, a wind cunningly winds about the mountains and breaks, warm and unclean, upon our mountain valley. Every nerve is set ajar; the conscience recognises, at a gust, a load of sins and negligences hitherto unknown; and the whole invalid world huddles into its private chambers, and silently recognises the empire of the *Fohn*.*

DAVOS IN WINTER

A mountain valley has, at the best, a certain prison-like effect on the imagination; but a mountain valley, an Alpine winter, and an invalid's weakness made up among them a prison of the most effective kind. The roads indeed are cleared, and at least one footpath dodging up the hill; but to these the health seeker is rigidly confined. There are for him no cross cuts over the field, no following of streams, no unguided rambles in the wood. His walks are cut and dry. In five or six different directions he can push as far, and no farther, than his strength permits; never deviating from the line laid down for him and beholding at each repetition the same field of wood and snow from the same corner of the road. This, of itself, would be a little trying to the patience in the course of months; but to this is added, by the heaped mantle of the snow, an almost utter absence of detail and an almost unbroken identity of colour. Snow, it is true, is not merely white. The sun touches it with roseate and golden lights. Its own crushed infinity of crystals, its own richness of tiny sculpture, fills it, when regarded near at hand, with wonderful depths of coloured shadow, and, though wintrily transformed, it is still water, and has watery tones of blue. But, when all is said, these fields of white and blots of crude black forest are but a trite and staring substitute for the infinite variety and pleasantness of the earth's face. Even a boulder, whose front is too precipitous to have retained the snow, seems, if you come upon it in your walk, a perfect gem of colour, reminds you almost painfully of other places, and brings into your head the delights of more Arcadian days—the path across the meadow, the hazel dell, the lilies on the stream, and the scents, the colours, and the whisper of the woods. And scents here are as rare as colours. Unless you get a gust of kitchen in passing some hotel, you shall smell nothing all day long but the faint and choking odour of frost. Sounds, too, are absent; not a bird pipes, not a bough waves, in the dead, windless atmosphere. If a sleigh goes by, the sleigh-bells ring, and that is all; you work all winter through to no other accompaniment but the crunching of your steps upon the frozen snow.

It is the curse of Alpine valleys to be each one village from one end to the other. Go where you please, houses will still be in sight, before and behind you, and to the right and left. Climb as high as an invalid is able, and it is only to spy new habitations nested in the wood. Nor is that all; for about the health resort the walks are besieged by single people walking rapidly with plaids about their shoulders, by sudden troops of German boys trying to learn to *jodel*, and by German couples silently and, as you venture to fancy, not quite happily, pursuing love's young dream. You may perhaps be an invalid who likes to make bad verses as he walks abroad. Alas! no muse will suffer this imminence of interruption—and at the second stampede of jodellers you find your modest inspiration fled. Or you may only have a taste for solitude: it may try your nerves to have some one always in front whom you are visibly overtaking, and some one always behind who is audibly overtaking you, to say nothing of a score or so who brush past you in an opposite direction. It may annoy you to take your walks and seats in public view. Alas! there is no help for it among the Alps. There are no recesses, as in Gorbio Valley by the oil-mill; no sacred solitude of olive gardens as on the Roccabruna-road; no nook as upon Saint Martin's Cape haunted by the voice of breakers, and fragrant with the threefold sweetness of the rosemary and the sea-pines and the sea.

For this publicity there is no cure and no alleviation; but the storms, of which you will complain so bitterly while they endure, chequer and by their contrast brighten the sameness of fair-weather scenes. When sun and storm contend together—when the thick clouds are broken up and pierced by arrows of golden daylight—there will be startling rearrangements and transfigurations of the mountain summits. A sun-dazzling spire of alps hangs suspended in mid-sky among awful glooms and blackness; or perhaps the edge of some great mountain shoulder will be designed in living gold, and appear for the duration of a glance bright like a constellation, and alone 'in the unapparent.'* You may think you know the figure on these hills; but when they are thus revealed, they belong no longer to the things of earth—meteors we should rather call them, appearances of sun and air that endure but a moment and return no more. Other variations are more lasting, as when, for instance, heavy and wet snow has fallen through some windless hours, and the thin, spiry, mountain pine-trees stand each stock-still and loaded with shining burthen. You may drive through a forest so disguised, the tongue-tied torrent struggling silently in the cleft of the ravine, and all still except the jingle of the sleigh-bells, and you shall fancy yourself in some untrodden northern territory—Lapland, Labrador, or Alaska.

Or, possibly, you arise very early in the morning; totter downstairs in a state of somnambulism; take the simulacrum of a meal by the glimmer of one lamp in the deserted coffee-room; and find yourself by seven o'clock outside in a belated moonlight and a freezing chill. The mail sleigh takes you up and carries you on, and you reach the top of the ascent in the first hour of the day. To trace the fires of the sunrise as they pass from peak to peak, to see the unlit tree-tops as they stand out soberly against the lighted sky, to be for twenty minutes in a wonderland of clear, fading shadows, disappearing vapours, solemn blooms of dawn, hills half glorified already with the day and still half confounded with the greyness of the western heaven—these will seem to repay you for the discomforts of that early start; but as the hour proceeds, and these enchantments vanish, you will find yourself upon the farther side in yet another Alpine valley, snow-white and coal-black, with such another long-drawn congeries of hamlets and such another senseless watercourse bickering along the foot. You have had your moment; but you have not changed the scene. The mountains are about you like a trap; you cannot foot it up a hillside and behold the sea as a great plain, but live in holes and corners, and can change only one for another.

ALPINE DIVERSIONS

There will be no lack of diversion in an Alpine sanatorium. The place is half Englished, to be sure, the local sheet appearing in double column text and translation; but it still remains half German; and hence we have a band which is able to play, and a company of actors able, as you will be told, to act. This last you will take on trust, for the players, unlike the local sheet, confine themselves to German; and though at the beginning of the winter they come with their wig-boxes to each hotel in turn, long before Christmas they have given up the English for a bad job. There will follow, perhaps, a skirmish between the two races; the German element seeking, in the interest of their actors, to raise a mysterious item, the *Kur-taxe* which figures heavily enough already in the weekly bills, the English element stoutly resisting. Meanwhile, in the English hotels, home-played farces, *tableaux-vivants*, and even balls enliven the evenings; a charity bazaar sheds genial consternation; Christmas and New Year are solemnised with Pantagruelian dinners, and from time to time the young folks carol and revolve untunefully enough through the figures of a singing quadrille. A magazine club supplies you with everything, from the *Quarterly* to the *Sunday at Home*. Grand tournaments are organised at chess, draughts, billiards, and whist. Once and again wandering artists drop into our mountain valley, coming you know not whence, going you cannot imagine whither, and belonging to every degree in the hierarchy of musical art, from the recognised performer who announces a concert for the evening, to the comic German family or solitary long-haired German baritone who surprises the guests at dinner-time with songs and a collection. They are all of them good to see; they, at least, are moving; they bring with them the sentiment of the open road; yesterday, perhaps, they were in Tyrol, and next week they will be far in Lombardy, while all we sick folk still simmer in our mountain prison. Some of them, too, are welcome as the flowers in May for their own sake; some of them may have a human voice; some may have that magic which transforms a wooden box into a song-bird, and what we jeeringly call a fiddle into what we mention with respect as a violin. From that grinding lilt, with which the blind man, seeking pence, accompanies the beat of paddle wheels across the ferry, there is surely a difference rather of kind than degree to that unearthly voice of singing that bewails and praises the destiny of man at the touch of the true virtuoso. Even that you may perhaps enjoy; and if you do so, you will own it impossible to enjoy it more keenly than here, 'im Schnee der Alpen.'* A hyacinth in a pot, a handful of primroses packed in moss, or a piece of music by some one who knows the way to the heart of a violin, are things that, in this invariable sameness of the snows and frosty air, surprise you like an adventure. It is droll, moreover, to compare the respect with which the invalids attend a concert, and the ready contempt with which they treat the dinner-time performers. Singing which they would hear with real enthusiasm—possibly with tears—from the corner of a drawing-room, is listened to with laughter when it is offered by an unknown professional and no money has been taken at the door.

Of skating little need be said; in so snowy a climate the rinks must be intelligently managed; their mismanagement will lead to many days of vexation and some petty quarrelling; but when all goes well, it is certainly curious, and perhaps rather unsafe, for the invalid to skate under a burning sun and walk back to his hotel in a sweat through long tracts of glare and passages of freezing shadow. But the peculiar outdoor sport of this district is tobogganing. A Scotsman may remember the low flat board, with the front wheels on a pivot, which was called a 'hurlie'; he may remember this contrivance laden with boys, as, laboriously started, it ran rattling down the brae, and was, now successfully, now unsuccessfully, steered round the corner at the foot; he may remember scented summer evenings passed in this diversion, and many a grazed skin, bloody cockscomb, and neglected lesson. The toboggan is to the hurlie what the sled is to the carriage; it is a hurlie upon runners; and if for a grating road you substitute a long declivity of beaten snow, you can imagine the giddy career of the tobogganist. The correct position is to sit; but the fantastic will sometimes sit, hindforemost, or dare the descent upon their belly or their back. A few steer with a pair of pointed sticks, but it is more classical to use the feet. If the weight be heavy and the track smooth the toboggan takes the bit between its teeth; and to steer a couple of full-sized friends in safety requires not only judgment but desperate exertion. On a very steep track, with a keen evening frost, you may have moments almost too appalling to be called enjoyment; the head goes, the world vanishes; your blind steed bounds below your weight; you reach the foot, with all the breath knocked out of your body, jarred and bewildered as though you had just been subjected to a railway accident. Another element of joyful horror is added by the formation of a train; one toboggan being tied to another, perhaps to the number of half a dozen, only the first rider being allowed to steer, and all the rest pledged to put up their feet and follow their leader, with heart in mouth, down the made descent. This, particularly if the track begins with a headlong plunge, is one of the most exhilarating follies in the world, and the tobogganing invalid is early reconciled to somersaults.

There is all manner of variety in the nature of the tracks, some miles in length, others but a few yards, and yet, like some short rivers, furious in their brevity. All degrees of skill and courage and taste may be suited in your neighbourhood. But perhaps the true way to toboggan is alone and at night. First comes the tedious climb, dragging your instrument behind you. Next a long breathing space, alone with snow and pine-woods, cold, silent, and solemn to the heart. Then you push off; the toboggan fetches way; she begins to feel the hill, to glide, to swim, to gallop. In a breath you are out from under the pine-trees, and a whole heavenful of stars reels and flashes overhead. Then comes a vicious effort; for by this time your wooden steed is speeding like the wind, and you are spinning round a corner, and the whole glittering valley and all the lights in all the great hotels lie for a moment at your feet; and the next you are racing once more in the shadow of the night, with close-shut teeth and beating heart. Yet a little while and you will be landed on the high road by the door of your own hotel. This, in an atmosphere tingling with forty degrees of frost, in a night made luminous with stars and snow, and girt with strange white mountains, teaches the pulse an unaccustomed tune and adds a new excitement to the life of man upon his planet.

THE STIMULATION OF THE ALPS

To anyone who should come from a southern sanatorium to the Alps, the row of sunburned faces round that table would present the first surprise. He would begin by looking for the invalids, and he would lose his pains, for not one out of five of even the bad cases bears the mark of sickness upon his face. The plump sunshine from above and its strong reverberation from below colour the skin like an Indian climate; the treatment, which consists mainly of the open air, exposes even the sickliest to tan, and a tableful of invalids comes, in a month or two, to resemble a tableful of hunters. But although he may be thus surprised at the first glance, his astonishment will grow greater as he experiences the effects of the climate upon himself. In many ways it is a trying business to reside upon the Alps: the stomach is exercised, the appetite often languishes, the liver may at times rebel; and, because you have come so far from metropolitan advantages, it does not follow that you shall recover. But one thing is undeniable—that is, that in the rare air, clear cold, and blinding light of Alpine winters, a man takes a certain troubled delight in his existence which can nowhere else be paralleled. He is perhaps no happier, but he is stingingly alive. It does not, perhaps, come out of him in work or exercise, yet he feels an enthusiasm of the blood unknown in more temperate climates. It may not be health, but it is fun.

There is nothing more difficult to communicate on paper than this baseless ardour, this stimulation of the brain, this sterile joyousness of spirits. You wake every morning, see the gold upon the snow peaks, become filled with courage, and bless God for your prolonged existence. The valleys are but a stride to you; you cast your shoe over the hill-tops; your ears and your heart sing; in the words of an unverified quotation from the Scottish psalms, you feel yourself fit 'on the wings of all the winds' to 'come flying all abroad.' Europe and your mind are too narrow for that flood of energy. Yet it is notable that you are hard to root out of bed; that you start forth singing indeed, on your walk, yet are unusually ready to turn home again; that the best of you is volatile; and that although the restlessness remains till night, the strength is early at an end. With all these heady jollities, you are half conscious of an underlying languor in the body; you prove not to be so well as you had fancied; you weary before you have well begun; and though you mount at morning with the lark, that is not precisely a song-bird's heart that you bring back with you when you return with aching limbs and peevish temper to your inn.

It is hard to say wherein it lies, but this joy of Alpine winters is its own reward. Baseless, in a sense, it is more than worth more permanent improvements. The dream of health is perfect while it lasts; and if, in trying to realise it, you speedily wear out the dear hallucination, still every day, and many times a day, you are conscious of a strength you scarce possess, and a delight in living as merry as it proves to be transient. The brightness—the levity and quiet of the air; the odd, stirring silence—more stirring than a tumult; the snow; the frost, the enchanted landscape: all have their part in the effect and on the memory, 'tous vous tapent sur la tête'; and yet when you have enumerated all, you have gone no nearer to explain or even to qualify the delicate exhilaration that you feel—delicate, you may say, and yet excessive, greater than can be said in prose, almost greater than an invalid can bear. There is a certain wine of France, known in England in some gaseous disguise, but when drunk in the land of its nativity, still as a pool, clean as river water, and as heady as verse. It is more than probable that in its noble natural condition this was the very wine of Anjou so beloved by Athos in the 'Musketeers.' Now, if the reader has ever washed down a liberal second breakfast with the wine in question, and gone forth on the back of these dilutions, into a sultry, sparkling noontide, he will have felt an influence almost as genial, although strangely grosser, than this fairy titillation of the nerves among the snow and sunshine of the Alps. That also is a mode, we need not say of intoxication, but of insobriety. Thus also a

man walks in a strong sunshine of the mind, and follows
smiling, insubstantial meditations. And, whether he be really so clever or so strong as he supposes, in either case he
will enjoy his chimæra while it lasts.

The influence of this giddy air displays itself in many
secondary ways. A certain sort of laboured pleasantry has
already been recognised, and many perhaps have been
remarked in these papers, as a sort peculiar to the climate.
People utter their judgments with a cannonade of syllables,
a big word is as good as a meal to them; and the turn of
a phrase goes further than humour or wisdom. By the
professional writer many sad vicissitudes have to be under-
gone. At first, he cannot write at all. The heart, it appears,
is unequal to the pressure of business, and the brain, left
without nourishment, goes into mild decline. Next, some
power of work returns to him, accompanied by jumping
headaches. Last, the spring is opened, and there pours at
once from his pen a world of blatant, hustling polysyllables,
and talk so high as, in the old joke, to be positively offensive
in hot weather. He writes it in good faith and with a sense
of inspiration; it is only when he comes to read what he
has written that surprise and disquiet seize upon his mind.
What is he to do, poor man? All his little fishes talk like
whales. This yeasty inflation, this stiff and strutting architecture of the sentence, has come upon him while he slept;
and it is not he, it is the Alps, that are to blame. He is
not, perhaps, alone, which somewhat comforts him. Nor is
he ill without a remedy. Some day, when the Spring returns,
he shall go down a little lower in this world, and remember
quieter inflections and more modest language. But here, in
the meantime, there seems to swim up some outline of a
new cerebral hygiene and a good time coming, when
experienced advisers shall send a man to the proper
measured level for the ode, the biography, the religious
tract; and a nook may be found, between the sea and
Chimborazo, where Mr Swinburne shall be able to write
more continently, and Mr Browning somewhat slower.

Is it a return of youth, or is it a congestion of the brain?
It is a sort of congestion, perhaps, that leads the invalid,

when all goes well, to face the new day with such a bubbling cheerfulness. It is certainly congestion that makes night hideous with visions, all the chambers of a many-storied caravanserai haunted with vociferous nightmares, and many wakeful people came down late for breakfast in the morning. Upon that theory the cynic may explain the whole affair—exhilaration, nightmares, pomp of tongue and all. But, on the other hand, the peculiar blessedness of boyhood may itself be but a symptom of the same complaint, for the two effects are strangely similar; and the frame of mind of the invalid upon the Alps is a sort of intermittent youth, with periods of lassitude. The fountain of Juventus does not play steadily in these parts; but there it plays, and possibly nowhere else.

EXPLANATORY NOTES

Volume numbers of Stevenson's works and letters refer to the Tusitala Edition unless otherwise stated.

Balfour = Graham Balfour, *The Life of Robert Louis Stevenson*, 2 vols. (1901).

Cevennes Journal = *R.L.S. The Cevennes Journal: Notes on a Journey Through the French Highlands*, ed. Gordon Golding; Notes by Jaques Blondel, Gordon Golding, and Jacques Poujol (1978).

Maixner = Paul Maixner (ed.) *Robert Louis Stevenson: The Critical Heritage* (1981).

Swearingen = Roger G. Swearingen, *The Prose Writings of Robert Louis Stevenson: A Guide* (1980).

2 *Thus sang . . . English boat*: from Marvell's 'Bermudas', where the line reads 'Thus sung they . . .'.

3 *Caleb and Joshua*: Numbers 13: 1–25.

5 *Sir Walter Grindlay Simpson*: a friend of R.L.S.'s from his student days in Edinburgh.

9 *barnacled*: bespectacled.

   Miss Howe or Miss Harlowe: characters in Richardson's *Clarissa Harlowe* (1748).

11 *C'est vite mais c'est long*: it is quick but it is long.

16 *French Huguenots . . . tribulation*: refers to the persecution of Protestants following the revocation of the Edict of Nantes in 1685.

17 *Mammon . . . Heaven*: Milton, *Paradise Lost*, I. 679.

20 *Murray*: a guidebook, forerunner of Baedeker.

21 *Cœnacula*: (facetious) banquets, from Lat. *cenaculum*, an eating-room.

32 *bread-berry*: bread soaked in water, seasoned or sweetened.

   swipes: weak beer, small beer.

   Lucretian maxim: see start of Bk. II, *De Rerum Natura*: 'It is sweet to see from what evils you are yourself exempt' (trans. Munro).

34 *Molière's farce*: *Les Précieuses ridicules*, Act I, Scene xiii.

38 *Voilà . . . pour vous débarbouiller*: here is the water to wash your face with.

    Waterloo Crackers: fireworks.

    Austerlitz: defeat of Napoleon by the Austrians and Russians in 1805.

    angels unawares: Hebrews, 13: 1.

42 *corks*: a betting game played with double-coloured corks.

43 *Alma and Spicheren*: a British charge in the Crimean War (1854) and Prussian charge in the Franco-Prussian War (1870).

52 *Mountain Daisy*: cf. Burns's 'Mountain Daisy'.

    Come away, Death: from *Twelfth Night*.

57 *Caudine Forks*: defeat of the Romans by the Samnites in 321 BC.

    Fletcher of Saltoun: a Scots patriot (1653–1716), who in 1703 urged the need to liberate Scotland from domination by the English ministry. He wrote speeches and pamphlets in opposition to the Union of 1707.

61 *Gaston Lafenestre*: artist friend of Stevenson's in Fontainebleau. The phrase means something like 'Danish gloomyheads!'

65 *Nanty Ewart*: captain of the smuggler's brig in Walter Scott's *Redgauntlet* (1824).

74 *Bazin . . . la croix de Malte*: Bazin, inn-keeper, accommodation. At the Cross of Malta.

    Zola's description . . . the Louvre: see *L'Assommoir*, ch. 3.

86 *Out of my country and myself I go*: quoted in Hazlitt, 'On Going on a Journey', but of unknown origin.

96 *zélatrice*: enthusiasm, zealousness.

    dizaine: about ten.

100 *aff-'n-aff*: 'half-and-half', a drink of mixed bitter beer and porter.

103 *Châtelet . . . Alcazar*: Paris theatres.

104 *Tenez . . . je vais vous le dire*: Look gentlemen, I am going to tell you what it is.

108 *Epilogue*: not included in the first edition. It appeared in *Scribner's Magazine* in August 1888 and was published in *Across the Plains* in 1892. The incident of which this is a

narration took place in 1875, and R.L.S.'s mother wrote in her diary: 'Lou arrives today with only a knapsack... looking well and strong. He was taken up as a vagabond & put in a dungeon for two hours—everything taken from him even his pocket handkerchief lest he commit suicide with it!' (Quoted in Swearingen, p. 124.)

110   *... des portraits.* No... No, you have the pictures. *Colporteur*: door-to-door salesman.

  ... ce n'est pas bien. No, it is not kind of you. It is not kind.

114   *je suppose... votre camarade*: I suppose we must release your comrade.

117   *procès-verbal*: official report, record of evidence.

118   *vous êtes libre!*: You can go!

123   *A Mountain Town in France*: not included in the first edition. It was written in 1879 and was originally intended to serve as the opening chapter of the *Travels*. Swearingen comments: 'Stevenson no doubt drafted this material on Le Monastier during his stay there in September 1878 and revised it in Edinburgh that Winter (see Swearingen, p. 34).

124   *bourées*: a lively dance of French origin (two bars in a beat).

  Il n'y a plus de jevnesse: There are no more young people.

127   *Pas bong... en Écosse*: Not bad priests here... good priests in Scotland.

128   *Où'st-ce que vous allez?*: Where are you going?

  Quoi....ce soir?: Well, will you return to Monastier this evening?

  patois: dialect.

131   *bourgeois... avec des chaises*: a group of gentlemen and women who were playing a game with chairs.

  qui s'amusait à faire ça: who amused himself in this way.

  C'est difficile... à expliquer: It is difficult to explain.

133   *Legitimists... Republicans*: the Legitimists supported the claim of the elder line of the Bourbons, then represented by the Count de Chambord (d. 1883); the Orleanists were adherents to the princes of Orleans, then represented by the Count de Paris. The Imperialists still favoured the son of Louis Napoleon. The Republicans were loyal to the Republic established after the Franco-Prussian War.

139 *Et vous marchez comme ça!*: And you proceed like that!

147 *dur comme un âne*: tough like a donkey, stubborn as a donkey.

150 *the Napoleon Bonaparte of wolves*: Blondel, Golding, and Poujol comment on this mysterious BEAST: 'For three years, from the spring of 1764 until June 1767, this mysterious 'Beast of Gevaudan' terrified several of the regions through which Stevenson travelled. Its favourite victims were women, young girls and little children, particularly where they were tending sheep in the field; their bodies were often found drained of blood and sometimes partially devoured. The Beast was quite active around Langogne, Cheylard l'Eveque and Luc, and instances of its attacks were reported as far away as Marvejols and Saint-Flour, from Vivarais to Auvergne.' (*Cevennes Journal*, pp. 139–40.) Many efforts were made to kill the Beast and several times were thought to have been successful, as in September 1765 when a large wolf was shot; but then the Beast struck again. Finally, in June 1767, Jean Chastel killed the Beast with a rifle shot. It weighed 110 pounds.

Élie Berthet: (1818–91), French novelist and author of a work of fiction on the Beast of Gevaudan.

151 *D'ou'st-ce-que vous venez?*: Where do you come from?

153 *Herbert Spencer*: (1820–1903), English philosopher and agnostic. R.L.S. classified his works among 'Books which have influenced me.'

155 *a little farther lend thy guiding hand*: Cf. the first line of Milton's *Samson Agonistes*, 'A little onward lend thy guiding hand'.

C'est que . . . il fait noir: The problem is, you see, that it's dark.

mais—c'est—de la peine: but—it is—very difficult.

156 *C'est . . . de la porte*: it isn't that . . . but I am not going out of the door.

C'est vrai . . . venez-vous?: It is true, that . . . Yes, it is true. And where do you come from?

farceuse: joker

157 *Filia barbara pater barbarior*: a cruel daughter, a more cruel father.

159 *Pastors of the Desert*: the book by Napoleon Peyrat which was to provide R.L.S. with much material for the descriptions of the Camisard revolt which he added to the Journal before

it appeared in the published form. Peyrat was not, however, Stevenson's only source, and his interest in the Camisards dated from at least as early as 1873.

161 *Balquhidder and Dunrossness*: remote parishes in West Perth and the Shetlands, both Protestant.

165 *Mountains and vales . . . that whistle?*: from Wordsworth's sonnet, 'Proud were ye mountains when in times of old'.

166 *the length of twopence every day of my life*: refers to drawings that R.L.S. bought as a child. He comments upon them in his essay 'A Penny Plain and Twopence Coloured', in *Memories and Portraits*.

167 *Marco Sadeler*: the Sadeler family were Belgian copper engravers in the sixteenth century. This probably refers to *Solitudo sive Vitae Patrum*, copperplate engravings by J. and R. Sadeler showing scenes in the life of hermits (see *Cevennes Journal*, p. 143).

170 *MM les retraitants*: men who stayed at the monastery for rest and reflection without taking the vows.

171 *Elizabeth Seton*: (1774–1821), a Roman Catholic convert who founded a number of schools and the Order of the Sisters of Mercy in the United States.

Cotton Mather: a Puritan pastor (1663–1728) born in Boston, author of *Magnalia Christi Americana*, an ecclesiastical history of Massachussetts.

shako: a kind of military headdress.

172 *Basil, Hilarion, Raphael, or Pacifique*: Basil the Great (329–79), a father of the Greek Church; St Hilarion (d. 371), a hermit of Palestine; Raphael (1614–93), a Benedictine monk and historian of Portugal; Pacifique (1574–1653), a Franciscan monk and missionary who founded convents in Persia and the Antilles.

Veuillot: Louis Veuillot (1813–83), a French polemical Catholic writer known for his ultra-Conservatism.

Chateaubriand: François-René Chateaubriand (1768–1848), a French romancer whose works include *The Spirit of Christianity and the Martyrs*.

173 *lay phalansteries*: a phalanstery is a brotherhood or association living under one roof. The experience to which R.L.S. refers is probably that with the group of artists at Grez. See

'Memories of Fontainbleau' in this collection. The term *phalanstère* was invented by the French Utopian socialist Charles Fourier, who had always appealed to the 'dreamer' in Stevenson (see Holmes, *Footsteps: Adventures of a Romantic Biographer* (1985), 39).

176 *L'Amour les comptera!*: 'How beautiful your girls are ... The god of love will value them!' from a comic opera by A. C. Lecocq; Giroflé and Girofla are the names of twin daughters of a Spanish grandee. The passage replaces one containing personal thoughts about prayer, and some of R.L.S.'s own prayers, that occurs in the *Cevennes Journal* (see Introduction).

178 *Gambetta's moderation*: Leon Gambetta (1838–82), a prominent French politician, one of the founders of the Third Republic.

Et vous ... croyance?: And you intend to die in this kind of belief?

179 *Gætulian lion*: see Horace, *Odes*, I. xxiii. 10.

180 *C'est mon conseil ... et comme prêtre*: It is my advice as an old soldier ... and that of the gentleman as a priest.

181 *La parole est à vous*: The word is yours.

183 *At God's green caravanserai*: in other editions, these lines are attributed to an 'Old Play'; in fact, they are by R.L.S. himself. His other habit with his own verses at the start of sections is to attribute them to 'W. P. Bannatyne' (see e.g. note to p. 191 below).

Hé ... cinq heures!: Hullo there! It's five o'clock!

186 *nor nymph nor faunus haunted*. cf. Milton, *Paradise Lost*, IV, 707–8.

187 *sensibly relish it*. from Montaigne, essay on 'Experience'.

191 *W. P. Bannatyne*: R.L.S. himself—see note to p. 183 above.

192 *stared at the Pacific*: from Keats's, 'On first looking into Chapman's *Homer*'.

the Grand Monarch: Louis XIV.

Camisards: name commonly applied to Protestant rebels in the Cevennes from about 1702 onwards. The war of the Camisards (1702–5) was occasioned by Louis XIV's decision to revoke the Edict of Nantes (under this edict Henry IV had granted tolerance to French Protestants). In the Cevennes, however, Protestantism remained very strong and there was resistance to Louis's decision—committed Protestants read the Bible aloud to their families and attended secret meetings in the 'Wilderness'. R.L.S. was fascinated by the Camisards with whom he found many parallels with the Scottish Covenanters (see Introduction).

193   *and Lord Roland*: Roland Laporte (born *c*.1675), prophet and leader of the Camisards.

Cavalier: Jean Cavalier (1680–1740), a young Camisard leader who had much engaged the interest of R.L.S. In his manuscript notebook there is a poem (much and often revised) 'John Cavalier', and in June 1881 he appears to have become interested in writing a study of him, a project which did not progress beyond the opening paragraph (see Swearingen, p. 59).

Castanet: André Castanet (1674–1705), a captain under Roland.

194   *Florentin*: a follower of a Roman Catholic monk from Saint-Florent, who, in response to the murder of some Catholics by the Camisards in Chamborigaud, led a group of men and murdered those Protestants suspected of helping the Camisards (see *Cevennes Journal*, pp. 150–1).

197   *patet dea*: 'appearing as a goddess'. Cf. Venus appearing to Aeneas, in Virgil, *Aeneid*, I. 405.

southern Covenanters . . . Archbishop Sharpe: the Covenanters were so called from the National Covenant (1638) in which the Scottish people expressed their grievances against Charles I's popish tendencies and religious innovations. A second Covenant was drawn up in 1643. See Gordon Donaldson, *Scotland: James V–James VII* (Edinburgh, 1965). Archbishop Sharpe (1613–79) of St Andrews, an Anglican primate, was murdered by the Covenanters in 1679.

Villars: Claude Louis Hector Villars (1653–1732), marshal of France, suppressed the insurrection of the Camisards in 1704.

198   *Lamoignon de Bavile*: (1648–1720) was made intendant of Languedoc shortly after the revocation of the Edict of Nantes and is known as a very cruel persecutor of the Camisards.

du Châyla: (d. 1702), another persecutor of the Camisards, known for his brutality. He had been a missionary in Siam before he became archpriest and *curé* in the Cevennes.

199   *Scavenger's daughter*: an instrument of torture invented by William Skevington at the Tower of London during Henry VIII's reign.

202 *Killiecrankie*: the pass of Killiecrankie in the Scottish Highlands is associated with the defeat of John Graham of
Claverhouse, Viscount Dundee, who was commissioned in
1678 to act against the Covenanting conventicles then meeting in south-western Scotland.

204 *Joani's band ... Salomon's*: Nicholas Joani, a soldier who led
a band of Camisards along the Tarn. Salomon Coudrec is
associated with him. Coudrec was captured and burnt alive
in March 1706.

Antony Watteau: Antoine Watteau (1684–1721), the French
genre painter whose most famous subject was the (aristo-
cratic) fête-champêtre or outdoor entertainments.

207 *Many are called ... and few chosen*: Matthew 12: 14.

Moravians: members of the sect of Moravian Brethren in
Bohemia, which grew up (before the Reformation) around
the teachings and inspiration of John Hus. The members
were often forced to emigrate, and in England they had
some influence over Wesley and the Methodists. The term
here refers to anyone not a member of the official Reformed
Church of France, and thus is interchangeable, to the old
man who is speaking, with Derbist.

Derbists: Plymouth Brethren who were founded by, among
others, John Darby (1800–82).

208 *Christian and Faithful*: this refers to *Pilgrim's Progress*, Part I,
ch. 11.

211 *Mauchline, Cumnock, or Carsphairn*: towns associated with the
history and persecution of the Covenanters in the south-
western districts of Scotland.

Prophet Peden: Alexander Peden (d. 1686), a well-known
Covenanting preacher, hence his name 'Prophet'. Before
being imprisoned on the Bass Rock he travelled throughout
Scotland and Ireland preaching.

212 *Black Camisard ... White Cross*: 'A White Camisard was
defined by Bishop Fletcher of Nimes in a letter dated
November 20, 1703, as a member of one of "several bands
of Catholics which pillage and kill those Protestants but
newly converted to Catholicism ... They come from the
Comtat, from Provence, and we thought they would be
useful to us, but up until now they have done nothing but
steal cows and refuse to march upon the black Camisards

[that is, the Protestant rebels]." (Andre Ducasse, *La Guerre des Camisards*, 238). The distinction between black and white Camisards turns up again in Histoire des Camisards published in London in 1744, and has often been used since to blame Catholic irregulars for those acts of banditry that the Protestant rebels may have committed. The Miquelets were lightly armed auxiliary troops, with a taste for pillage, served as reinforcements for dragon regiments . . . . The cadets of the White Cross were so named "because of the white cross worn on their hats as a sign of recognition" '. (*Cevennes Journal*, Notes, 156).

219   *Naaman*: 2 Kings 5: 18.

      a royal grace of toleration: Louis XVI's edict of 1787 granting toleration, whereby non-Catholics were given the right to register their births, deaths, and marriages. Non-Catholic religious services, however, were not sanctioned.

220   *Cependant . . . dehors!*: Nevertheless . . . to sleep outside!

221   *Sir Cloudesley Shovel*: a British admiral (1650–1707) and commander-in-chief of the English Fleet in the attempted assault on Toulon in 1707. In the War of the Camisards he was given responsibility for bringing British aid to the rebels. 'Two ships were detached from his service to land troops near Sete, but returned without having attempted an attack. The menace of landing, however, combined with Cavalier's lowland offensive, seriously delayed the execution of Baville's plan for burning the Upper Cevennes in October 1703' (*Cevennes Journal*, p. 158 notes).

      Julien: a mercenary who was sent into the high Cevennes to devastate the country by burning.

222   *Pippa*: refers to Browning's poem, 'Pippa Passes'.

231   *The difference to me!*: Wordsworth, 'She dwelt among untrodden ways' (one of the 'Lucy' poems).

235   *Roads*: this, R.L.S.'s first published essay, appeared in the *Portfolio* in December 1873 (see Swearingen, p. 12).

      Mount Chimborazo: an inactive volcano in the Andes.

      in the great city pent: Coleridge, 'This Lime-Tree Bower My prison'.

237   *grata protervitas*: frowardness (Horace, *Odes*, I. xix. 7).

railroad . . . though a difficult country: 'Compare Blake, in the *Marriage of Heaven and Hell*: "Improvement makes straight roads; but the crooked roads, without improvement, are roads of Genius." ' (R.L.S.'s own footnote.)

239 *fresh sentiment of the road*: from Walt Whitman, Leaves of Grass, another book included by R.L.S. in 'Books which have influenced me.'

241 *Werther*: Goethe: *The Sorrows of Young Werther* (1774).

243 *Ordered South*: originally published in *Macmillan's Magazine*, 30 May 1874.

244 *persiennes*: outside window-blinds, shutters.

245 *Bethesda*: John 5: 4.

249 *Hazlitt . . . one of his essays*: 'On Personal Identity in Winterslow'.

252 *Etienne de la Boetie*: friend of Montaigne; see the latter's essay, 'Experience'.

253 *NOTE*: not contained in the first-published version of the essay, but was included in the version appearing in *Virginibus Puerisque* (1881) and in that in the Tusitala edition.

255 *Walking Tours*: accepted for publication by Leslie Stephen in February 1876, it appeared in the *Cornhill Magazine* in June 1876. See Swearingen, p. 23.

256 *I wish to vegetate like the country*: see Hazlitt's 'On Going on a Journey', in *Table Talk* (1821).

and go on singing: another allusion to Bunyan's *Pilgrim's Progress*, here to Christian when his burden had fallen from his shoulders at the sight of the cross.

260 *deprive him of his covetousness*: from Milton, *Areopagitica*. The quotation should read 'bereave' not 'deprive'.

Héloïse: *La Nouvelle Héloïse* (1761), a romance by Rousseau.

261 *happy thinking*: see Burns's 'The Rigs o' Barley'.

265 *Forest Notes*: published in the *Cornhill Magazine* in May 1876, having been written during the summer of 1875.

266 *Le seigneur . . . au loin roule*: The Lord of the Manor shuts up his peasants as though there were a door and hinges from the heaven to the ground. Everything is his, the ancient forest, the bird in the air, the fish in the stream, the beast in the thicket, the water which flows, the bell whose sound rolls into the distance.

267   *among the hounds*: ' "Deux poures varlez qui n'ont nulz gages et qui gissoient la nuit avec les chiens." See Champollion-Figeac's *Louis et Charles d'Orléans*, i. 63, and for my lord's English horn, *ibid*. 96.' (Stevenson's note.)

268   *De Retz*: Gilles de Retz or de Rais (*c*.1396–1440), maréchal de France, who was executed for kidnapping and murdering children.

276   *En voiture . . . Mesdames*: Take your seats, ladies and gentlemen.

     Il y a de l'eau: There is the water.

280   *à fond . . . piqueurs*: at top speed, monsieur, and with twelve huntsmen.

284   *sont admirées . . . libet*: are admired with surprise by travellers who write forthwith with Horace, 'How can a remote crag and an empty forest prompt in me a sense of wonder?'

289   *Millet*: Jean-François Millet (1814–75), a painter famous for his studies of peasant life, member of the Barbizon School. His pictures include *The Sower* (1850); *The Gleaners* (1857), and *The Peasant Leaning on his Hoe* (1863). *The Angelus*, painted in 1858–9, was much reproduced in the nineteenth century.

     Rousseau: Pierre-Étienne-Theodore Rousseau (1812–67), landscape painter of the Barbizon School.

296   *Petit Cénacle*: name given to a group of extreme Romantics, led by Petrus Borel (1809–59).

     Murger: Henry Murger (1822–61), author of sketches of Parisian artistic life, *Scènes de la vie de Bohème*, the basis of Puccini's *La Bohème*.

307   *Swiss Notes*: these essays were published between February and March 1881 in the *Pall Mall Gazette*. There is a fifth essay, not reprinted, in subsequent editions/collections, called, 'The Misgivings of Convalescence'.

312   *the Föhn*: a hot, dry, south wind blowing down the north side of the Alps.

315   *in the unapparent*: from Shelley, *Adonais*—'The inheritors of unfulfilled renown | Rose from their thrones, built beyond mortal thought, | Far in the Unapparent.'

317   *im Schnee der Alpen*: in the Alpine Snow.

320   *come flying all abroad*: cf. Psalm 18: 10, 'He rode upon the cherubims, and did fly; he came flying upon the wings of the winds'.

THE WORLD'S CLASSICS

A Select List

HANS ANDERSEN: Fairy Tales
Translated by L. W. Kingsland
Introduction by Naomi Lewis
Illustrated by Vilhelm Pedersen and Lorenz Frølich

LUDOVICO ARIOSTO: Orlando Furioso
Translated by Guido Waldman

ARISTOTLE: The Nicomachean Ethics
Translated by David Ross

JANE AUSTEN: Emma
Edited by James Kinsley and David Lodge

HONORÉ DE BALZAC: Père Goriot
Translated and Edited by A. J. Krailsheimer

CHARLES BAUDELAIRE: The Flowers of Evil
Translated by James McGowan
Introduction by Jonathan Culler

R. D. BLACKMORE: Lorna Doone
Edited by Sally Shuttleworth

MARY ELIZABETH BRADDON: Lady Audley's Secret
Edited by David Skilton

CHARLOTTE BRONTË: Jane Eyre
Edited by Margaret Smith

EMILY BRONTË: Wuthering Heights
Edited by Ian Jack

GEORG BÜCHNER:
Danton's Death, Leonce and Lena, Woyzeck
Translated by Victor Price

ÉMILE ZOLA:
The Attack on the Mill and Other Stories
Translated by Douglas Parmée

Nana
Translated and Edited by Douglas Parmée